PHOTOGRAPHY
IN VIRGINIA

Jeffrey Ruggles

Photography
In Virginia

by Jeffrey Ruggles

Virginia Historical Society
Richmond 2008

Published in conjunction with the exhibition
Photography in Virginia
Virginia Historical Society

© 2008 by the Virginia Historical Society

Designed by Sara D. Bowersox

ISBN 978-0-945015-30-7

Printed in China

Published by Virginia Historical Society
428 North Boulevard
Richmond, VA 23220
www.vahistorical.org

ILLUSTRATIONS:
All Virginia Historical Society unless otherwise credited

TITLE PAGE
Upper left: Children 1900, detail, *Hampton University Archives* (see p. 209)
Upper middle: Woman photographer, detail (see p. 144)
Upper right: O'Sullivan View, detail (see p. 41)
Center left: Harrisonburg carte de visite, detail (see p. 70)
Center: Camera obscura, *Thomas Jefferson Foundation* (see p. 3)
Center right: Jurors 1867, detail, *Valentine Richmond History Center* (see p. 98)
Lower left: Tidewater Knitting Mill, detail (see p. 116)
Lower middle: Gilbert Hunt, detail (see p. 22)
Lower right: Potato blossom princess, detail, *Library of Virginia* (see p. 178)

TABLE OF CONTENTS
President Harding and his wife (see p. 111)

FOREWORD
A Snow Scene, detail (see p. 103)

INTRODUCTION
Family at Washington's Tomb, detail (see p. 21)

NOTES
Turn-of-the-century handbill, detail (see p. 77)

ACKNOWLEDGEMENTS
The Association buyer (see p. 121)

INDEX
German Village (see p. 113)

TABLE OF CONTENTS

FOREWORD

If the one constant of history is change, the years since the introduction of practical photography in 1839 have been marked by the emergence of an increasingly visual culture. If the written word dominated from the Reformation through the Industrial Revolution, in the post-industrial era images gradually have attained at least equal status. Contemporary conversations are as likely to begin "Did you see?" as "Did you read?"

In 2000, the Virginia Historical Society organized an exhibition titled *The Virginia Landscape.* It examined the Virginia experience as reflected in landscape paintings across three centuries. *Photography in Virginia* not only explores a medium in which the experiences of Virginians have been captured since 1841, but also documents—for the first time in detail—the constant evolution of the photographic process as practiced in the commonwealth. The world of photography has been revolutionized by the digital image. It can be disseminated immediately, in infinite numbers, to the whole world, but as the result of a process fundamentally different from that initiated by Louis Daguerre and William Fox Talbot. The constant continues to be change.

The Virginia Historical Society has collected photographs for more than a century, but rather incidentally as gifts and never purchased. Even in the 1960s, the VHS was not certain that glass plate negatives were fit for its archival mission. Today we fully recognize the importance of photographs as a key component of the historical record. The information a photograph contains, or the feelings it evokes, can be precise or vague, conclusive or ambiguous. For the biographer, there is nothing like a portrait; for the architectural historian, it can settle an argument. Photographs made for one purpose—this exhibition shows the enormous range of them—can be useful for an entirely different reason, even generations after the images were created.

Photographs are reproduced in publications in the Virginia Historical Society's library. Others are kept in the manuscripts department with family papers. Most, however, are in the museum department, which is charged with continuing to collect photographs that tell the history of Virginia and its inhabitants. Exhibitions are team efforts, but in this one the chief thanks must go to the exhibition's curator and the author of this companion book, Jeffrey Ruggles, our talented curator of prints and photographs.

CHARLES F. BRYAN, JR.
PRESIDENT AND CEO

INTRODUCTION

Photography is one of the significant legacies of the nineteenth century. In recent years a number of books have related the history of photography from an international perspective quite effectively. This study takes another approach and looks instead at one state's experience with photography. Rather than a trans-Atlantic tale of discoveries and first successes that jumps from place to place, this account stays with the locals as they adopt innovation from elsewhere. It is a kind of case study of the history of the medium as practiced on a regional stage.

Photography in Virginia covers work made within the state from the 1840s to about 1970. As a picture book, it is okay to browse from the middle. The rule for inclusion has been that the photograph must have been taken within the borders of Virginia. The majority are previously unpublished. The photographers include both Virginians and those just passing through. The aim has been to include all the sections of the state, but the representation is admittedly imperfect.

Virginia's photography began by 1841, two years after Daguerre announced his process, when a daguerreotypist advertised in Richmond. For this project the significance of the Civil War was the profusion of photography. The late nineteenth century saw the growth of photography as a cottage industry, with each community served by an operator. In the early 1900s photography evolved from a practice limited to trained technicians to a popular medium, accessible at first to skilled amateurs and eventually by the 1960s to virtually everybody. Over the twentieth century, too, in large part from necessity, most professional practice became specialized.

A thesis of this book is that about 1890 a critical mass of technical advances came together, and photography became essentially the modern practice that many readers—at least those born before 1975—can remember. That period in photography is now identified, by the light of the rising digital sun that marks its close, as the analog era. Its long century lasted from 1890 to 2005. From the vantage of the twenty-first century, it is clear that the emergence of digital media starting at the end of the twentieth century has been not just an incremental but a fundamental change.

Photographs are historical documents, in the sense that they record what was in front of the lens at a specific time and place, and have become the primary visual evidence used in publications and in moving pictures. By knowing more about the process of creation—how photographs were originally used, or the purpose for which they were made—we are better able to interpret them as documents. And of course as a collection of visual documents, this book in its own way is also a historical portrait of Virginia.

PHOTOGRAPHY
IN VIRGINIA

Woman and child
Daguerreotype, quarter-plate, c. 1845–50
Subjects unidentified. *Valentine Richmond History Center, V.30.33*

CHAPTER ONE

EARLY PHOTOGRAPHY IN VIRGINIA

Photography did not burst onto the scene in Virginia as it did in France. In Paris, Louis Daguerre's invention made a dramatic entrance in January 1839, when the prominent scientist François Arago announced the discovery to the Académie des Sciences. At the event brilliant examples were shown, and the cognoscenti marveled. By contrast, photography as introduced to Virginians was an imperfect art practiced by itinerants. From rented rooms these "professors" made plates that were not always successful in showing an image, and when they did sometimes soon faded.

A number of cultural strands of the late eighteenth and early nineteenth centuries came together in photography. The era of scientific investigation was underway with discoveries in chemistry and the properties of light. Among scientists and gentlemen scholars there was great interest in the nature of vision, and in optics and in optical instruments that could magnify, refract, and serve as an aid to recording. The broader public was paying ever more attention to visual phenomena and to pictures of all kinds. For the class that could afford to have portraits, visiting artists usually produced them. Then came the itinerant daguerreotypers, who took the airs of artists, advertised like showmen, and acted like salesmen.

THE CAMERA OBSCURA AT MONTICELLO

Some of the components of photography were present in Virginia long before 1839. The "camera obscura" was based on an optical principle known to Aristotle, that in a darkened room a pinhole opening would project the light of the outside scene onto the surface opposite. The earliest full description appeared in the tenth century in the writings of the Arabian scholar Alhazen. By the Renaissance, a por-

Camera obscura, 1793
The camera obscura used a lens to project an image onto a ground-glass screen at the back of a chamber. It was like seeing an image through a modern camera but without a way of capturing and preserving the images. This portable camera obscura is thought to be the instrument fabricated by David Rittenhouse of Philadelphia and acquired by Thomas Jefferson in 1793.
Thomas Jefferson Foundation

table camera obscura had been fabricated, using a lens to capture the image and with the viewer sitting inside a tent-like chamber. In the late 1600s a portable camera obscura was developed that was an optical instrument, a wooden box in which a lens at one end projected an image onto a ground glass at the other end.

The camera obscura became a craze in the early 1700s. Portable instruments served as an aid to sketching for artists and as an amusement for the moneyed. By the early 1800s, a century later, the image of the world as seen through a lens was becoming familiar to many educated people. Of the inventors of photography, Daguerre and William Henry Fox Talbot especially were driven by the vision of capturing and making permanent the image on the ground glass of the camera obscura.[1]

One Virginian with an active interest in optical devices was Thomas Jefferson, one of the great collectors of his time.[2] In addition to a telescope, a hand magnifier, a solar microscope, prisms, and a perspective glass, Jefferson over time acquired two camera obscuras and another related device. The latter was a scioptric ball, purchased in London in 1786 and which he referred to as an "Artificial eye in brass."[3] It was a lens mounted in a metal sphere atop a stand that looked like a candlestick-holder. Set in the window of a darkened room, the scioptric ball could covert the chamber into a camera obscura.

In 1793, while serving in Philadelphia, Jefferson borrowed a box-type camera obscura from its builder, David Rittenhouse, an inventor and astronomer, so his daughter Mary could "take a few lessons in drawing from nature."[4] The next year he purchased the instrument from Rittenhouse. This is possibly the same one that his granddaughter Cornelia Jefferson Randolph used at Monticello in the 1820s and that is part of the Monticello collection today.

Jefferson's third camera obscura was purchased for him in 1805 in London by geographer William Tatham. Its location is not known today. It was described as "A Camera Obscura, with extra Glasses constructed in the best manner by Adams," and it folded into a compact package when not in use. Jefferson seems to have acquired it to entertain his daughter's family.[5]

SAINT-MÉMIN AND THE PHYSIONOTRACE

Virginia had long been a place artists passed through without settling. A portrait painter would lease quarters at a crossroads, or circulate to the homes of a particular social set, and stay until the market for his services was saturated. The sorts of ancillary business that might help to anchor an artist community, such as publishers who needed engravings, did not take hold in Virginia until the mid-nineteenth century.

One artistic traveler was the French portraitist, Charles-Balthazar-Julien Févret de Saint-Mémin (1770–1852), who worked in Richmond in the period 1807–08. He is well known for his profile portraits, which he executed in two formats, drawings and engravings. The drawings, almost always presented in

Thomas Jefferson
Engraving, by Charles-Balthazar-Julien Févret de Saint-Mémin, 1805
Saint-Mémin used a mechanical device called the physionotrace to sketch Jefferson from life in 1803. With the assistance of a mechanism called a pantograph, the artist transferred the drawing at a smaller scale to an engraving plate. He issued a first edition of this print in 1804 that was oval in shape, and the round second edition the following year. *Virginia Historical Society*

octagonal wood frames, are in chalk or crayon on paper that was often tinted pink. Saint-Mémin was advertising in Richmond newspapers in July 1807 and apparently stayed into spring of the following year. He arrived in Richmond when the town was full of visitors for the Aaron Burr treason trial, which took place in August-September 1807.[6]

In less than a year Saint-Mémin made portraits of over 120 individuals. He typically delivered, as recorded in an 1808 invoice, "a likeness in chalk, copperplate, and 12 engravings," the prints being nearly identical to the drawing.[7] He was able to achieve such high production through the use of a machine, the "physionotrace." This device was derived from another mechanism of that period, the "pantograph." The pantograph was a copying machine—Jefferson had one—made of rods hinged together in the shape of two parallelograms. As the operator moved a dry pen, or stylus, to trace the lines of an original drawing, the motion was transmitted by the rod-parallelograms to a marking stylus, a pencil or other drawing instrument, to make an exact copy on another sheet. The pantograph could be adjusted so that the copy was either larger or smaller than the source, yet still proportional.

The exact functioning of the physionotrace, the machine used by Saint-Mémin, is not known. None survives, and there is only a single sketch of one. It seems to have been a panel about five feet by two feet, mounted on two legs and then standing like an easel on a third leg. The panel held a modified pantograph. The operator, instead of moving a dry stylus to control the motion of the marking stylus, looked through an eyepiece—without a lens, it seems to have been more a viewing hole with a cross-hair—and presumably moved the point of the cross-hair over the lines of the subject. "The machine," according to Appleton's, "only gave the outline, the finishing being done in one case with crayon, and in the other with the graven and roulette."[8]

Machinery helped not only to capture the image but also to multiply it. Using either the physionotrace, adjusted to function as a pantograph, or a separate pantograph, Saint-Mémin was able to copy each drawing at a much reduced size to an engraving plate with great fidelity.

PROFESSOR JOHN WILLIAM DRAPER AT HAMPDEN-SYDNEY

In 1839, the year photography became publicly known, at least one resident of Virginia knew enough to fully appreciate the discoveries. John William Draper (1811–1882) was twenty-eight years old and in his third year as a professor at Hampden-Sydney College. He was not an inventor of photography, but his experiments brought him tantalizingly close, and he was among the most important of the first wave of photographic practitioners.

Draper was English born and raised. His studies in chemistry at London University ended when his family moved to Mecklenburg County, Virginia, in 1832. Living in Christiansburg (not the present city of that name, but today's Chase City), he conducted scientific experiments and maintained his subscriptions to British journals. After London, however, Draper did at times feel isolated in Virginia, as if he were "in the depths of forests, alike unused to music, to poetry, or to philosophy." His biographer Donald Fleming writes that he "kept to the end of his life the sense of belonging to the European intellectual community, the sense, it would almost seem at times, of being in exile." Draper

John William Draper (1811–1882)
National Museum of American History, Smithsonian Institution

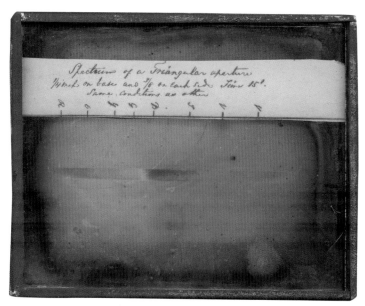

Light spectrum
Daguerreotype, by John William Draper, c. 1840
In his Virginia experiments, Draper recorded the refraction of white light into the colors of the spectrum on light-sensitive paper but was not able to preserve his result. Using a daguerreotype, after he moved to New York, Draper was able to preserve the results. His notes state: "Spectrum of a Triangular aperture/ 1/4 inch on base and 3/8 on each side/ Time 15' [minutes]. Same conditions as other." The letters read from bottom: R [red] O [orange] Y [yellow] G [green] B [blue] I [? indigo?] V [violet] V [violet]. *Smithsonian Institution, National Museum of American History, Photographic History Collection*

published eight research papers from 1834 to 1836. In 1835–36 he studied at the University of Pennsylvania and earned his degree in March 1836.[9]

Returning to Virginia as a M.D., he became associated with the Mineralogical Society of Virginia, which led to a teaching position at Hampden-Sydney College in Prince Edward County. In fall 1836 Draper became professor of chemistry and natural philosophy (that is, physics). At Hampden-Sydney, Draper continued to perform experiments, mostly related to the effects of light on chemical reactions. One area of study was the "action of the spectrum on silver salts," which were known to be light sensitive. A valuable discovery was that paper made light sensitive by absorbing silver salt solution was significantly more affected by blue light than by red or green light.[10]

Draper conducted tests on light passing through various chemical solutions, utilizing a prism and light-sensitized paper, and discovered different patterns of visible light absorption. A good portion of his investigations centered on the differing properties and behavior of individual colors of light. A camera lens, for example, that is optically uncorrected acts similarly to a prism and refracts the light passing through it, such that each color comes into focus at a slightly varying distance from the lens. Opticians in this period were learning to make corrected, or achromatic, lenses, designed so that the different colors of visible light would

focus together as white light. Draper learned that one could compensate for a non-achromatic camera lens—one that was optically uncorrected—by focusing for the blue light that most affected the light-sensitive paper.[11]

Much of Draper's pre-1839 research became, after the introduction of the daguerreotype, directly applicable to problems in making portraits. In 1863 Draper wrote that "I wish you had seen the Journal of the Franklin Inst of Phila from about 1836 to 1839 and so been acquainted with what I wrote on the Chemical action of light before any person in America had turned attention to the subject or Daguerre or Talbot had published anything."[12] For example, "from considering the difficulty of getting an impression from colored surfaces as red or green," he realized "the necessity of enlarging the aperture of the lens, and diminishing its focus [that is, its focal length], so as to have the image as bright as possible; for it was plain that in no other way landscapes could be taken or silhouettes replaced by portraits."[13]

Prior to 1839 Draper had temporarily captured camera obscura images on light sensitive paper, but like the similar experiments of Thomas Wedgwood some forty years earlier, the images faded away when exposed to light because they were unfixed. Draper knew of Herschel's discovery of "hyposulphite of soda," which became the fixer used to preserve images, but when Draper tried it he "found it removed the black as well as the white parts . . . probably owing to my having used too strong a solution."[14]

Draper, like few other experimenters at the time, was within reach of all the elements necessary to make photography work. What he seems to have lacked, as a scientist working simultaneously in a number of directions, was the intense vision of capturing the camera image that drove inventors like Daguerre and Talbot. In Draper's own description of his near miss, he does not seem nearly as single-minded as they, as suggested by his use of "amused": "I had long known what had been done," wrote Draper, "by Wedgwood and Davy, had amused myself with repeating some of their experiments, and had even unsuccessfully tried the use of Hyposulphite of soda. . . ."[15]

Through his journal subscriptions, Draper stayed in touch with the European scene as announcements regarding the photographic process unfolded during 1839. Plates produced by Daguerre's method were shown at the Académie des Sciences in Paris on 7 January. This first revelation was not specific about the process, but it nonetheless prompted the English experimenter William Fox Talbot to hurriedly submit his results to print. A description of Talbot's method was published in a London journal in late January, and several other articles followed. Enough detail was included for Draper to attempt in spring 1839 to repeat Talbot's process. He did not have great success, however, which he blamed

Earliest Virginia camera
This camera was discovered in the physics lab at Hampden-Sydney College in the early 1930s by a student, Howard C. Cobbs. It is an early design, modeled after Daguerre's 1839 camera. No older camera of Virginia provenance is known. Because Daguerre's description did not reach the U.S. until Sept. 1839, after John W. Draper had moved to New York, Draper probably did not use the camera when he taught at the college 1836–39. Possibly Draper acquired it in New York and sent it to Hampden-Sydney, where his double brother-in-law, Daniel Gardner, filled his former post 1839–42. Draper could have delivered and demonstrated the camera himself on a visit to family. The camera was loaned to the Smithsonian in 1940 and returned to Hampden-Sydney in 2006. *Atkinson Museum, Hampden-Sydney College*

on "insufficient sensitiveness in the bromine paper." At that point Draper said he "waited anxiously for the divulging of Daguerre's process, respecting which statements were beginning to be made in the papers."[16]

Specifically Draper may have been referring to artist and inventor Samuel Morse's letter on "The Daguerreotipe," written from Paris on 9 March 1839 and copied widely in the American press. Draper might have seen it in the May 1839 issue of Edmund Ruffin's Virginia-based journal of agriculture, *The Farmer's Register*. The daguerreotype process was publicly presented in Paris in August 1839, and the technical description reached the United States in September.[17]

At the dawn of American photography, Draper did indeed begin to make daguerreotypes. By then, however, he had left Virginia, having accepted an appointment as professor of chemistry and botany at the University of the City of New York (today's New York University). In New York Draper became an associate of Morse and an important technical contributor to the early practice of photography in America. His knowledge of light, silver salts, and ways to make lenses faster was immediately relevant. Draper was among the first to make a successful portrait, including perhaps the earliest photographic portrait image extant, of his sister Dorothy.[18]

THE DAGUERREOTYPE IN VIRGINIA

Photography arrived in the U.S. in fall 1839. Boston, New York, and Philadelphia were the initial centers, and from those places it spread, reaching the District of Columbia by March 1840. That month at the Medical College Hall in Washington, in connection with an exhibition of "sun-painted pictures," an advertisement promised "a lecture on the art of Daguerreotype" and demonstrations "performed by means of a complete apparatus."[19]

Almost all early U.S. photography took the form of the daguerreotype. The method had been publicly revealed in France and was not protected by patent. Materials and courses of instruction were soon available. As a medium it was vivid and alluring, although eventually it proved limited in versatility. Like modern slide film, the actual material that was loaded into the camera for the shot was processed into the final daguerreotype. A copper plate was coated with silver, cleaned and polished, sensitized in iodine vapor, exposed, developed in mercury vapor, fixed, and washed, then mounted under glass. The image was reversed left to right. The English experimenter Talbot's process of paper negative to paper positive, although the basis for future methods, was little practiced in the U.S.

For most places outside the big eastern cities, the early years of photography were the era of the itinerant. In July 1841, "Daguerreotype Miniatures" were advertised in Richmond, the earliest such notice found for Virginia. The advertisement made a virtue of the flopping of the image: "The time required for sitting is just two minutes, and develops every feature and expression of the countenance as correctly as if reflected in a mirror." Prices were substantial at $5 and $6.[20] Not long after, in October 1841, the daguerreotypist Paulsen thanked "the citizens of Richmond for the patronage he has received in this city, and informs them that he will remain during the present week."[21]

The itinerant daguerreotypers, like the earlier portraitists in oils or Saint-Mémin employing his mechanism, probably gauged the length of a stay to the response: how long those who desired a portrait and could afford it kept coming forward. Practitioners sometimes billed their appearances like a theatrical company, using attention-grabbing headers, subtitles with story-hooks, selected clips from reviews, and warnings of imminent departure dates. As a whole, the initial forays of the itinerants may not have always been wonderfully successful in their results, for there is an absence of glowing reports of the early daguerreotypes. Paulsen in October 1841 probably provided his guarantee out of necessity: "Likenesses are made Perfect and satisfactory, or no charge."[22]

In December 1841 J. M. Edwards and T. N. Starr announced themselves as "the pupils, and one of them late assistant of Professor Morse of New York." The *Richmond Compiler* described them as "polite, obliging, and competent," and observed, "The painter's art may present the human face with a livelier glow, with the warmth of coloring, but his art may err: The impressions of the Daguerreotype are as unerring as truth itself."[23] Just over a year later in Richmond, in March 1843, J. M. Emerson addressed the *Compiler's* critique by providing "Daguereo-

type Miniatures with the colors. Not only is the skin of a natural appearance, but the actual color is given to the face." Taking advantage of the presence of the legislature, Emerson announced the move of "his apparatus to one of the Committee Rooms of the Capitol, where he will remain until the close of the Session." Moving on to Petersburg not long after in May 1843, Emerson was advertising "an accurate and durable Likeness by the Daguerreotype process," but only for a short time. "Mr. E has engagements at other places, which call him away soon."[24]

In Norfolk, J. D. Keeler advertised "Photographic Likenesses by the Daguerreotype Process" in October 1843. "He has taken a room at the corner of Main and Talbot streets." The *Norfolk American Beacon* commented, "Some of them might be taken for miniatures beautifully painted on ivory. . . . A frame, containing a number of his specimens, may be seen in the Reading Room during this day." Keeler's notice warned, "His stay in Norfolk will be for a short time only."[25]

In September 1844, James Burney advertised to "the citizens of Lynchburg" that "he will remain for a few days" and "is prepared to take Daguerreotype Portraits superior to any that have ever been taken in this place, and equal to any in the world." Presenting samples of work was already standard procedure: "He has a variety of specimens on hand, and invites ladies and gentlemen to call and examine them."[26] Doubtless many places in Virginia were introduced to photography by such itinerants who went unrecorded.

Galleries, as daguerreotype studios were called, began to be established in the state during the mid-to-late 1840s. Where an itinerant might have worked in a single room with a window, resident daguerreotypers installed improved facilities. Galleries took their name from a public room separate from the posing room, typically a well-appointed Victorian parlor for waiting where sample

Small portrait and Locket
Daguerreotype, 1 inch diameter, c. 1846–56
Locket, gold alloy, 1.75 inch diameter (contains two facing daguerreotypes), c. 1846–56
A small portrait such as this one of Judith Harrison (Tomlin) Coalter (1807–1859) might be mounted in a broach or pin, displayed in a tiny frame, or kept in a locket like the one illustrated. The daguerreotype supplanted the painted miniature as the art of choice for personal keepsakes. *Virginia Historical Society, Gift of Mrs. John Worth McAlister*

Unidentified subject by Unknown
Daguerreotype, quarter-plate, c. 1845–50
As is the case with most surviving American daguerreotypes, neither the subject of this portrait nor the daguerreotyper is identified. Typical too is that there is no information about its provenance, such as the family in which it was passed down. All that can be said is that because this particular portrait is in a Virginia collection, there is a good chance that the subject was a Virginian. *Virginia Historical Society*

Town view of Lynchburg
Daguerreotype, whole-plate, c. 1848–52
The view from Daniels Hill looks east toward the covered bridge across the James River, with the James River & Kanawha Canal at left in front of the river, Madison Heights rising to the left beyond, and Percivals Island downstream. The only daguerreotypist associated with Lynchburg who is known to have made whole-plate landscapes was Jesse Whitehurst, who advertised one of Richmond in 1848. *Valentine Richmond History Center 61.218.1*

work was displayed. Galleries were not evenly spread across Virginia but congregated in the larger towns, in Norfolk, Lynchburg, and Petersburg, with the highest concentration in Richmond. Almost all state travel passed through those hubs, where the river and canal routes and the railroad lines that began opening in the late 1830s converged. Later many communities, even small ones, had a resident photographer, but not in the daguerreotype era. It was not as if this concentration was an inconvenience: posing for a portrait was a rare event for most, and itinerant photographers continued to work rural areas.[27]

While it is not surprising that the early daguerreotype period would have been unsettled, to a significant degree the changeableness of the trade never ceased. Only a handful of daguerreotypers sustained themselves in one place for any period of time, and galleries that stayed open under the same name tended to have a lot of staff turnover.[28] But if daguerreotypists had in common a kind of wanderlust in their DNA, in other respects they came from different backgrounds. One of the first to operate a Virginia gallery for as long as two years was Henry Bryant, who was in Richmond 1844–46. From the Hartford, Connecticut, area, Bryant was a portrait painter turned itinerant daguerrean. In 1844 he came south with James D. Willard, a partner from Hartford. Willard & Bryant worked two weeks in Charleston, in western Virginia, after which the partners split. Bryant came to Richmond later that year and opened at 89 Main Street.[29]

A daguerreotypist who came to the trade from another direction was F. W. Burwell. In April 1845 Burwell rented rooms at Main and Talbot streets, Norfolk, offering "Daguerreotype Portraits." At the same address a few months later in July 1845, offer-

Ann and Maria Hall
Daguerreotype, sixth-plate, c. 1849
The sisters were from Culpeper, Virginia, a place that did not have a resident daguerreotyper. The Halls may have visited a gallery in Charlottesville or Alexandria, or an itinerant may have passed through Culpeper, perhaps setting up on court day. *Virginia Historical Society, Gift of Mrs. John R. Norris*

White Sulphur Springs
Daguerreotype, c. 1845–50.
The view of the resort, today the Greenbrier in West Virginia, has been attributed to James Presley Ball (1825–1904). Ball was an early African American photographer who wrote that he "acquired the art of Daguereotyping" at the resort in 1845. The attribution to Ball, while not impossible, is probably wishful thinking. The maker could have just as easily been his teacher, John B. Bailey, or another itinerant daguerreotyper for whom the mineral springs resorts would have been an attractive location in the summer months. *University of Virginia Special Collections, Mss 11531*

ing "Daguerreotype Likenesses in Colors, For a Few Days Only," were Bryant & Burwell. Most likely the Bryant was Henry, the artist out of Richmond. Burwell in years following became a prominent Norfolk watchmaker and jeweler, and one imagines he was skilled at preparing the plate and finishing cases. However he may have lacked the picture-making ability and élan of the artist Bryant.[30]

Another sort of career was that of James Presley Ball (1825–1904), a black daguerrean. He was born in Virginia and raised in Cincinnati. The only account of the Virginia phase of his career was provided by Ball himself in 1855 for the published guide to his moving panorama. In 1845 Ball "met at the White Sulphur Springs, Va., Mr. John B. Bailey, a colored gentleman" who was also free. Likely Ball was working at the resort during the summer season when numerous jobs opened up. From Bailey, Ball "acquired the art of Daguereotyping. This was the turning point of his fortune." That fall he returned to Cincinnati and opened a daguerreotype gallery. However there was little business so Ball "removed in the spring of '46 to Pittsburgh, and from thence to Richmond, Va. where he arrived with his apparatus, a small supply of materials, and a single shilling. This last he paid to the carter who hauled his heavy trunk, and found himself penniless. Nothing disheartened, he applied, and obtained employment in the dining room of a hotel, where he remained until he had accumulated a capital of one hundred dollars, with which he took and furnished a room near the capitol house. The tide now turned. The Virginians rushed in crowds to his room; all classes, white and black, bond and free sought to have their lineaments, stamped, by the artist who painted with the Sun's rays." With that note of success, Ball's Virginia chapter closed. "Again he returned to Ohio, and traveled nearly two years practicing his art." In his long career, Ball went on to open successful galleries in Cincinnati and Montana.[31]

The section of Main Street in Richmond that was the primary locus for daguerreotypists was just down the hill from Capitol Square. Ball might have obtained his supplies from S. M. Zachrisson, a chemist and druggist on Shockoe Hill. Under the heading "Attention! Daguerreotype Artists," in early 1846 Zachrisson offered "a full supply of every kind of article used in Daguerreotype, viz: Plates, Cases, Chloride of Iodine, Chloride of Gold, Hyposulphate Soda, Bromine Iodine, Distilled Mercury, Quickstuff, &c. &c." In late 1846 O. A. Strecker of Richmond offered "Daguerreotype Plates and cases, of medium and quarter size."[32]

By the late 1840s other communities around the state had gained resident galleries. W. A. Retzer came from Philadelphia, and after working in the partnership of Van Loan & Retzer in Richmond in February 1845, he went out on

Buena Vista
Daguerreotype, half-plate, hand-colored, c. 1850–56
Because daguerreotypes were not easily produced in the field, and doubtless also because of losses in the Civil War and since, there are few surviving antebellum photographic images of Virginia estates and their residents. Buena Vista—since 1873 known as La Vista—still stands in Spotsylvania County. *Virginia Historical Society*

Wren Building
Daguerreotype, half-plate, c. 1856
This view is the only photograph of the second Wren Building at the College of William and Mary, built 1710 and burnt in 1859.
Swem Library, Special Collections

Advertising cut
From the original wood-engraving, or cut, short for wood-cut, copies were made by first making a negative mold of the engraving in plaster, and then using the mold to cast in lead. One copy in lead, called a stereotype, could be made for each Whitehurst gallery, so each could advertise with the same image in the local newspaper.
Lynchburg Virginian, 14 May 1849.

his own. In May 1846 Retzer advertised "Daguerreotype Miniatures" in Lynchburg. In 1847 Retzer's Daguerrian Gallery informed the citizens of Charlottesville that its pictures were "warranted durable, and will exist for ages." A Charlottesville report from 1853 stated "Our old friend, Mr. Robert S. Jones, has become the successor of Mr. Retzer. . . . Mr. Jones was the pupil of Retzer for a considerable time, and spent a greater portion of the last summer in perfecting himself in the north." In Fredericksburg, William Burke's Daguerreotype Room in 1852 was over the *Herald's* newspaper office, where "he has a fine light." Burke promised "to produce the most characteristic and pleasing resemblance."[33]

The 1850 Census recorded two daguerreans in Winchester, John F. Baker and John W. Slager, and Kagey was listed there in an 1851 directory. Two daguerreotypers were located on King Street in Alexandria in 1851, George R. Blacklock near Pitt Street and E. L. Brockett at the corner of Royal. In June 1853 on King Street—apparently the only address an Alexandria daguerreotyper could have—a new "Sky-Light Gallery" was operated by F. B. Bailey, and Brockett continued "to take Daguerreotypes in the most elegant style of the art." By August, however, D. Haas had bought out Brockett's Alexandria Daguerrean Gallery. Two years later in August 1855 galleries were operated by N. S. Bennett, who had just won a silver medal, and by R. A. Carden, both of whom were on King near Royal.[34]

The daguerreotype was at its height in the U.S. from 1849 to 1854, with an estimated 3 million daguerreotypes made annually. The year 1853 may have been the crest of the daguerreotype's popularity. In the U.S. Census for 1850, there were nineteen people listed as working as daguerreotypists in Virginia. As a rough estimate, if each of those daguerreotypists made ten plates a day for 300 days a year, that would total about 60,000 daguerreotypes made in Virginia in the year.[35]

JESSE WHITEHURST AND HIS GALLERIES

Of Virginia daguerreans, the leading entrepreneur was Jesse Harrison Whitehurst (1819–1875). His operations grew to include four Virginia galleries and four out of state. Whitehurst "has extended the field of his operations," claimed an advertisement with justification in 1851, "over more ground than any other Daguerreotypist in the country."[36]

Whitehurst was from Princess Anne County (modern Virginia Beach). According to an 1875 obituary, he moved to Norfolk at age fifteen and learned cabinet-making. An 1853 account says that Whitehurst went to New York in 1843 to learn to daguerreotype and "through books and study, obtained knowledge enough of the art to commence for himself—which he did successfully in Charleston, S.C. In the fall of 1843, he opened a gallery in Norfolk." The obituary states that "Whitehurst was the first to introduce daguerrean work in Norfolk, in 1843, over J. M. Freeman's store, Main street." Both of these accounts, however, probably relied on information from Whitehurst himself, which might thereby have been colored.[37]

Whitehurst's early enterprise is not well documented. No records for 1843 or 1844 have been found. The 1853 account states that he opened his Richmond gallery in January 1844, but the first confirmed record for Whitehurst is a Richmond advertisement from June 1845. In it he states he "will continue a short time longer" at his Richmond rooms, words that imply he did not yet see that location as fixed. Indications are that for the first few years he worked as an itinerant, as many did, supported by Whitehurst's own reference to "the liberal patronage which he has received,

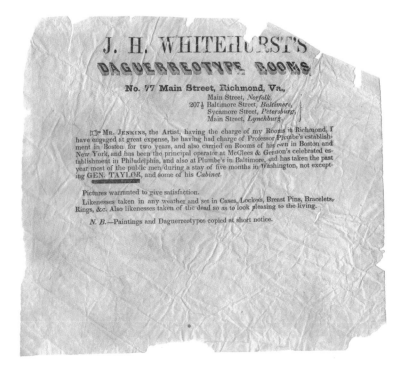

Willie Anne Anderson
Daguerreotype, sixth-plate, by Whitehurst Gallery, c. 1845–50
The subject was from a Louisa County family. Of the various Whitehurst locations, the portrait was likely made in the Richmond gallery.
Virginia Historical Society. Gift of J. Madison Macon, IV

Richmond handbill
Paper, 6.7 x 7 in.
By its reference to Zachary Taylor as president, the text dates from March 1849 to July 1850. During the several years that the British-born Solon Jenkins was an operator for Whitehurst in Richmond, he periodically went to Washington to make portraits of "the public men." A small bill such as this one may have been handed out at a fair or other public event.
Virginia Historical Society

in both Northern and Southern cities." In September 1845, three months after the Richmond notice, a Norfolk advertisement announces that "he has again returned and is prepared to serve" patrons. If Whitehurst's language is precise, he had not only returned to his home town for a second appearance, but was returning again for at least a third appearance. In that Norfolk notice, too, the final lines state, "Also 170 1-2 Main St., opposite the Banks, Richmond Va., for a short time only." Rather than give up his Richmond location when he shifted to Norfolk, Whitehurst kept the space. It was an early step in building his chain, although he may not have envisioned such at the time. [38]

In 1848 Whitehurst called his Richmond branch "the oldest gallery in the state," so it could well have been his first. By then he had moved to 77 Main Street, several blocks downhill from the main locus of daguerreotypers in the city. It is not known when Whitehurst established his Norfolk gallery on a regular basis. The earliest notice found is from January 1848, when it was located at Newton's Row, on the south side of Main Street. Whitehurst operated with the two galleries, Richmond and Norfolk, until late 1848. By then he employed eight assistants between them and had accumulated sufficient economic standing to expand. In November

of that year he moved to open new galleries in Petersburg and Lynchburg. [39]

In Petersburg Whitehurst purchased a building on Sycamore Street and renovated it—"neither sparing pains nor expense"—by installing a "splendid sky-light" and "running a stair-way and making an entrance from the street." In Lynchburg Whitehurst took over the gallery of Peter E. Gibbs. Gibbs in August 1848 announced he was "having fitted up" a "Large Sky Light Gallery." In early November 1848, his new space not yet completed, Gibbs reported that he had "spent some time" in Whitehurst's Richmond gallery, "for the purpose of improving himself in the art of daguerreotyping." Meanwhile, Whitehurst in his Petersburg notices announced that he would be present in that city on two days, the 5th and 15th of November. Between those dates he apparently traveled to Lynchburg and made a convincing argument to Gibbs, probably fortified by a financial investment. A mid-November advertisement announced that Whitehurst "has taken the house . . . occupied by Mr. P. E. Gibbs" and "is now putting it in thorough repair, and erecting a large Sky Light." Gibbs became Whitehurst's manager in Lynchburg. [40]

Whitehurst looked to expand his trade beyond only standard portraits and advertised "likenesses of infant Children, Corpses, copying of Paintings, Daguerre-

Tarifa Witherspoon
Daguerreotype, sixth-plate, by Whitehurst Gallery, c. 1848–56 Because the subject was from a Petersburg family, it seems probable that the image was made in Whitehurst's Petersburg gallery. *Virginia Historical Society, Gift of Mrs. Robert Pemberton*

Whitehurst and photographers
Salt print, 11 x 14 inches, c. 1855–57
The photograph came from an album assembled by John R. Johnston, who was a colorist and painter for Whitehurst's Baltimore gallery in the late 1850s. Among those recognizable are the three Vannerson brothers from Richmond: in the back row, second from left is Lucian and fifth from left is Adrian, and in the front row, third from left is Julian. By his central position, it seems likely that the man seated behind the table is entrepreneur Jesse Whitehurst, of whom no other portrait is known. *Courtesy of Vintage Works Ltd.*

otypes, &c." He established a "Great Depot of Daguerreotype materials at the Richmond Gallery," probably as stock for the other Virginia galleries and also offered "for sale at New York prices." The new galleries must have been paying for themselves rather quickly. In the latter half of 1849, Whitehurst opened a gallery in Baltimore, a considerably larger city than any in Virginia. He probably knew Baltimore from his days as a traveling daguerreotyper and because it was linked to Hampton Roads by regular steamer service.[41]

At the beginning of 1850, and including the Baltimore gallery, Whitehurst reported that he employed twenty-one assistants, and his shops "were taking at the rate of 20,000 Likenesses annually." With this level of business activity supporting him, Whitehurst in 1850 opened new galleries in Washington, D.C., and New York City. That August he advertised in Richmond, "Eight No. 1 Daguerreotypists wanted by the first of October." Both of these high-profile locations would have required a sizable investment to launch. New York offered much potential for financial return if successful. In Washington it was not so much profit but prestige that might be acquired. Galleries in both cities could attract the famous to sit and benefit the whole chain.[42]

Whitehurst is remembered more as an entrepreneur than as a photographer. If several views that were probably his had not been lost, his reputation might be different. In 1848 the Richmond gallery invited the public to view "a splendid Daguerreotype of over 250 persons, including the beautiful Engine and Fire Company of No. 5, on one of the largest daguerreotype plates ever used, which were taken instantaneously as they passed up Main Street." Such a plate would have required a special extra large camera and lens; another report indicates that it was Whitehurst using this camera, and that he had become proficient at oversize plates. In September 1850 Whitehurst made "twelve splendid views of the Falls of the Niagara on double whole size plates." A whole plate was 6 x 8 inches, so a double plate could have been as large as 8 x 12 inches. The Niagara views became his exhibition at the Crystal Palace, the Great Exhibition of 1851 at London; one observer called the display "a grand conception of Mr. Whitehurst's." At the 1853 American Fair in New York City, wrote a critic, "Whitehurst has a few good pictures in a large and passable collection; he has ten pictures illustrating the Falls of Niagara, which are very well executed."[43]

With a large chain there were ups and downs. The New York gallery was at 349 Broadway, an excellent corner location, but Whitehurst had misfortune when it suffered a fire in 1852. Insurance policies in this period would not cover such loss; in August 1852 Whitehurst sold the gallery to Jeremiah Gurney. In January 1853 Whitehurst opened a gallery in Wilmington, N.C., located in Mozart

Young girl
Daguerreotype, half-plate, handcolored, by Whitehurst Gallery, c. 1851–54 The subject is unidentified. *Virginia Historical Society, Gift of Virginia Stuart Waller Davis*

Hall, Front Street. First hired to run the gallery was Benjamin F. Harrison, and then in 1854 M. M. Mallon came to run it.[44]

Whitehurst's chain seems to have been more closely managed than that of John Plumbe, Jr., the only other American chain of any size. Once Whitehurst opened his Baltimore gallery, he made it his base of operations. His job became one of dealing with property, contracting for materials, and hiring and teaching operators. In September 1851 H. H. Snelling of New York noted the "number of western and southern Daguerreans, who have come eastward for the purpose of purchasing their winter's supply of materials," including "Whitehurst of Baltimore." Whitehurst's galleries served as a training ground for much young talent. He was probably traveling much of the time, for one advertisement stated that he visited each gallery every quarter. He seems to have had a variety of local arrangements. In one Petersburg advertisement Whitehurst was listed as "sole proprietor," but without some sort of profit-sharing there would have been insufficient motivation for his managers to be active or honest. By June 1852 his Lynchburg operator, Peter Gibbs, was listed as the proprietor in advertisements, and by 1853, although Whitehurst kept Lynchburg on his list of locations, Gibbs was advertising under his own name.[45]

A task that Whitehurst seems to have performed himself was writing the copy for his advertisements. He always had an angle or a one-up for the competition. In 1845 he offered "Colored Daguerreotype portraits," taken in "clear, cloudy and even in stormy weather." In 1848 he was pitching a "Splendid Sky Light" and "Electro Daguerreotyping," the latter described as an "Electro Galvanic Process." These came together in the heading "Splendid Sky-light Electro Daguerreotypes."[46] Additionally in 1848 Whitehurst commissioned an artist to make a wood engraving of a studio interior, which he duplicated in stereotype and distributed around the chain to use as an illustration in each location's advertising.[47]

In 1850 Whitehurst cautioned "all Daguerreotypists against using his Rotary Background, as a patent for the same has been applied for."[48] That year too he announced the "important discovery" of the "Ivory Daguerreotype." By 1852–53 he was calling attention to the "Grand and Free Exhibition!" available at the galleries, "comprising likenesses of the most prominent individuals of the age."[49] Beginning in 1853 he asked, "What higher testimony of merit can be given for the superior excellence of works of art than Medals?" The advertisements recounted the medals and prizes won, with headings "Whitehurst's Medals" and "Whitehurst Again Triumphant" for a gold medal in Maryland, and, after two medals at the 1853 World's Fair in London, "Another Premium" from the Crystal Palace at New York.[50] He began to run favorable quotes from publications such as the

Baltimore Clipper: "Whitehurst's Pictures are unequalled. Their particular excellence lies in the richness of the light thrown upon them, and in the gracefulness of posture." And then there was another round of varieties, the ivory daguerreotype, the mammoth daguerreotype, and the stereoscopic, or solid, daguerreotype.[51]

By the later 1850s the photography trade had grown to include more than just the daguerreotype. The old business model for a portrait gallery had flourished when the competition was the miniature painter and that trade's relatively high price for a portrait. New popular galleries engaged in price-cutting and generally required higher volume to compensate for the lower prices. Adapting was not always easy. "His attention was too much drawn from the work in hand," the 1875 account said, "to other and larger operations, his daguerrean business commenced declining." Whitehurst's empire receded and "finally was abandoned."[52]

In January 1855 he closed the Wilmington gallery. By 1856 the proprietor of the Petersburg gallery was N. M. Wevere. In June 1856 the manager of the Norfolk gallery was Fowler, who had been sent down from Baltimore. A small ad for the Norfolk gallery appeared as late as November 1857, but a year later, when the 1859 Norfolk directory was compiled, Whitehurst's location had been taken over by a different firm, Burwell & Hobday. In Richmond Albert Litch was manager of Whitehurst's in February 1857. By 1859 the location had been taken over by a different photographer, J. H. Watson. Whitehurst kept the Baltimore gallery open until 1863. In his late career he left photography altogether. At his death in 1875 he had recently "located several (before undiscovered) rich guano islands in the Caribbean Sea, after years of intense and severe examination."[53]

WILLIAM A. PRATT

William A. Pratt (1818–1879) was a different sort of big-thinking Virginia daguerreotypist. Born in England, in 1832 Pratt came with his family to the District of Columbia, where they settled in Alexandria. He studied architecture and civil engineering and at eighteen worked as an engineer on the Chesapeake and Ohio Canal. In the early 1840s Pratt lived in Baltimore and was a superintendent at Green Mount cemetery. Established in 1839, Green Mount was Baltimore's version of the era's new park like cemeteries, with structures designed in revival styles that expressed the romanticism of the era—very much Pratt's taste in his own architectural work.

The earliest record that links Pratt to photography is from March 1846, when he was awarded U. S. Patent #4423 for a daguerreotype coloring process. The patent listed his address, presumably at the time of application, as Alexandria, District of Columbia. The complexity of the procedure described in the patent indicates that Pratt had been working with daguerreotypes for some time by then.

There is reason to think that Pratt gained his experience through John Plumbe, Jr.'s daguerreotype operations. Plumbe (1809–1857) was a key figure in early American photography, an entrepreneur whose chain of studios in their time ranged farther than Jesse Whitehurst's. Plumbe was born in Britain like Pratt and nine years older. He learned to daguerreotype in Boston, opening his first gallery and school there in 1841. Probably working with graduates of his train-

ing program, Plumbe set up a string of galleries in other cities, including one as far away as Dubuque, Iowa Territory, operated by his brother Richard Plumbe. At his New York branch Plumbe developed a manufacturing capability for daguerreotype materials. Paired with the intangible of the Plumbe brand name, the distribution of equipment and supplies was probably the most tangible element to the chain.[54]

At the greatest extent there were some twenty-five galleries affiliated with Plumbe. The Plumbe gallery in Petersburg, the only one in Virginia to last for any time, operated c. 1845–47. In late 1844 the Plumbe National Daguerrean Gallery opened in Washington, the first resident gallery in the city to survive more than a year, and Plumbe moved his base of operations there. Plumbe had reasons beyond business for locating in the capital. His great cause was advocating a transcontinental railroad, which proximity to Congress and the government could facilitate.[55]

Either or both of Plumbe's galleries in Washington and Baltimore are likely places for William Pratt to have learned the daguerreotype trade. There is no direct evidence, but there are hints of connections. A Plumbe advertisement from September 1845 lists an Alexandria location, at the Lyceum, about the time that Pratt applied for his patent from the same city. Then, Pratt opened a gallery in Richmond in 1846 at 139 Main Street. A Plumbe publication from January 1847 lists that street address as an affiliate of a Plumbe publishing venture. There are indications that Pratt may have purchased supplies from Plumbe's distribution center. However Pratt never advertised any connection to Plumbe, whose ambitious enterprises began to falter in 1847 and came apart by 1848.[56]

Pratt had a ten-year run as a Richmond daguerreotypist. Although he always put his starting date at 1846, no record has been found before 1848. Pratt's rise

Old man
Daguerreotype, sixth-plate, by William A. Pratt, c. 1846–51. The subject is unidentified.
Collection of Richard L. Bland

was steady. In the Richmond personal property tax records, Pratt is not listed in 1846 or 1847. He first appears in 1848 as owning a gold watch, the exemplary status gadget of the time. In 1849 and 1850 Pratt is listed as owning a gold watch and one slave over twelve years old. Pratt's first address, 139 Main Street, was centrally located in the printing and publishing district below Capitol Square. Pratt's 1848 advertisements include an engraving of the building, probably after Pratt's own rendering, shown with the sign "Virginia Daguerrian Gallery." He did good business and in an 1853 advertisement claimed to have made over 35,000 portraits, an average of about 5,000 per year.[57]

Pratt was able to think creatively and nurture big ideas, which no doubt marked him as a character. He seems to have been persuasive in conversation. Among Pratt's better-known portraits is one of Edgar Allen Poe in September 1849. Pratt probably told the tale of its taking more than once:

> "I knew him well, and he had often promised me to sit for a picture, but had never done so. One morning—in September, I think—I was standing at my street door when he came along and spoke to me. I reminded him of his unfulfilled promise, for which he made some excuse. I said, 'Come upstairs now.' He replied, 'Why, I am not dressed for it.' 'Never mind that,' said I; 'I'll gladly take you just as you are.' He came up, and I took that picture."[58]

As evidenced by his 1846 patent, Pratt was interested in innovation. In 1848 he advertised the "Celerotype"—"purchased for us at a very heavy outlay"—which enabled the portrait to be "taken in an incredibly short time." In late 1850 Pratt announced he had rights to the Talbotype, another name for the calotype, a paper print from a paper negative; and to the Hyalotype, an image on glass for use in a magic lantern. There is no evidence that either ever amounted to more than a novelty item in Virginia. Pratt continued to develop his own techniques: in 1851 he wrote about "producing his medallion pictures," which involved masking the plate during exposure by shooting through an oval vignette.[59]

While running the daguerreotype gallery, on the side Pratt worked in architecture and design. In 1847 he drew plans for a new Richmond cemetery, including "roads, paths, and ponds." His proposal

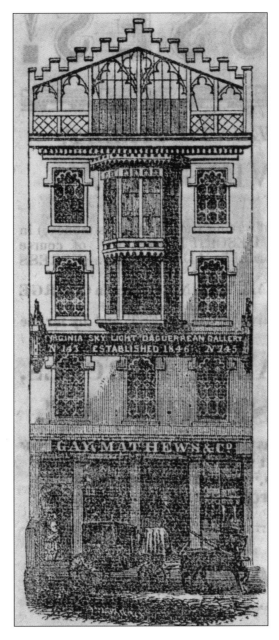

Pratt's gallery, 145 Main Street
Engraving, *Elliot & Nye's* Virginia Directory, 1852
William A. Pratt himself designed the "Gothic Window" for his new gallery location. Its thirty-foot height and contiguous skylight made the studio room bright, and the distinctive look made the location a Richmond landmark. *Virginia Historical Society*

was too expensive for the cemetery developers, so they hired another designer who provided a more feasible plan and the name, Hollywood Cemetery. In the late 1840s Pratt designed and built a pair of houses on North Fifth Street in Richmond in a style he called "Cottage ornée," one of which he used for a dwelling. Thus when his gallery was ready for a new space, the renovation was "from drawings designed and executed by the proprietor." The move took place in February 1851 and went a few doors up the hill to 145 Main Street.[60]

Pratt's new "Virginia Sky Light Daguerrean Gallery" was the acme of its kind in Virginia and worthy of a few words of description. The gallery occupied the second, third, and fourth floors of the building. Up a flight of stairs, "the visitor is ushered into a superb reception room" the width of the building, with a semi-circular back wall where daguerreotypes were displayed. "Three windows light up the surface of the curved wall; each point of which is equally well adapted to show pictures." The "lower sashes of the windows are of crimson and yellow stained glass," the walls covered in black velvet, and the décor of the room includes "statuettes, curtains, divans (of crimson velvet), carpets, mirrors." To the rear of this room was "a staircase, leading to the operating rooms above," and back further was "a Ladies' retiring room, which has been fitted up and furnished with taste."[61]

The floor had apparently been removed at the fourth level to open a high-ceiling room for "the distinguishing feature of Mr. Pratt's Gallery": "The immense bay window which forms the principal ornament in front, is eight feet wide by about 16 feet in height, and in combination with the gothic screen work above, also filled with glass, forms our operating light, which is thirty feet from the floor of the room and runs back about ten feet. This window projects two feet into the street, and forms a conspicuous object in connection with the parapet above from nearly every point of the city." The new slogan for the gallery became "At the Sign of the Gothic Window." In a letter to *The Photographic Art Journal*, Pratt boasted that he had "the objects most to be desired in a Daguerrean establishment, viz.: Publicity, an immense northern window in combination with a sky-light, a fine operating room in the third-story, surrounded by the necessary offices for cleaning, buffing, &c., and a show room, which in all my travels I have not seen surpassed except in point of size."[62]

Once he had the new gallery open, Pratt did not rest on his laurels. About four months later, he left the gallery in the hands of John S. Grubb, a comrade from Alexandria, and traveled to the Crystal Palace in London. The showpieces that Pratt displayed at that 1851 exhibition probably reflected his John Plumbe connection. In May 1846, at the Great National Fair in Washington, Plumbe had demonstrated how to make the most of an opportunity to show to the public. The Fair was a large exhibition of American-produced goods, at which Plumbe, drawing upon work from a number of his galleries, presented a group of more than 300 daguerreotypes. The well-known Plumbe views of the U.S. Capitol, Patent Office, and White House may have been a part of this exhibition. In particular, Plumbe was assembling multiple daguerreotypes into groups for display. The many portraits of senators and representatives were collected in "Six frames, each containing thirty-six pictures." Another piece was "One large frame containing twenty-eight views of public buildings in New York and twenty portraits" of distinguished figures from the city.[63]

Daguerreotypers were always eager to display portraits of famous people in their galleries, and politicians soon realized that such exhibits were good for recognition. This symbiotic relationship worked not only at the national capital but also at the state level. In 1848 Pratt advertised a "free exhibition of statesmen and heroes" of the Mexican War, which he almost certainly acquired rather than photographed himself. In time Pratt did create his own assemblages. Two important pieces, now unfortunately lost, were the Virginia Legislature of 1850–51 and the Virginia Constitutional Convention of 1850–51. These probably comprised small individual portraits mounted together into a single frame.[64]

In 1850 Pratt produced "three frames enclosing jointly twenty-six portraits upon plates" that may have been, in his lifetime, the most viewed of any of his pictures. They were Pratt's entry to the Great Exhibition at the London Crystal Palace. At that exhibition, American daguerreotypes as a group won special praise and helped atone for the perceived weaknesses of the U.S. in other departments. "Every observer must be struck by the beauty of their execution," stated the jury. "Were we to particularize the individual excellences of the pictures exhibited we should far exceed the limits of space." The photography writer H. H. Snelling commented:

> W. A. Pratt & Co., of Richmond, Va. sends a grand national gallery of pictures which will be much admired for the artistic taste displayed in their arrangement as well as for their excellence as Daguerreotypes. The centre picture is a full size portrait of the Governor of Virginia. This is surrounded by portraits of the most distinguished men of that State; the whole forming a tout ensemble of excellent arrangement and superior Daguerrean skill.

Of the seven American daguerreotypers represented at the Crystal Palace, two were Virginians, Whitehurst and Pratt.[65]

The American daguerreotypes were submitted to London for the exhibition at the beginning of 1851. Some months later, around June, Pratt went himself to the Crystal Palace, and then to Paris. While there, he toured "European Galleries. I visited nearly all in England and in Paris, and found them, generally speaking, below mediocrity." In Paris he obtained "a new and beautiful coloring style called Heliotype"—the process not easily identifiable, because that name was so often

Miss Talcott
Daguerreotype, half-plate, by William A. Pratt, 1846–51
As a whole, the daguerreotypes identified as made at 139 Main Street, Pratt's first gallery, are more imaginatively posed and lit, suggesting that Pratt himself took them rather than his assistants. The subject was one of the daughters of Andrew and Harriet Randolph (Hackley) Talcott. *Virginia Historical Society*

used in photography—"with all the effect of the most exquisite miniature." He appears also to have made arrangements to import French daguerreotype plates, which he was offering for sale in 1852.[66]

Back in Virginia, Pratt embarked in January 1852 on a new project. A few days after the General Assembly convened, Pratt invited legislators to sit for him, "that he may add your portrait to his collection of the Convention and Legislatures of the Old Dominion." "Five minutes of your time is sufficient," the advertisement stated, suggesting that "the morning is the best time."[67]

A month into the session, Pratt stated that "we are now engaged at and have partially completed, the present Assembly" and renewed his call "to those who have not yet sat." He planned "a complete picture" of the legislature "in a splendid frame, valued at two hundred dollars." In return for their "kindness in sitting for him," Pratt would conduct a drawing for the finished piece among the members of the legislature, "without cost to the lot holders."[68] In late March 1852, Pratt announced that the drawing for "The Picture of the General Assembly," which he described as "covering nearly 10 square feet of Silver," would take place on 31 March. He continued to ask if "those who have not yet sat" would "favor us with a call," suggesting he still lacked portraits for some of the legislators. In the end almost all did sit.[69]

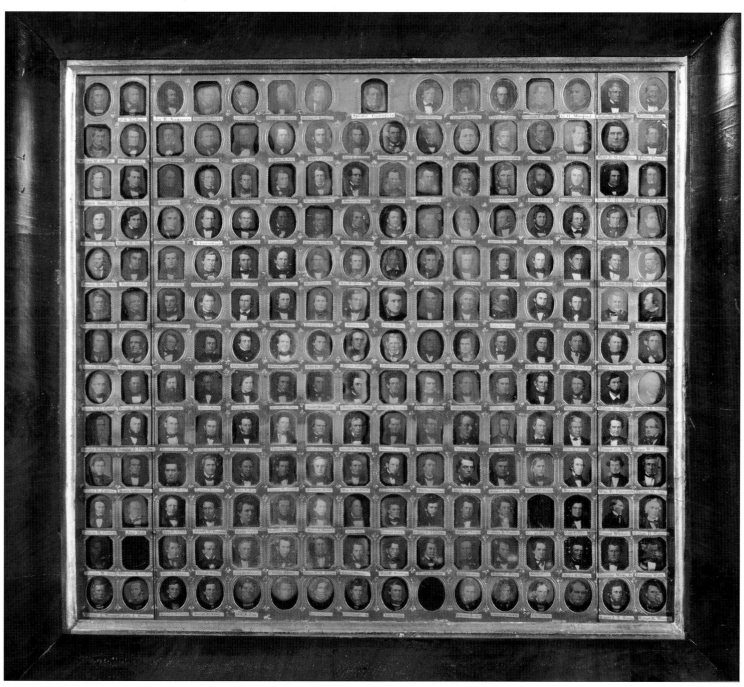

Virginia General Assembly

Composite, wood frame with 204 daguerreotypes under a single gilt metal mat, individual plates 1.5 x 1.25 in., by William A. Pratt, 1852

Beginning in January 1852, Pratt invited the legislators who were then in session in Richmond to visit his gallery, and by the end of March the assemblage had been completed. The two columns of portraits to the left and the two columns to the right represent the Senate, and the twelve middle columns the House of Delegates. *Virginia Historical Society, Purchased with funds provided by Elizabeth and L. Dudley Walker, Hunter Andrews, Anne and Elmo Cross, John Davies, Clive DuVal, Elmon Gray, Ed Holland, W. Tayloe Murphy, Jr., Panny Rhodes, Elliot Schewel, and others.*

In following years Pratt became involved in projects that took him away from an active role in photography. He built a singular house in 1853. Perched on the brow of Gambles Hill in Richmond, the famous Pratt's Castle was made of wood covered in formed sheet metal.[70] In 1855 Pratt became involved in efforts by University of Virginia alumni to obtain a copy of the painting the "School of Athens." Pratt traveled to Paris to pick up the painting. The connections gained through this project led to Pratt's appointment as superintendent of buildings and grounds at the University of Virginia in 1856.[71]

In May 1856 Pratt sold the Richmond gallery to Richard S. Sanxay and James F. Chalmers. In a note to the public about his successors, Pratt said that "the satisfaction which my pictures have given is mainly ascribable to their efforts—having personally done but little in the business for some years past." The gallery remained open until about 1858.[72]

PHOTOGRAPHY ON GLASS AND PAPER

Comparing 1840s prints made from paper negatives to daguerreotypes, it was evident that the paper prints were not as sharp. Waxing or oiling paper negatives to make them more translucent improved sharpness but did not bring equivalence. Seeking better results, experimenters looked to glass as a negative support. They ran into difficulties, however, finding an emulsion that would stick to the glass evenly, bind the silver salts, and remain transparent.

In the late 1840s "albumen," an emulsion made from egg whites, was found to work well on glass, but the negatives were too slow, taking many minutes for an exposure. In 1851 a better emulsion, "collodion," was reported by the British researcher Frederick Scott Archer. This discovery introduced the "wet plate" process. Collodion is made of gun-cotton—cotton soaked in an acidic solution—mixed with alcohol and ether, which forms a sticky clear material. The wet plate process, like that of the daguerreotype, required chemical preparation of the plate just before exposure and then immediate development. Different than the daguerreotype, however, the glass negative could be used to make multiple copies of the image.[73]

The sensitized paper used to make contact prints from paper negatives was adopted to make

positives from wet plate negatives. It was prepared by floating the sheet in salt and silver solutions. Today such a positive is called a "salt print"; in the 1850s it was called a "photograph."

Along with the photograph, a second adaptation of the wet plate process had a wide impact in the United States. The "ambrotype" was a glass negative mounted over a black backing that caused the image to reverse and look positive. Ambrotypes were similar to daguerreotypes in many respects: they were mostly used for portraits and were mounted into cases for presentation. Thus they had the advantage of a familiar look, while being less expensive to produce but also the disadvantage of being one-of-a-kind.[74]

Charles Ellet, Jr.
Daguerreotype, uncased, sixth-plate, attributed to William A. Pratt, c. 1846
The portrait of Charles Ellet, Jr., is from a framed assemblage of twenty-seven daguerreotypes, since taken apart, that was commissioned about 1846 by Joseph Carrington Cabell. Titled "James River and Kanawha Canal Directors and Employees," the set commemorated Cabell's associates during the period he headed the canal company. Ellet (1810–1862) served as the canal's chief engineer from 1836 to 1839 and became a renowned civil engineer. Cabell's assemblage is attributed to Pratt based on timing, interest, and format. *Virginia Historical Society, Gift of Mrs. Robert K. Campbell*

A portrait on glass
Ambrotype, quarter-plate, hand-colored, c. 1856–61
In an ambrotype, the glass negative that was exposed in the camera is placed against a black backing, which causes the image to reverse to positive. The subjects are John Gershom Granbury (1833–1895) and Mary Ann Granbury (1831–1908). Few Virginia ambrotypes have a gallery mark. Uncertainty about the Cutting patent probably left the unlicensed photographer unwilling to make a target of himself as a maker of an ambrotype. Even if the patent was weak, as most believed, no one wanted to be forced to hire a lawyer to avoid liability. *Virginia Historical Society, Gift of Julian Hastings Granbery*

John Moncure Daniel
Ambrotype, half-plate, by Whitehurst Gallery, c. 1861
Daniel (1825–1865) was no stranger to controversy
during his career as a journalist, diplomat, and editor of
the *Richmond Examiner* during the Civil War. *Valentine
Richmond History Center, x53.1.71*

The Licensed Ambrotype
Ambrotype, quarter-plate, by Peter E. Gibbs, c. 1856–61
The subjects are W. S Pendleton, left, and Robert Stanard (1833–1861). Imprinted
on the bottom edge of the mat is "Ambrotype by P. E. Gibbs Rich^d / Patent July 4 &
11 1856." *Virginia Historical Society, Gift of Ellen Beverley Wooldridge*

> **Stop!** Mr. M. P. Simons, not quite so fast, but wait until a jury of your peers shall decide (which will soon take place) whether you can continue making your Imitation Ambrotypes, before you bragg so high.
>
> The public are informed that the genuine Ambrotype can only be obtained at my Gallery, where I guarantee to furnish better Ambrotypes than he that boasts so much, in every instance, or no charge made. Gallery Corinthian Hall. P. E. GIBB,
> de 31 Ambrotypist.

"Stop! Mr. M. P. Simons"
Advertisement by Peter E. Gibbs. *Richmond Dispatch,* 11 Jan. 1856

> **Imitation Ambrotypes, as Mr. Gibbs** calls them, are liked by all who see them much better than the genuine article. Mr. Gibbs, however, is an exception to this rule. He says that they are not so good. We will now see whether he really believes what he says, by putting him to the test. The test shall be a forfeit of $100, that he cannot make a superior Ambrotype of any subject than we can. But we would like this to be understood, that if we beat him, he must not talk any more about infringements, but be satisfied with the opinion of the judge, that there is no infringement. To us it seems quite ridiculous in Mr. Gibbs to say that ours is only an imitation, and then to accuse us of an infringement.
> ja 8 M. P. SIMONS, Ambrotypist.

"Imitation Ambrotypes"
Advertisement by Montgomery P. Simons. *Richmond Dispatch,* 10 Jan. 1856

In a few years the new mediums of the photograph and the ambrotype knocked the daguerreotype out of the market. The main year of transition in Virginia was 1855. At the beginning of the year, state galleries advertised only daguerreotypes. In April, Whitehurst's introduced "Photographs on paper, in oil colors," and other galleries followed, such as R. A. Carden in Alexandria, who in August 1855 announced that he had "become proficient in the new Photographic process." With the ambrotype there was a complication to its adoption. In July 1854 James A. Cutting of Boston was awarded an ambrotype patent, and galleries were expected to purchase a license to produce them. There was much (justified) feeling among photographers that too many rights had been assigned to the patent and that Cutting's agents were claiming control over procedures he did not originate. This led to contention in many places, which in Virginia became quite public.[75]

Because the name ambrotype, although not coined until early 1855, was associated with the patent, galleries avoided using that term. In April 1855, M. P. Simons in Richmond began to advertise "Cabinet Size Daguerreotypes," which were probably ambrotypes. At that time the word daguerreotype was used generically for any kind of photograph. By September Osborne was advertising the "new style of Daguerreotype," and Powers & Duke used the same phrase.[76]

In August 1855, the Lynchburg gallery Gibbs & Keagy offered "Patent Ambrotypes." They had purchased a license to make them by Cutting's method, which they pointed out was "owned in this place by Gibbs & Keagy only." Peter E. Gibbs, it will be recalled, had initially opened a gallery in Lynchburg, had agreed to be taken over by Whitehurst and to be an operator for the chain, and then had purchased the gallery back. A "native Virginian," after seven years in Lynchburg he moved to Richmond about the beginning of October 1855. Gibbs saw opportunity because no one had acquired the Richmond rights to Cutting's patent.[77]

At his arrival in Richmond, Gibbs presumably circulated the message that he held the license from Cutting. The city galleries reacted through their advertising. Powers & Duke did "not pretend to humbug the people with Ambrotypes or Glass-Pictures, hermetically sealed between two glasses, but they are still taking their world-renowned Flesh Tint Daguerreotypes."[78] Reading between the lines, one wonders if Powers & Duke were not still making ambrotypes. M. P. Simons, who had avoided the term ambrotype before, responded most directly. In October he advertised "Ambrotypes and colored Photographs," in November "Ambrotypes for Children," and in early December "Ambrotypes for Christmas and New Year's Presents."[79]

Montgomery Pike Simons (c. 1816–1877), who emerged as the challenger to the patent, began as a daguerrean in Philadelphia in the early 1840s. He was active there as a casemaker, an inventor of a coloring method, and as a daguerreotyper whose portraits were used for engravings. After a season in Charleston, S.C., Simons moved to Richmond in 1851 and opened a gallery. Never bashful, in 1852 he became involved in an advertising back-and-forth with another gallery, Moulson's, after Simons's attempt "to hold these cadets in the art up to public eye." Simons wrote to "suggest the propriety and fairness of the operator's name being attached" to a daguerreotype "for two reasons—first, that the public may know from where caricatures may be had; and second, that they may avoid them when they wish a daguerreotype." In Richmond Simons is probably best known for the "Passions Series" daguerreotypes, a study of expression produced in January 1853 in collaboration with Richmond scion Mann S. Valentine II and the painter William Hubard.[80]

A letter from Simons appeared in *The Photographic Art Journal* in November 1855 regarding the ambrotype patent: "if you will get Mr. Cutting's claim from the patent office reports, 1854 (I have one before me), you will find that two glasses can be used, and cemented together with any varnish except balsam of fir; I use two glasses and cement them together with a varnish which I think has many advantages of the patented balsam; it is not so sticky and unpleasant to use, it dries quicker and the tone which it imparts to the picture is quite as good."[81] Clearly Simons was not about to give in to Gibbs's claim of rights over his ambrotypes. On 20 December 1855 he declared in the *Dispatch,* "All those who have attempted to prevent Simons from making his beautifully colored Ambrotypes, have failed in the undertaking, and it is well for the public that they did."[82]

Over the next few weeks, the *Richmond Dispatch* was the vehicle for a dialogue about ambrotype rights. Gibbs responded with an advertisement the next day, 21 December: "A Humbug, Verily—One that pretends to have what he has not. But not so with Gibbs and his Ambrotypes."[83] Simons returned the next day, the 22nd, with topical humor: "No Speaker yet Elected.—Notwithstanding this

Family at Washington's Tomb
Ambrotype, quarter-plate, hand-colored, c. 1856–61
Ambrotypes taken outdoors are not common. Perhaps an itinerant stationed himself at Mount Vernon during the busy season. Visitation at Washington's home and tomb increased in the late 1850s. Members of the Davidson family appear in this view: John Ellis Davidson, Mr. and Mrs. Joseph R. Davidson, a Davidson family member, Joseph E. Davidson, and Charles Crawford.
Virginia Historical Society

great calamity to the nation, Simons is still making his beautiful Ambrotypes, and no thanks to a speaker; for they all speak for themselves, and tell the public not to be humbugged by 'patent stamp.'"[84] (By the last phrase, Simons referred to the stamp that Gibbs pressed into the mat of his ambrotypes with his name and "Patent July 11 1854.")

Simons's message had thrown down a gauntlet. Gibbs's next, on 31 December, addressed him directly: "Stop! Mr. M. P. Simons, not quite so fast, but wait until a jury of your peers shall decide (which will soon take place) whether you can continue making your Imitation Ambrotypes, before you bragg so high."[85] The week that followed was apparently when a hearing before a judge of the U.S. District Court took place. Simons's next reply on 8 January seems to make reference to the arguments made in that hearing: "Imitation Ambrotypes, as Mr. Gibbs calls them, are liked by all who see them much better that the genuine article." Simons challenged Gibbs to an ambrotype contest, with a stake of $100. "To us it seems quite ridiculous in Mr. Gibbs to say that ours is only an imitation, and then to accuse us of an infringement."[86]

Gibbs replied to this advertisement the next day, 9 January, with the longest notice of the exchange, "Beaten At His Own Game." Gibbs noted that "three months since" he had come to the city "a stranger," but that thanks to "the liberality of one M. P. Simons, he has been made known" to "a large portion of the community." In it Gibbs, along with passing along some gossip, such as the bad faith of Pratt's "gift enterprise of $30,000," which Simons had

participated in, restated his argument: "the Ambrotype is a patent picture, the right of which I have bought, legally, and paid for. M. P. Simons is trying to deprive me of it, thereby disregarding the laws of his country and infringe the rights of his fellow man."[87]

Simons's next-day reply, "To Mr. P. E. Gibbs," referred to "the ungentlemanly card of yours," with its "slanderous attacks," without responding otherwise.[88] Two days later Gibbs published a note from his lawyer stating "no judge has decided that Mr. Simons is not infringing your Ambrotype patent."[89] Simons's reply on the 14th asked "if any Judge has said that I was?" and pointed out that the judge "refused to grant the injunction which you plead so hard for."[90]

By this time, several weeks into it, previous advertisements from Simons and Gibbs were reappearing in the *Dispatch* daily but out of order. The public was probably more aware that a controversy existed than what it was about.

Appearing at the Metropolitan Theater while the advertisements ran was the Julian Opera Troupe, a blackface minstrel group that used topical skits to keep the show fresh. For the 15 January show, their advertisement noted, along with "the best Fancy Dancer in the world," the troupe would "appear in a Grand Portraiture Contest."[91]

Simons reported on the case in a letter to *The Photographic Art Journal:* "His bill desired to restrain me from making ambrotypes and cementing them between two glasses. My answer was, that there was nothing new or novel in the patent, and, if the patent was good, that I did not use balsam, and, therefore, did not infringe his rights." The judge, said Simons, "decided in my favor, by refusing to grant the injunction."[92]

The main contest was finished in January 1856. Late that month it was noted that "J. H. Whitehurst having purchased an equal interest with P. E. Gibbs in his Ambrotype patent for the city of Richmond, is now prepared to make these popu-

Group of women
Tintype, quarter-plate, c. 1857–70
The subjects are unidentified. By 1857 some Virginia galleries were offering the melainotype, a proprietary name for a tintype. By whatever name, the plate was black-enameled iron, not tin. *Virginia Historical Society, Gift of J. Madison Macon, IV*

Gilbert Hunt
Salt print, by Smith & Vannerson, 1860
The Smith & Vannerson partnership began and ended in 1860. The inscription on the mount reads (with gaps): "is the portrait of Gilbert Hunt, a faithful colored man . . . [res]cued many persons from the burning theatre in Rich[mond] . . . year 1811. *Virginia Historical Society*

Across The Brigge. Looking East.

Natural Bridge
Albumen print, by E. P. Mathews, c. 1859
Inscribed on the mount are the words: "Across The Brigge. Looking East." The print is from a group of five, all similar, one of which is credited and dated. The view is of the fenced-in crossing over the top of Natural Bridge, with the Natural Bridge Hotel beyond, in Rockbridge County. *Virginia Historical Society*

lar and imperishable double glass Pictures." The effect of the patent tussle was mixed. In Lynchburg, Keagy continued to advertise "Patent Ambrotypes" through April 1856 but after that dropped the phrase to emphasize quality and beauty. At the other, unlicensed Lynchburg gallery, N. S. Tanner had started advertising "Vitrotypes on Glass," ambrotypes by another name, well before the patent was shown to be unenforceable and stayed with vitrotypes into June 1856. In Norfolk, Hankins and Clark advertised as a "Daguerreotype, Photograph, and Ambrotype Gallery" beginning in April 1856. In Richmond M. P. Simons continued advertising ambrotypes until September 1856, when he moved back to Philadelphia and Powers took over his gallery space.[93]

A few years after the ambrotype, another refinement of the wet plate process came to Virginia with much less fuss. The "tintype" put the emulsion onto an iron plate painted black, so the reversing effect required no additional parts. The

format was brought to market in 1856 by two different Ohio producers, one of whom called it the "melainotype," and the other the "ferrotype." The name tintype was popularly used for both, though they contained no tin. The chemical process was much the same as for the ambrotype; the thin metal sheets had the advantages of being more durable, readily mailed, and easily trimmed to fit lockets and other mounts. The image quality of the best tintypes was not as good, however, of that of a well-made image on glass or paper.[94]

In Petersburg, George W. Minnis advertised only the daguerreotype at his gallery in April 1855. By April 1856 he was offering the "Daguerreotype, Ambrotype, or Photograph as desired." In August 1857, Minnis listed those three items, plus the oil photograph and the melainotype. By February 1858 the sphereotype was listed (its nature not known), but the daguerreotype was not.[95]

The daguerreotype was an attractive format, but the new ones were less expensive. In the long run the mediums on rigid surfaces like metal or glass could not compete against paper. Of them the tintype had the longest survival, extending into the early twentieth century, and glass positives had a niche role as magic lantern slides. Of course negatives continued to be shot on glass, but that was not a final product. Paper with its multiplication factor and its adaptability became the dominant medium. A few daguerreotypers stuck it out to the beginning of the Civil War. The ambrotype made it through the war but did not last much past it.

City Point, July 1864
Albumen print on album page, by Andrew J. Russell, 1864
The printed title states: "No. 107. Depot Building and Wharves of the City Point Railroad."
Virginia Historical Society

CHAPTER TWO

CIVIL WAR

In 1860 the photography trade, which had just weathered a large transition five years earlier, was on the verge of a new round of changes. Formats that had become popular in Europe were poised to enter the American market. Following the election of 1860, however, the country split in two and so did the photographic experience for North and South. In the North the new formats became standard, and photography boomed. In the South photography faced reduced circumstances and mostly kept to the older methods.

Virginia was the largest Atlantic state when the Civil War began and the only Confederate state to border Pennsylvania or Ohio. West was Kentucky and north was Maryland, both border states that stayed in the Union. Virginia itself was full of the mixed opinions that characterized border states. When fighting began in 1861, Virginia became divided. The largest portion went Confederate, though parts came under Union control for the duration. The northwest seceded and became a new state. Other areas changed hands as armies moved back and forth.

Photography around the state followed partly the northern pattern and partly the southern. There was no single tale for photographers but rather many. Both sides utilized photography for military purposes. Wartime photography in the field was almost entirely from the Union side, including the entrepreneurial programs of Mathew Brady and others that were both patriotic and commercial in nature. In the Confederate strongholds the primary wartime expression was portraits of leaders, reflecting an outlook on the war's conduct that centered on personalities.

The wet-plate outdoors
Ambrotype, sixth-plate, 1859
The ambrotype was essentially a wet-plate negative, sensitized just before exposure and developed immediately after. The technical requirements made photographing away from a gallery harder to do. This scene, by tradition of the donor family, descendents of one of the militiamen, is of the Richmond Grays at "the 'Death-watch' of John Brown's execution." Brown was hanged at Charlestown, Virginia (today W.Va.), 2 Dec. 1859. The photographer may have accompanied the militia from Richmond. *Virginia Historical Society. Gift of Mrs. Wallace C. Saunders*

PHOTOGRAPHIC FORMATS IN '60–61

Leading up to the war, the shakeout of galleries whose business model had been formed around the economics of the daguerreotype had run its course. Competition had brought the cost of the least-expensive portraits down considerably. "The apparent volatility of the profession," writes Keith Davis, "was magnified by the threat of a fluctuating economy; only a few years earlier, for example, the Panic of 1857 had forced many photographers into bankruptcy and created a lingering climate of financial insecurity." In the late 1850s ambrotypes were the standard trade, with tintypes, usually called melainotypes, and photographs, that is, paper prints, also widely available. Photographs could be provided "plain," but in their advertising galleries emphasized such enhancements as "oil colors, water colors, and India ink."[1]

Improvements from Europe sufficiently upgraded the "plain" photograph for it to become the medium of choice in the North by 1861. In 1850, the French entrepreneur Louis-Désiré Blanquet-Evrard experimented with "albumen," made from egg-whites and previously tried as an emulsion for negatives. He discovered that it was well-suited as an emulsion for printing papers. Because the glossy emulsion kept the image on the surface of the paper, the image in an albumen print was sharper than in a salt print. A new system became the photographic standard: glass-collodion negatives made by the wet plate process, contact printed on albumen paper. Manufacturers began to provide pre-coated albumen paper that a photographer had only to sensitize with silver-salt solution.[2]

The formats that incorporated albumen prints and became widespread in the U.S. in the 1860s had emerged in Europe in the 1850s. Among the most popular was the "carte de visite." A format based on the calling card, the carte de visite was introduced in the early 1850s in France as an albumen print about 2½ x 3½ inches mounted on board. With the Paris photographer André-Adolphe-Eugè Disderi as its most prominent producer, the carte de visite flourished, especially in Paris beginning 1859 and in London in 1860. "Twelve months ago they were almost unknown," wrote *Humphrey's Journal* of New York in October 1862. "Now they fill one or more volumes on every center-table, and overshadow the contents of every card basket."[3] Among the earliest cartes de visite in Virginia was a "beautiful photograph of Piccolomoni," noted by the *Richmond Whig* in January 1859. To publicize the European singer's upcoming performance, her portrait was presented to the newspaper. Similar ones were on sale at a music store for 25 cents.[4]

At the Crystal Palace exhibition of 1851, one of the new sensations was the "stereoscope." This was an era when the quirks of human vision were a subject of inquiry. An optical device that took advantage of one such trick of the eyes, the effect of binocular vision, was the stereoscope. Photographs taken from slightly offset positions were mounted together and viewed side-by-side through the stereoscope, a binocular viewer, to create a 3-D effect. In Virginia, M. P. Simons of Richmond had produced daguerreotype stereos, but these were expensive, utilizing a special case fitted with built-in viewing lenses. Albumen prints were ideal for stereo when mounted onto a card, for their sharpness made the effect work wonderfully. Titles and captions were printed on the cards, called "stereographs."

A European boom in stereo ensued in the late 1850s. By early 1860 wholesalers of stereo views were advertising in Virginia, seeking local dealers. To Norfolk, the London Stereoscopic Company promoted their "Unparalleled Assortment at prices which defy successful competition." A notice appeared in Williamsburg for the "American and Foreign Stereoscopic Emporium," operated by E. Anthony, the New York importer and manufacturer of photographic materials. In addition to seeking the trade of retailers, Anthony offered views and viewers by mail and solicited "First class stereoscopic Negatives" from photographers. Only one prewar Virginia retailer has been noted, a Richmond optician and dealer in microscopes, telescopes, and opera glasses, who advertised through July 1861 "The finest collection of Stereoscopes and Stereoscopic Pictures."[5]

The carte de visite did emerge in Confederate Virginia during the war, but the stereograph did not, and neither did two other formats that arrived in the U.S. about this time. The "Imperial" was a photograph considerably larger than

previous maximums. Whole-plate daguerreotypes and ambrotypes were rarely larger than 6 x 8 inches, and Imperials typically used negatives of 17 x 21 inches to make a contact print. No Imperials are known from Virginia prior to 1861. A medium that predated photography was the "magic lantern," also called "Dissolving Views" and a precursor to the modern projector. New to the magic lantern in the late 1850s were photographic glass slides that could be projected, with improved gas light for brighter illumination. Such an exhibition played in Alexandria in May 1860, Marsh & Kaye's "Photographs of Famous Places, Beautiful Statuary, and Landscapes in the Moon," described as "the first of the kind ever exhibited in this country." However it was also the last of its kind seen in Virginia for a few years.[6]

PORTRAITS OF SOLDIERS

In 1861 the prime subject for a photograph was a soldier in uniform. The genre of men in uniform was a well-represented tradition in Virginia portraiture. Militia units were linked to the glories of the American Revolution and War of 1812. Membership conferred status and enabled social mobility. A member would not have gained all that he signed up for until he was photographed in full trappings. One imagines that a good portion of the Virginians who served had posed in uniform well before the Civil War began.

Virginia militia units went into action in late 1859 in response to the John Brown-led raid on Harpers Ferry. That incident influenced the Virginia Assembly in early 1860 when it moved to reopen the state armory. The 1861 mobilization after Fort Sumter in April and Virginia's vote to secede activated militia organizations and set off recruitment drives. The developments sparked a portrait boom among hometown Virginia galleries. Another wave of portrait-making was set off when events brought soldiers from other states to Virginia. For a soldier who left home without leaving behind a portrait, a second chance to sit came once they arrived at military camp. Because of the state's position, it was occupied by soldiers arriving from both northern and southern states in two opposing armies. The impulse for mementos took in both sides. Within Virginia there were likely as many or more Union soldiers portrayed in camp as Confederate. Significant Union army encampments were located in northern

Virginia and Alexandria, and around Fort Monroe and the lower Peninsula.

"The photographers who are not fighting men," reported the *American Journal of Photography* in May 1861, "are doing a thriving business; a fact which appears very reasonable when we remember that each of the hundred thousand men going from home, perhaps on a very long journey, leaves at least one who loves him. The photograph for many will prove the last pledge of affection." In September the *Journal* reported that "photographers in the neighborhood of military recruiting are even doing better than usual."[7]

In the case of Union soldiers, "the photographer accompanies the army wherever it goes." One imagines that there were at least some Confederate itinerants at the camps, too, but there is no direct evidence from Virginia. Because the southerners spent most of the war defending their home ground, they had access to home

galleries. Soldiers on leave may have primarily patronized a gallery in a nearby town. From all indications, the ambrotype was the primary medium for photography in Confederate territory. On the Union side, reports varied. Coleman Sellers reported in 1862 that "the majority of the pictures made for soldiers in camp, or as they pass through any town, are ambrotypes. This is because their movements are too uncertain to allow for the delay of paper pictures; besides many of them have a liking for the fancy cases in which their portraits are enclosed—and in addition to all this, they are so cheap." On the other hand, *Humphrey's Journal* stated "most of these pictures are taken on the Melainotype Plate for the reason that it is light, durable, and easily sent in a letter." Because tintype plates were manufactured in Ohio and New York, the access of southern photographers to that medium would have been greater earlier in the war while blanks remained in stock than later.[8]

Cased portrait, small
Ambrotype, one-ninth plate, hand-colored, c. 1861–64
The Confederate soldier is unidentified. *Virginia Historical Society*

Cased portrait, medium
Ambrotype, one-sixth plate, hand-colored, c. 1861–64
Brothers Fred, Richard, and William Anderson all served as Confederate soldiers. Richard, center, survived; Fred was killed in action; and William died after the war from wounds. *Virginia Historical Society, Gift of J. Madison Macon IV*

The main Confederate army camps in late spring–early summer 1861 were in the suburbs of Richmond and in northern Virginia. No photographers are known to have been at the northern Virginia camps. Located in the west of Richmond on Broad Street, Camp Lee was a main instructional facility, and nearby Richmond College also became a training camp. Soldiers at these facilities could go into the city for portraits. Richmond had always been the main center for photography in the state and remained so during the Confederate period.

In Richmond there were three main galleries and at least two smaller ones. Of the latter, one arrived with the Confederate government in 1861, A. J. Riddle from Georgia, who opened Riddle's Ambrotype Gallery at 151 Main St. A second smaller operator was Peter E. Gibbs, the protector of the ambrotype patent in 1856–57. Gibbs's gallery was in the western part of town, and he resided in Sydney, an early west end suburb.[9]

The seventh and last annual exhibition of the Virginia Mechanics' Institute took place in October 1860, and as it happens the awards went to what would become the three main Richmond galleries during the war. For the third-best display, Rees & Co. was awarded a second-class diploma. Charles R. Rees was operating in Richmond by August 1859 and in 1860 took over Pratt's former gallery (of the Gothic window) at 145 Main. Previously Rees had run a New York City gallery in 1853–54. His advertisements offered "Photographs and Ambrotypes," "done artistically and at a reasonable price." In February 1861 he announced with topicality that the gallery had "just received eight hundred dollars' worth of Union and Disunion, Oval Velvet, Pearl, and a great variety of other Fancy Cases, all of which will be sold at panic prices."[10]

Cased portrait, large
Ambrotype, one-quarter plate, hand-colored, c. 1861–64
The Confederate soldier is John Harmer Gilmer, Jr. *Virginia Historical Society, Gift of J. Madison Macon IV*

Southern tintype
Tintype, one-sixteenth plate oval, c. 1861–65
Because the suppliers of blanks were northern, the number of southern tintypes was limited. The subject, Gen. John Pegram (1832–1865), courted Hetty Cary, a famous belle from Baltimore, and their Jan. 1865 wedding was a big event at a time Richmond society had little else to celebrate. Less than three weeks later he was killed in battle. *Virginia Historical Society, Gift of J. Rieman McIntosh*

For second best at the exhibition, Smith & Vannerson was awarded the first-class diploma. Julian Vannerson (1826–after 1873) was raised in Richmond and owned a hat store there in 1846. According to a family account, his older brother, Adrian (1821–1878), trained in Whitehurst's Richmond gallery, and Julian followed him into the trade there. Another brother, Lucien, also joined the Whitehurst chain. In the early 1850s Julian Vannerson was the photographer at Whitehurst's gallery in Washington. He opened his own gallery in 1855 on Pennsylvania Avenue, but the venture did not succeed. In 1856 he was associated with the Washington gallery of James McClees; in 1857 he joined George W. Minnis in Petersburg; and he appears in District of Columbia directories in 1858 and 1860 as a daguerreotypist at McClees's address.[11]

In Washington Vannerson made portraits of many important people, so when he returned to Richmond in 1860 he was something of a big fish. He and a partner opened as Smith & Vannerson at "Whitehurst's old Gallery," 77 Main Street. In November 1860 Smith & Vannerson were "producing the finest Photographs ever offered to the public of this city." They offered ambrotypes "as low as fifty cents" when the cut-rate price was twenty-five cents. By December 1860

Smith's name no longer appeared in the advertisement: "If you want a sound and cheap Photograph or Ambrotype, go to Vannerson's, No. 77 Main st."[12]

The top prize from the Mechanics' Institute, the certificate of silver medal, was presented "To G. W. Minnis, for finest display of Photographs." By 1860 George W. Minnis was a veteran photographer. After studying with Marcus Root of Philadelphia, he opened his first gallery in Petersburg in 1847. In the 1850s Minnis opened and moved on from branch galleries in Richmond and Lynchburg. In 1857 he opened in Richmond again, where the Minnis gallery in February 1861 invited "Members of the Convention, the House of Delegates, and the Senate of Virginia" to "examine the various and beautiful styles of portraiture."[13]

Other Virginia galleries close enough to camps to have made Confederate soldier portraits in 1861 included those in Winchester, Norfolk, and Fredericksburg. In Fredericksburg, E. Francis Cox advertised his "New Ambrotype Gallery" on Main Street in March 1860. Nathaniel Routzahn had opened a gallery in Winchester in 1855 and kept it open until at least 1863.[14]

Alexandria was occupied by northern forces in May 1861, and throughout the war it served important military and political functions for the Union. It was

A soldier's child
Ambrotype, one-ninth plate on ruby glass, hand-colored, c. 1860–62
A Virginia soldier found this portrait after the June 1862 battle at Port Republic, Virginia, lying between a fallen Confederate soldier and a fallen Union soldier. *Museum of the Confederacy*

A soldier's wife
Tintype, one-sixteenth plate, hand-colored, c. 1861–65
The subject, Lucy Elizabeth Edwards of King George County, was married to Pvt. William Balthrope Edwards, 30th Virginia Infantry. The small cased portrait was likely the soldier's memento of his wife during his service. *Museum of the Confederacy*

Slave in uniform
Ambrotype, one-sixth plate, c. 1861–64
It is unusual to see an African American in a Confederate uniform, and the painted backdrop of a camp is also rare. Marlboro Jones was the slave of Capt. Randal F. Jones of Georgia. Capt. Jones was mortally wounded at Trevilian Station, Virginia, in June 1864. *Museum of the Confederacy*

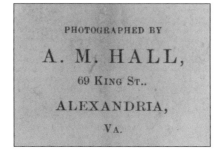

Card from a Confederate town
Carte de visite, by William Roads, c. 1861–65
Roads seems to have kept his Charlottesville gallery open through the war. Because the town had no special military value, it avoided combat. *Virginia Historical Society*

From a Union-occupied city
Carte de visite, by Augustus M. Hall, c. 1861–65
Alexandria was occupied early by Union forces and became a key support base for federal operations. *Virginia Historical Society*

From a Union camp
Carte de visite, by John Jones, c. 1862–64
The photographer was based at Rendezvous of Distribution, a large Union convalescent camp in Alexandria. Inscribed on the reverse: "Dear Mother, I now present you my picture. I should like to get a letter from you. I have [two] years to stay in the [army] and then I will come out to see you and bring my wife." *Virginia Historical Society*

home to army camps and hospitals, and its wharves and railroad facilities distributed war materials and supplies. The Union version of the Virginia state government was based in Alexandria. The *Local News* commented on "the changed appearance of King street," which "now assumes the appearance of the avenue of a populous city," like "those Eastern marts on whose thoroughfares many nations mingle in common traffic. The various regiments exhibit . . . the peculiar military costumes of half of the nations of the world." The newspaper continued, "The streets show little novelties, each of which attracts crowds. . . . At another corner, a large stereoscope gives wondrous views, showing to the astonished eye whole cities in a little box." So Union had the city become that the abolitionist singing group, the Hutchinson family, could offer a concert there in January 1862.[15]

With many soldiers present in the town, Alexandria hosted probably the largest congregation of photographers in the state. In January 1862, discussing "Daguerrean Galleries" (and using "saloon" in a photographic sense), the *Local News* remarked that "the change which has come over Alexandria has brought with it in place of the three saloons which formerly were ample for all wants, some twenty similar establishments, all of which seem to be busy."[16]

The galleries of Nahum S. Bennett and Henry Woolf were probably included in those pre-existing "three saloons." Woolf had moved to Alexandria from Washington and in February 1861 was offering "Ambrotypes, Daguereotypes, and Photographs."[17] A directory listing from 1864–65 suggests that, whatever his sympathies, Woolf remained in Alexandria for the duration. Other photographers were new arrivals: in October 1861 John H. Devaughan announced his Ambrotype Gallery. James W. Gillingham advertised his Ambrotype Gallery in June 1862 and in 1863 obtained a permit from the provost marshal's office to photograph at an army camp.[18]

Many Union camps in 1861 were located in the Virginia portion of the District of Columbia that had been retroceded to the state in 1846, called then Alexandria County and today Arlington. Colemen Sellers reported in May 1862 that "an unnamed photographer from New York state 'has been for some time driving a brisk business at the camps below Washington,' making ambrotypes and stereographs. It was reported that 'the soldiers are very good customers as long as their money holds out.'" Sellers commented that "photography, in a

From a Union-occupied city
Carte de visite, by E. W. Beckwith, c. 1861–65
The federal bugler is identified as Munroe Nichols.
Pamplin Historical Park

business point of view, has been benefitted by our troubles. The dealers in photographic stock and instruments are at their wit's end to meet their orders, and all the galleries are crowded with visitors."[19] A dozen photographers were associated with the Bergstresser brothers, tintypers from Pennsylvania, according to permits found by the archivist Josephine Cobb. The *New York Tribune* in August 1862 found the Bergstressers "near General Burnside's headquarters at Fredericksburg" and reported that "they have followed the army for more than a year and have taken, the Lord only knows how many thousand portraits."[20]

A second place in Virginia where there were significant Union army encampments was the Peninsula, modern Hampton and Newport News. The Union's possession of Fort Monroe, at Old Point Comfort on the tip of the Peninsula, was the key to the blockade of Hampton Roads and to control of the Chesapeake Bay. In 1862 that stronghold was the starting point for the Peninsula campaign against Richmond. The army's Camp Hamilton was located near the fort in modern Phoebus, and other camps were established at Newport News, occupied in May 1861. Photographers given passes to Camp Hamilton included Harris & King of Philadelphia, Horace Fosdick (1864), William Crouch (1863–65), and Harris Crandall to bring in ambrotype materials from Baltimore. Balch & Weeks worked the Newport News camps in 1864. Certain northern photographers specialized in hometown soldiers: "G. H. Houghton of Brattleboro, Vermont, made scores of outstanding images with the Vermont regiments in McClellan's army on the Peninsula, then took them home to sell to friends and loved ones."[21]

After the Peninsula campaign came to its unsuccessful conclusion, federal forces continued to occupy Williamsburg and Yorktown. The Union encampment at Yorktown in early 1863 was served by a "Mammoth Gallery on the Square, next door to the church." In March 1863 it offered ambrotypes. By April, the gallery was under the name Warren & Barney and offered a full line of "Photographs!!, Cartes de Visite, Ambrotypes, Malenotypes, &c. taken in superior style and finish."[22]

Across Hampton Roads, Norfolk before the war usually supported three or four galleries, of which the main ones in 1860 were Burwell & Hobday and Hankin & Clark. In May 1862 the Confederates withdrew from Norfolk, and Union forces occupied the city. By December 1863 B. F. Evans & Son occupied the gallery at 14

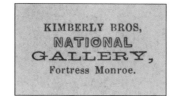

From a Union fort
Carte de visite, by Cross, c. 1862–64
The photographer was based at Fort Richardson, in Alexandria County (modern Arlington). The artilleryman is unidentified.
Pamplin Historical Park

From a Union fort
Carte de visite, by Kimberly Brothers, Fort Monroe, c. 1862–65
After Union forces occupied Norfolk, Kimberly Brothers opened a National Gallery there too.
Virginia Historical Society

From a Union camp
Carte de visite, by Harris & King, c. 1862–64
The photographers' Monitor Gallery was at Camp Hamilton, located on the bay side of Old Point Comfort. The federal sergeant is unidentified. *Pamplin Historical Park*

WHITE OAK CHURCH, VA.

Entered according to act of Congress, in the year 1863, by Weittle & Hall, in the Clerk's Office of the District Court of the District of Columbia.

Ambrotype gallery
Carte de visite, by Weittle & Hall, 1863
White Oak Church still stands in Stafford County, near Falmouth and across the Rappahannock from Fredericksburg. Nearby was a large federal winter camp in 1862–63. The building also served as a hospital. Until the Civil War, the Primitive Baptist congregation seems to have included both black and white members. *Pamplin Historical Park*

B. F. ÉVANS & SON,
14 MAIN STREET,
Norfolk, Va.

From a Union-occupied city
Carte de visite, by B. F. Evans, Norfolk, c. 1862–65. *Virginia Historical Society*

Confederates in the field
Ambrotype, half-plate, c. 1861–62
There are very few examples of outdoors Confederate photography in the Virginia theater. This view of soldiers from a Texas unit, identified by the sign on the door for the "Wigfall mess," was probably made at the Confederate winter camp of 1861–62 near Manassas. *Museum of the Confederacy*

Tom Rutter, working for James Coleman, and Johnson, working for W. B. Jackson.[25]

As well as the many thousands of portraits of soldiers, there were portraits of other people too, some made in Virginia and some brought to Virginia. "A very large number of soldiers get their 'pictures' taken and send them home to their friends. Friends at home in return send their portraits to the soldiers, and in this way an immense transportation business has been done by the Post Office." In July 1861, in the aftermath of the Confederate victory at Bull Run, the *Richmond Daily Dispatch* wrote of "the excitement in the city" that came after the "anxiety . . . subsided." The "relics of the battle," the article stated, "were brought down last evening. Not the least interesting among these were daguerreotype likenesses of females, found in the pockets or haversacks of those who expected to whip the 'rebels.'"[26]

E. Main, near Market Square, where Burwell & Hobday had been located in 1860. Evans had a permit to bring in ambrotype supplies from Baltimore and offered "Photographs, Ambrotypes, and every other style of life's simile."[23] The following month, January 1864, Burwell returned to town. F. W. Burwell's Photographic Gallery opened at "his new and extensive suite of rooms" at 63 Main Street. He noted that he "formerly conducted the Picture business in Norfolk" and that another prewar Norfolk photographer, T. W. Clark, was also working at the gallery. "His Sky Light is constructed in accordance with the most modern improvements, and his chemicals and other materials many of them of his own manufacture, he will guarantee are inferior to none now in use." Burwell also had a permit to bring in chemicals from New York to Norfolk.[24]

Other locations around the state that became Union camps long enough for photographers to operate included Brandy Station, the army's winter encampment in Culpeper County (1863–64), and City Point, the James River supply base (1864–65). In 1864–65, Alexander Kern was "Photographist at General Hospital, City Point," with five employees. On the James River, L. C. Dillon operated at City Point and Varina Landing, and Philip E. Kennedy was at Deep Bottom. On the Appomattox, Charles Harris was with the Naval Brigade at Point of Rocks. Of some twenty-two photographers listed at Bermuda Hundred, upriver from City Point between the James and the Appomattox, two were identified as "colored":

A brief story published in the *Soldiers' Journal,* a Union Alexandria newspaper, was undoubtedly sentimental and possibly fictional. Nonetheless the context in 1864 was only too real, namely the deaths of many thousands of soldiers in the Virginia theater:

Touch Not My Sister's Picture.—The following incident was related by a rebel prisoner to an attendant, who by many acts of kindness had won his confidence: 'I was searching for spoils among the dead and dying upon a deserted battle-field, when I discovered a small gold locket upon the person of a dying boy, apparently about fifteen years of age. As I endeavored to loose it from his grasp, he opened his languid eyes and implored me, by all that was good and pure, by the memory of my own mother, not to rob him of his sister's picture. Oh! It was her last gift, I promised her, when she kissed my cheek at parting, that I would always, wear it next my heart, in life or death. Then, as if throwing his whole soul into the plea, he exclaimed:—Oh! Touch not my sister's picture! As the last words faltered upon his tongue, his voice hushed in death. By the dim light of the stars I hastily scooped a shallow grave, and buried him with his sister's picture lying upon his breast.'[27]

Entered according to Act of Congress, in the year 1862, by Gardner & Gibson, in the Clerk's Office of the District Court of the District of Columbia.

NORTHERN ENTREPRENEURS

In March 1861, as open conflict became ever more likely, the *American Journal of Photography* discussed the potential military role of photography. The French had decided that "a moveable photographic establishment shall be attached to each regiment," the *Journal* noted. "Great topographic and historiographic advantages are expected," not least that "those who stay at home" would be able "to know almost as much about a battle as the soldiers." If "there must be battles," said the *Journal*, "a battle scene is a fine subject for an artist—painter, historian or photographer. We hope to see a photograph of the next battle." In May 1861 the *Journal* gave this advice: "we recommend the photographer who finds himself in the midst of great facts, to out with his camera, make ready,—take aim,—and send on his capture to Frank Leslie."[28]

The "travelling-army-portrait-maker" was one type of northern photographic entrepreneur. Although mostly lacking that class of operator, the Confederates had the equivalent when a soldier obtained a portrait from a town gallery. Another kind of entrepreneur was the view-maker, epitomized by Mathew Brady. The *American Journal of Photography* had suggested "perhaps there will be a photographic corps appointed for the grand army in the land of cotton. We trust some of our good friends in Dixie will get such offices." But there was never a southern counterpart to the northern photographic corps.[29]

Bull Run and bridge

Stereograph, by G. N. Barnard, "Photographic Incidents of the War," 1862
After Confederate forces pulled back from northern Virginia in early 1862, Union photographers gained access to the battle sites of 1861. George Barnard was probably still nominally working for Brady when he made the negative, but Alexander Gardner, Brady's Washington manager, was already acting to assert control over material, and the copyright notice is in the name of "Gardner & Gibson." This stereograph was issued after Gardner and his group had split with Brady, under the imprint of Gardner's Gallery, with E. & H. T. Anthony, N.Y., as wholesale agents. *Virginia Historical Society*

In practice, the itinerant portrait-makers to the soldiers were a kind of merchant, much like the sutlers who set up shop at encampments. The view-makers on the other hand operated at the command level, on a par with Signal Corps or intelligence officers. They performed functions that were often important to generals, particularly as an avenue to public recognition. Brady became the most famous of the entrepreneurs who photographed the Civil War, but he was hardly the only go-getter involved. In truth these ventures operated with enterprising individuals at every level, including the men in the field who were not so much employees as independent contractors.[30]

Large format view
Albumen print, by Barnard & Gibson, 1862
Compared to Brady, Alexander Gardner seems to have more actively encouraged the use of larger negatives, especially 8 x 10 inch. George N. Barnard and James F. Gibson both left Brady with Gardner. This view shows fortifications abandoned by Confederate troops near Centreville, with winter quarters visible beyond. The logs had the semblance of cannons at a distance and were dubbed "Quaker guns."
Virginia Historical Society

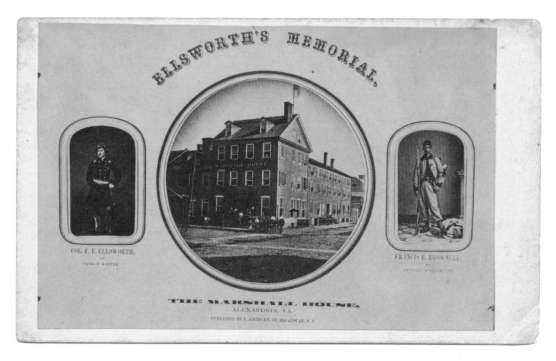

For the Union cause
Carte de visite, copy by Montgomery P. Simons, c. 1861
Col. Elmer Ellsworth was an early Union martyr, killed in May 1861 at the Marshall House in Alexandria. "Ellsworth's Memorial" was originally issued by E. Anthony, the N.Y. photographic publisher, likely in 1861 when interest was high. Patriotic fervor seems to have trumped any copyright issues when M. P. Simons, who had moved back to Philadelphia from Richmond, copied and issued the image under his own imprint.
Virginia Historical Society

Brady imprint
Carte de visite, "Brady's Album Gallery," 1862
Views of officers and units, issued in the small formats of carte de visite and stereograph, were the Brady Gallery's wartime forte. This card's label, with inscribed corrections by a participant, identifies the subject as Capt. Robertson's Battery of Horse Artillery, near Richmond, 20 June 1862, at the end of the Peninsula Campaign. *Virginia Historical Society*

The three men who did the most to launch the photographic coverage of the war were Brady, Anthony, and Gardner. Each had his role. Mathew Brady had built a wide reputation since the 1840s through his New York and Washington, D.C., galleries, his portrait collections, and participation in publishing ventures. Edward Anthony was the leading supplier of materials to the American photographic trade, had recently begun to distribute stereocards, and was about to start producing cartes de visite. Alexander Gardner had opened Brady's Washington gallery in 1858 and continued to manage it, and before that had helped the Brady operations make the transition into wet-plate photography.[31]

Brady was a long-time associate of Anthony, going back to 1840s New York City. Beginning in 1847 they operated their businesses for several years out of the same Broadway building. In the early 1840s Anthony had operated a "National Miniature Gallery" of well-known people, and thus he would have had full appreciation for Brady's ability to attract the powerful and famous and gather their portraits. In addition Anthony began as early as 1842 to adapt photographic imagery to prints for large-scale distribution. Anthony needed Brady as a picture source for his popular cards, and Brady needed Anthony because, with the ups and downs of trade, one of Brady's chief assets was his line of credit with Anthony's supply house. Gardner was a practical businessman in ways that Brady was not, and at the outbreak of the war he worked out an agreement with Anthony to copy portraits from inventory and provide negatives of new work. It might have been Brady who thought to have wagons equipped for mobile

photography; it was likely Gardner who came up with a practical design and arranged the fabrication.[32]

To photograph the war in the field was a speculative venture with an initial investment and continuing expenses. Income would be dependent upon the distribution of new formats at an uncertain moment. The participants jumped into it with patriotic fervor. In July 1861, the Union army moved to displace Confederate forces positioned thirty miles west of Washington at Centreville, Virginia. To record the expected success, Brady set out with two wagons and a crew. When the federal troops were thrown back at the battle of Bull Run in severe disorder, Brady's wagons were caught up in the hellbent retreat. He was fortunate to have escaped capture and to have suffered only the loss of equipment and no personnel.

After that inauspicious start, as William Frassanito has written, "Not one authentic photograph has ever emerged that would support claims suggesting that

CAMP WINF

Entered according to act of Congress, by GARDNER & Ga

any photographer took views on the battlefield in 1861." For the remainder of the year, photographers worked around the encampments of the Union army and in Union-occupied Alexandria. Different from the portrait-makers, who took individuals, the Brady crews worked with officers to photograph whole units. "The groupings of entire regiments and divisions," wrote *Humphrey's Journal* in 1861, "within a space of a couple of feet square, present some of the most curious effects as yet produced in photography." Field photography in Virginia began in March 1862, when George N. Barnard and James F. Gibson, working for Brady, went out to the Manassas/Centreville area after Confederate forces withdrew. Barnard and Gibson recorded the Confederate Quaker guns—logs that at a distance would be seen as cannon.[33]

In April 1862 under Gen. George B. McClellan the Union army initiated the Peninsula campaign, starting from the tip at Fort Monroe and advancing toward Richmond. Photographic coverage began in May 1862 when James F. Gibson and John Wood photographed the army's Camp Winfield Scott, Union positions at Yorktown, and the base on the Pamunkey River at Cumberland landing. Comparing Gibson's work on this campaign to that of Timothy O'Sullivan's earlier in 1862 on the South Carolina coast, Frassanito finds O'Sullivan's work to "depict relatively static views" and to record "images only after locales had been secured." Gibson's photographs, on the other hand, "were recorded in the midst of an active field campaign in which no one knew when or where the next blow would fall." Gibson

Panoramic view

Five albumen prints mounted together, 5.75 x 20 inches, by Gardner & Gibson, 1862

Alexander Gardner was not locked into formats and tried different ways of presenting photographs. Camp Winfield Scott, near Yorktown, was established early in the 1862 Peninsula campaign. For a later camp in that campaign at Cumberland Landing, the negatives are extant for a similar panoramic view, but no contemporary prints are known. *Virginia Historical Society, Gift of Le Duc Family*

photographed closely after the battles at Fair Oaks in early June and at Savage's Station in late June, both only a few miles east of Richmond. At Savage's Station, he portrayed wounded soldiers at a field hospital who, a day or two later, were probably among those abandoned when the army rapidly shifted its position.[34]

During the Peninsula campaign Alexander Gardner took a leave from the Brady firm and became a photographer attached to the army. One imagines patriotism had more to do with this move than commercialism. "Given the honorary title of captain, Gardner served loyally in McClellan's 'military family,'" writes Keith Davis. "In this period he specialized in the photographic duplication of maps and drawings for the army's topographic engineers." An extant photographed map from this time is credited to Gibson, so he too must

SCOTT, YORKTOWN, VA.

he Clerk's Office of the District Court of the United States for the District of Columbia.

have been attached in some way to the army. Gardner remained with the army until July, when he "either joined or replaced" Gibson "in the vicinity of the James River."[35]

Other Brady photographers who worked on the Peninsula in the period June to August 1862 included George Barnard at Fair Oaks, Yorktown, and Hampton in June and July and John Wood and David B. Woodbury. The *Southern Illustrated News* commented on this campaign in a piece called "Difficult Photography": "The Yankees, when they moved upon Richmond by way of the Peninsula, brought with them the most delicate and perfect photographic apparatus, and made beautiful pictures of Williamsburg, Yorktown, Westover, and other places. It is understood that the artist had a great many orders for a picture of the Confederate capital, which he was unable to fill, for the reason that it was found impossible to take Richmond."[36]

Timothy O'Sullivan photographed in Virginia for the first time in mid-1862, accompanying the forces under Gen. Pope from Manassas to Warrenton, the Culpeper area, and the battle of Cedar Mountain in early August. When Pope's army returned to Manassas at the end of August, it suffered a new defeat there on the same battlefield, a loss that like the first was too overwhelming to permit documentation.[37]

Following Second Manassas, the Army of Northern Virginia under Gen. Lee moved north, leading to a major battle at Sharpsburg, Maryland, not far from Harper's Ferry, along Antietam Creek. When reports reached Washington, Alexander Gardner rushed to the site with John F. Gibson. They arrived before all the dead were buried, and their photographs were the first of the war to show corpses on the battlefield. Americans had become familiar with photographs of the deceased as a means of remembrance, but the usual style was to represent the subject with sensitivity, as if asleep. Gardner's Antietam photographs showed death without nicety. When displayed by Brady at his New York gallery, there was significant public notice. "Very fine views of Battle Fields," judged *Humphrey's Journal*. "They offer to the eyes the dreadful actualities." The *New York Times* wrote that if Brady "has not brought bodies and laid them in our door-yards and along streets, he has done something very like it."[38]

Even as the photographic coverage of the war achieved notice, Brady's financial difficulties began to surface around November 1862. That month Gardner photographed at the Union camp at Warrenton, then in February 1863 at the supply center at Aquia Creek. These images were distributed by Brady. However by spring 1863 Gardner cut his connection with Brady. Keith Davis states that "he reclaimed many of the war views made during his tenure with Brady, evidently in lieu of unpaid wages or other obligations." Gardner took with him a number of the photographers who had been working for Brady, including O'Sullivan, Gibson, and Barnard, and established his own studio. In addition, Gardner attracted a number of fellow Scots: his brother James, John Reekie, and David Knox.[39]

"Why should he monopolize this department?" asked *Humphrey's Journal* about Brady in September 1861. "We have plenty of other artists as good as he is. . . . Let other artists exhibit a little of Mr. Brady's enterprise, and furnish the public with more views." Gardner and the others who left Brady never specified their reasons. Management of the operation was no doubt one item. Brady had run a high-profile portrait gallery successfully, but that was different from covering a war. Men who had camped with the army were likely to have opinions about management from afar that took all the credit. Recognition was surely a key issue: instead of the line "Photo by Brady" applied to every image, Gardner gave credit to the photographer.[40]

If at the outset the photographers in the field had been employees of Brady, their permission to accompany the army initially negotiated by Brady, that operating model does not seem to have persisted beyond 1862. Gardner and his group appear to have worked under a more fluid, less hierarchical system. As the photographers accumulated comrades and contacts in the army, they were more able to make arrangements on their own, perhaps exchanging photographic services for hosting, such as to copy maps at short notice or to provide prints to officers or to newspapers. This official or semi-official status may have been sufficient to qualify for a rations issue and horse-feed and to travel and camp with a unit. The

historian Susan E. Williams states that one view-maker, Egbert G. Fowx, "contact printed in the field and sold his prints to soldiers." Later in the war Brady too used photographers who were not his employees but contracted by the day.[41]

The most active among the photographers working with Gardner was Timothy O'Sullivan. O'Sullivan later described his position as "three years as photographer attached to Head Quar Army of the Potomac." He spent much of the war in northern Virginia. In December 1862 he was at Falmouth, the Union position facing Fredericksburg across the Rappahannock, and he returned there in March-April 1863. Gardner, O'Sullivan, and Gibson all went to Gettysburg in July. From August to November 1863, O'Sullivan moved around the Virginia Piedmont, the rolling hills east of the Blue Ridge, at Bealton, Warrenton, Culpeper, along the Orange & Alexandria Railroad, and Auburn. As the armies settled into camps for the winter, O'Sullivan left the field, probably spending the off-season at Gardner's gallery to identify negatives and make prints.[42]

In his studies of northern field photography, William Frassanito estimates that 75–80 percent of the images were shot using a stereo camera. Typically a stereo negative was two 3 1/2 inch square images side-by-side to make 3 1/2 x 7 inches. The stereograph was the format that did best at the beginning of the war. Later, a contact print of a stereo negative would be trimmed to make two cartes de

Preparing plates in the field
Stereo glass negative, 1864
At the Union encampment after Cold Harbor, a photographer, probably Guy Fowx, holds a glass plate as he sits by his photographic wagon. Left of him appear to be bottles of chemicals. Because he is working with the plate in daylight, he might be cleaning the surface to ready it for coating. Light-sensitive procedures were undertaken standing in the dark-chamber at the back of the wagon. *Library of Congress, Prints and Photographs Division, LC-B811-2447*

O'Sullivan portrait
Glass negative, by Timothy O'Sullivan, 1862
For simply posing an officer in front of a tent, this image has an active design. The reason in part is because it is a scan from a glass negative, rather than from a print, which has introduced some visual elements: at the left is a light patch where tape or glue remains on the glass; at the bottom a ragged edge of peeling emulsion is visible; and on the ground are up-and-down chemical streaks. Col. Alfred Duffie, 1st Rhode Island Cavalry, poses in July 1862 near Manassas. *Library of Congress, Prints and Photographs Division, LC-B811-644*

O'Sullivan View
Albumen print, by Timothy O'Sullivan, 1863
O'Sullivan left Brady, with whom he began his career, to join Gardner. O'Sullivan had a great ability to identify a subject and organize a picture. His images are interesting visually and have a clear point of view. Similar to Eugène Atget, the French photographer, the quality of O'Sullivan's vision becomes apparent not necessarily in any single image but upon viewing many. This view is of a Union encampment by the residence of Dr. Murray, known as the Castle, near Auburn in Fauquier County.
Virginia Historical Society

O'Sullivan View
Albumen print, by Timothy O'Sullivan, 1863
Union tents near the town of Culpeper, Nov. 1863. *Virginia Historical Society*

visite, once that format gained popularity. Depending on the subject, the 2 1/2 x 3 1/2 inch carte de visite image could be made as a horizontal or as a vertical from the square stereo frame. Ways of offering photographic prints of larger sizes for sale seem to have been developed later in the war, and in particular by Alexander Gardner. Beginning in 1863 he offered 8 x 10 inch prints on mounts imprinted with captions under the title "Incidents of the War."

CONFEDERATE PHOTOGRAPHY

A good deal less photography was produced on the Confederate side in Virginia than on the federal. Of southern photographs, the great majority were portraits. Only a small proportion were made outside a gallery setting.

A standard view of southern Civil War photography, as stated by Frederic E. Ray, is that "the blockade so restricted the necessary imported chemicals and supplies that Confederate artists could no longer afford the highly speculative business of taking outdoor war views. After 1861 they almost exclusively used their carefully husbanded materials for the indoor portrait work that made their livelihood." Several writers from the period reached that conclusion too. In January 1862 *Humphrey's Journal* declared "the Photographic Art down South has completely died out in consequence of the war. The miserable rebels are shut up like a rat in a hole."[43]

The description of southern photography as missing in action has become widely accepted. Historian Keith Davis folds in with the materials shortage another factor: "The combined effects of the blockade and the deteriorating Confederate economy gave Confederate photographers 'nothing to work with, and nobody to work for.'" Basic staples of life were selling for prices high enough that every household became cautious about making unnecessary purchases. In October 1861 the *American Journal of Photography* similarly cited both points: "in the Southern states of the Union, photography like most other artistic and industrial pursuits, for lack of materials wherewith to work, and for lack of patrons, is well nigh a lost art."[44]

Was the art of photography lost in Virginia? Virginians at the time would not have thought so. They would have complained about the price, but the material deficiencies were neither decisive nor the only relevant factors, at least not until the last year of the war brought severe shortages. What northern observers thought was lacking might not have been something that southerners wished to have.

Consider first the formats that were used in the Confederacy. Virtually all Confederate photography was shot with sensitized glass-plates, exposed to be a negative for a photograph, or slightly underexposed to be seen as a positive for an ambrotype. For this process the necessary components were glass, collodion emulsion (made of gun cotton, ether, and alcohol), and silver salt solution, plus the developing chemicals. For making paper-positives, the blockade did restrict access to albumen paper, which was generally purchased in factory-prepared boxes with the emulsion applied. The default paper medium was the salt print. Salt prints required paper, chemicals, and usually a toner, which was a chemical like gold chloride.[45]

Here the *American Journal of Photography* overstated its case in 1861. "The people of the South," said the Journal, "are yet not progressed far enough to have the cunning for manufacturing daguerreotype cases, glass, paper, or pho-

Riddle card portrait
Carte de visite, by A. J. Riddle, c. 1861–63
A. J. Riddle came to Richmond about the time that the Confederate government did. By mid-1864 he had been appointed as Chief Photographer, Dept. of Tennessee. The portrait subject is Launcelot Blackford. *Virginia Historical Society*

Rees case portrait

Ambrotype, one-half plate, by Charles R. Rees, c. 1861–65
Most ambrotypes continued to lack a photographer's mark. Images by Rees are distinctive for the column prop, as seen in this portrait of Private Blair. Rees was located at 145 Main St., the gallery that featured Pratt's Gothic window. *Museum of the Confederacy*

tographic chemicals." Glass had been manufactured in Virginia since it was Jamestown's first industry 250 years earlier. During the Civil War, when it came to replacing the windows in a large building, glass may have been relatively less available and more expensive than usual, but little enough glass was used in photography that a higher price would not have impeded work. Plate glass continued to be available in Richmond.[46]

Certain types of paper became scarce in the South rather quickly. The *Richmond Examiner* commented in January 1862 that "Thousand upon thousands of dollars invested in printing materials are now lying idle and unproductive for want of paper. No other branch of business in the South has suffered more than the printing business, and that mainly for the want of paper."[47] Still, if there was not enough paper to meet all demands, there was a good quantity of paper about. Most affected were large consumers of cheap paper like the *Richmond Christian Advocate,* a publication that was short as early as September 1861. But the same month the *Advocate* could not find paper, Franklin Paper Mill in Richmond was offering "Envelope, Manilla, Wrapping, News and Book Paper."[48] In October 1863 the Wholesale Paper Warehouse in Richmond offered "by late arrivals from Nassau" a variety of papers and boards.[49] For a price, better paper was probably always available, and the total quantity that photographs required was small enough that shortages should not have been a decisive factor.

A more critical area of shortages may have been in photographic chemicals. The south had no producers of such products. Yet England or France would have been a ready source for any chemicals, or indeed for any sort of photographic supplies, and as high-value, low-bulk products, photographic materials would have been ideal cargo for a blockade-runner. How much did galleries anticipate the effects of a war and stock up on the material usually acquired from New York City or other northern cities? There was a window in 1861, as passion was building but before borders were closed. In June 1861 N. S. Tanner in Lynchburg advertised, "Five hundred dollars worth of Stock, for Ambrotypes, Melainotypes and Photographs. Just received direct from the South. Which Enables the Proprietor to Fill all Orders for Pictures in any Style of the Art."[50]

When, in December 1861, Rees's Gallery in Richmond advertised "For sale all kinds of Photograph and Ambrotype Materials, and Chemicals," one presumes the gallery had enough beyond its own needs to sell.[51] In September 1863, the Richmond auctioneer Fowle offered "the stock of a photographer." Included in the lots were a number of photographic chemicals: "Nitrate of Silver, Chloride of Gold, Hypo Sulph. Soda, Chloride of Lead, With a great variety of chemicals, suited to the trade." The items did not sell at that time, for Fowle offered the same list again on 12 October, and then again in May 1864. Among the items still available in May were "Nitrate of silver" and "Chloride of Gold," two basic chemicals. No doubt the asking prices were inflation-driven as all in Richmond were—nonetheless chemicals were to be had. The fact that photography was being produced in Confederate Virginia through at least 1864 suggests that some quantity of materials was available.[52]

According to the standard analysis, the other main deficit in Confederate photography was the lack of patrons. One potential measure of activity that would seem to support this notion is that advertising by photographers in the Confederate areas of Virginia tailed off after 1861 and by late 1862 was seldom seen. However the decline might have been for other reasons besides the amount of business. The circumstances of wartime might have made advertising less relevant. Few new galleries were opening that needed advertising to become known. For existing galleries, people were in the grip of strong feelings and either had a reason to sit for a portrait or would put it off. To the war-bound soldier, the cost of the sitting was not a deciding factor. The reduced advertising activity, then, while indicative of changed conditions, might not directly reflect the level of business in photography.[53]

Regarding views in the field, the particular area in which southern photography was most lacking in comparison to northern, a considerable part of the explanation probably lies in the structure of the commercial economy, the network of wholesale suppliers and retail outlets. In the North, Currier & Ives was only the most prominent of a number of image producers who by the 1850s were distributing their products widely. These producers of lithography, mezzotints, and other kinds of prints were a separate category from the illustrated periodicals such as *Harper's* and *Leslie's* that arose in the 1850s. Producers and distributors worked out of the large eastern seaboard cities from Baltimore north and such newer interior cities as Cincinnati and Chicago. In cities and towns there were retailers who stocked these pictures, traveling salesmen, publications offering prints as subscription benefits, and in sum a functioning system to distribute pictures. The new development of 1860 was that E. & H. T. Anthony Co. and a few other firms were introducing photographic images in the formats of stereographs into this distribution system. Then in 1861 the carte de visite became the hot picture product in vogue.

Thus an entrepreneur who proposed to photograph the Civil War, such as Mathew Brady, knew that there was a way to get the images before the public. Success was not guaranteed, but a clear shot at it was available. By comparison, the experience of Edward Beyer in Virginia revealed that the state lacked such a system. In 1854 Beyer, an artist from Germany, came to Virginia and spent three years sketching and painting the landscape, especially of the central mountainous region and the resorts at the springs. In 1855–56 he conceived the notion of issuing a set of lithographs of these landscapes, which became the well-known *Album of Virginia.* Beyer solicited subscriptions from the public, either for the complete set of forty prints, or singly for one of the five parts of eight prints each that appeared from April 1857 through mid-1858. Beyer did not discover any sort of statewide network that he could tap into and instead had to create his own distribution system. He and his wife traveled to many of the principal towns, seeking a newspaper office that was sympathetic, or local storekeepers who might represent them, or a bookstore that occasionally would offer images, or even a home decorating shop that offered framed prints. There was no existing structure for distributing Beyer's editions of lithographic prints and no Virginia-based wholesaler or distributor of images.[54]

As little as Virginia possessed of a picture-distribution system, what existed was more than the other southern states possessed because Virginia at least had towns and cities where there was a concentrated commercial presence. Even so the state did not have anything like the pool of energetic strivers that populated northern communities. Had there been an entrepreneur with the intention to create images and distribute to the C.S.A., he would have faced a large task to establish outlets even without a war. "Some of our photographers should repair to the scenes of the late battles, and take views of the fortifications, camps, etc.," commented the *Richmond Whig* shortly after the Seven Days' battle turned back the Union army's Peninsula campaign. If that sentiment had been expressed more often and more strongly, some photographer might have sought to do it. No producer of views in lithography or any other print format succeeded at distributing their products across the South either.[55]

Another question altogether, despite the *Whig's* call for views, is whether anyone in the South would have wished to have documentary photographs of the war. In the North, the discourse of the press and public was on the path to the free-for-all model of the current day, with a range of opinion published and a great many topics open for discussion (much more true of today than then, of course). Southern states, on the other hand, had placed legal limits on public discourse since the 1830s. Whether sent by mail or spoken in a public forum, antislavery

CHS. R. REES & CO.
PHOTOGRAPHIC
ARTISTS,
Richmond, Va.

Rees card portrait
Carte de visite, by Charles R. Rees, c. 1861–65
By one account, Charles R. Rees made the gallery's ambrotypes, and his brother Edwin J. the cartes de visite. The soldier is unidentified, by provenance possibly a Page or a Woolfolk. *Virginia Historical Society*

Belle Isle

Albumen print, 2.5 x 4 in., by Rees, c. 1863

The view is a rare Confederate field photograph, one of several exposures made at the time. Viewed from a bluff on the island, the open-air prison for federal soldiers was surrounded by the James River. Visible beyond is the Capitol, on the horizon left-center; two shapes right-center that are the Gallego Mills; and the Richmond & Petersburg railroad bridge. This small print may have been made from the original negative that was lost in 1865. *Valentine Richmond History Center*

Libby Prison

Stereograph, original by Rees, c. 1863

This piece is in the stereo format but lacks stereo effect; the same image, a copy of Rees's view, is printed on both the left and right side. The label on the back states, "From the original Photograph, taken August 23, 1863—The negative having been destroyed by fire on the memorable morning of 3rd April, 1865." *Valentine Richmond History Center*

Vannerson portrait and wartime imprint
Carte de visite, by Julian Vannerson, c. 1862–65
Vannerson's signature portrait style is a vignetted bust on an oval print. The mount in this case is not cardboard but more of a thick paper, probably what was available. The subject is Major Powhatan Ellis. *Virginia Historical Society*

Minnis portrait and imprint
Carte de visite, by George W. Minnis
No carte de visite with a definite wartime date and a Minnis ink imprint has been seen. (A few with an embossed imprint are known.) The credit line "Minnis & Cowell" may have reflected an informal rather than a formal arrangement. This card with its fancy imprint most likely dates to just after the war when Minnis reopened in 1865–66. The subject, Philip Haxall, was of the flour-mill family and later wed belle Mary Triplett. *Virginia Historical Society*

Where Rees's gallery stood
Albumen print on mount, possibly by Guy Fowx, 1865.
The view looks west on Main Street, with the Custom House—between 10th and 11th streets—visible at right rear. A map of the Burnt District shows that, north of Main, the eastern extent of the fire was between 13th and 14th streets. That burnt edge was at the far end of the buildings to the right in the image. Thus the ruins to the left where the men are seated include the site of Rees's gallery.
Virginia Historical Society

Federal photography unit
Glass negative, 1865
This big copy camera and darkroom set-up are identified as the quarters of the photographers attached to the Engineer Corps at Petersburg. Note the contact print frames leaning against the cabin. Likely the chief production was copies of maps. *Library of Congress, Prints and Photographs Division, LC-B8184-7347 (detail)*

opinion was not permitted, and even mild opposition brought a severe social price. Other topics did not require explicit law to be proscribed. Despite the occasional calls for battlefield views, there is no reason to suppose that many southerners would have wished to be exposed to, or to have circulated, the documentary information of photographs, with the chance of being possibly off-message.

The Confederacy was not opposed to all art and did embrace one particular kind of photograph: portraits of leaders. These were head shots, with occasionally a half-figure or full-figure, usually in uniform. The standard format included no background, no connection to any particular time or place—these were idealized busts. They were in keeping with a worldview that personalized the armies in the field with leaders' names attached to brigades and regiments.

By August 1861 the first batches of cartes de visite of southern leaders were received in Richmond. Such New York publishers as E. & H. T. Anthony utilized prewar portraits for their issues, obtained from galleries such as Brady's. The *Richmond Daily Dispatch* reported that the bookseller West & Johnson had "received a lot of beautiful photographic likenesses of President Davis and Lady, and Generals Beauregard, Johnston, Lee, Magruder and Huger." The newspaper commented that "the pictures bear the imprint of a New York firm, showing that the Yankees are determined to make money out of our Generals in private, if they cannot beat them in public." The Richmond bookseller George Bigood offered cartes de visite of leaders in September, and J. W. Randolph had them by October, advertising their availability into February 1862.[56]

In the same vein of portraiture, the *Southern Illustrated News* featured wood engravings of military leaders on its front page from September 1862 to February 1864. The engravings were mostly derived from photographs (and demonstrated the South's shortage of good engravers). As a steady flow of Confederate leaders posed for photographs in galleries, updated portraits became available, many distinguished from antebellum versions by war-beards and grayer hair. Virginia-produced cartes de visite were first mentioned in 1863, in the *Southern Illustrated News*. In June five titles from Rees & Co. were cited, and then in August an article appeared on the subject. Titled "Pictures of Our Generals," it reported on albums designed to hold cartes de visite, newly "introduced into Yankeedom and filled with the Generals of Lincolndom." The vision of an album full of portraits stirred the article writer's patriotic feeling: "But neither Europe, and least of all, Lincolndom, have material equal to that possessed by the Southern Confederacy wherewith to fill their Albums, for what country on the face of the habitable globe, save the young Confederacy, can boast of such illustrious heroes as Stone-

A Confederate photographer
Salt print, by Daniel Bendann, from Richmond Light Infantry Blues album, 1856
The subject, Richard S. Sanxay, had managed Pratt's gallery, and after becoming an owner in 1856 operated the business for several years. Sanxay served with the Blues for the first part of the war until called upon as a photographer. *Virginia Historical Society*

wall Jackson and Robert E. Lee?" The article then devolved into a puff for the carte de visite series issued by Minnis & Cowell of Richmond, listing thirteen titles: "There is not a child in our land who would not dwell in admiration for hours upon the features of any one of these great heroes."[57]

In raw numbers the quantity of Confederate cartes de visite issued during the war may not have been that great. But enough did appear to make an impression: in March 1864 the New Richmond Theatre announced that "an entirely new Farce" was in preparation "entitled the Carte De Visite."[58]

CONFEDERATE PHOTOGRAPHY IN RICHMOND

Because the city was the seat of the Confederacy, the state of Virginia was never more "Richmond-centric" than during the Civil War. The principal photographers active in Richmond were Minnis, Vannerson, and Rees.[59]

Charles R. Rees did not advertise after April 1861. Nonetheless, based on 1863–64 tax returns, Rees's gallery was the most active in the city: the gross receipts were over two times larger than any other Richmond photographer. In November 1861 Rees gained unsought press attention when a runaway horse "attached to a covered vehicle made a furious run down Main street." It was about "to plunge into West & Johnston's bookstore, but brought up with a smash against Rees's daguerrean show case in front." After the collision, "pictures were scattered about promiscuously in the sidewalk, the likenesses of several distinguished individuals being extinguished for time, as well as those of some smaller fry." In January 1863 Rees was hiring: "Wanted—A No. 1 white Cook, Washer, and Ironer." Until May 1863, he owned two horses, a sign of his prosperity. That month the horses were requisitioned, for which he was paid $440 for one grey mare and $500 for one bay horse.[60]

In June 1863, the *Southern Illustrated News* was "indebted to Messrs. Charles R. Rees & Co., Photographic Artists, Richmond, for carte de visite photographs," including "a picture of Beast Butler, copied from an original taken in New Orleans." In August 1863 Rees made several views of Libby Prison, one of the only examples of Confederate field photography from Virginia. It was probably one of Rees's views that a Union prisoner referred to in a December 1863 letter: "To-day I bought of one of the guards the inclosed photograph of Libby. Cost $5 in Confederate money." Probably in the same time period, Rees also made two views of Belle Isle prison camp. Whether these views had an official purpose is not known.[61]

Tax records indicate that Rees continued in business through at least April 1864. His trade may have dipped once Union forces closed in on the Richmond-Petersburg area in summer 1864 and the siege of Petersburg began. In August 1864, a notice appeared: "Wanted, a Situation, by an experienced Photographer, acquainted with all branches of the business," and stating "Apply to C. R. Rees & Co." Perhaps the seeker was not Rees but an assistant, his services no longer required. During the Evacuation Fire, Rees's gallery burned. It is likely that no more than a small portion, if any, of his negatives survived.[62]

Julian Vannerson was likely busy at his gallery in 1861 as soldiers arrived in Richmond. Probably because his brother John T. served as captain of the unit, in November 1861 Julian became a recruiting agent for a company of the "Young Guard," the 15th Regiment Virginia Volunteers. In early 1862 Vannerson was one of three men running a recruiting office at 17th and Marshall streets "for the purpose of raising one hundred men, either for infantry or artillery service, as the vote of the company may decide." In February 1862 a fire at his gallery caused "much damage," and Vannerson's loss was "about $200—no insurance."[63]

A Vannerson portrait of Gen. Joseph E. Johnston was the source for a November 1862 engraving in the *Southern Illustrated News*. Confederate tax records show that his gross sales for the first half of 1863 were $4,800 and that he maintained about the same level of business through April 1864. In January 1864 he was commissioned by the government to photograph an officer at General Hospital No. 4 and the next month to take another at General Hospital No. 1. In early 1864 Vannerson made portraits of Gen. Robert E. Lee for sculptor Edward V. Valentine to work from in London. In April-May 1864 Vannerson worked as a contract photographer for the Confederate government. His brother John T. was wounded in both legs at Spotsylvania Court House on 16 May 1864, and the need to care for him may be a reason that Vannerson left the government at the end of May.[64]

When George W. Minnis opened in Richmond, a rival gossiped that "they say that Minnis makes very poor Pho." Many who learned as daguerreotypers did have trouble adapting to paper photographs. Minnis solved any deficiency by hiring D. T. Cowell for the Richmond gallery, which had won the top prize at the 1860 Mechanics' Institute fair. Minnis also had "permanently in his employ the very best of artists in oil colors, water colors, and India ink," including "the artistic pencil of Mr. King," a contributor to the *Southern Illustrated News* and in 1862 "long connected to the Minnis Gallery."[65]

Of all the galleries, Minnis attracted the most Confederate leaders to pose, due as much or more to Cowell as Minnis. In March 1863 the *Southern Illustrated News,* "determined to give our readers as truthful and accurate likenesses of the heroes of the present war as it is possible to obtain," was finally able "to secure, through the politeness of Mr. Cowel, the gentlemanly artist of the Minnis' gallery, an admirable picture of Gen. Hill, taken only a few weeks ago." Then in July 1863, the *Southern Illustrated News* addressed those who "have insinuated that

the picture of Gen. Jackson, which we have announced to accompany our Book is not a bona fide likeness of the lamented hero." The newspaper wished to announce that the picture was taken for us by Mr. D. T. Cowell, of the Minnis Gallery. Through the kindness of a friend we were enabled to procure for Mr. Cowell a letter of introduction to Gen. Jackson, who, immediately upon the arrival of the artist at his headquarters at Fredericksburg, consented to sit for the picture. Three different photographs were taken at the time, one of which was spoiled by the shaking of the instrument. . . . The three negatives are now in the possession of Mr. Cowell, who will . . . furnish all who wish photographs for the purpose of framing.[66]

The name of the business never changed from the G. W. Minnis Gallery, but the credits on the firm's cartes de visite became Minnis & Cowell, a change that also took place in the credits carried by the *Southern Illustrated News* beginning in August 1863. The tax records for the gallery from September 1863 and February 1864 show it to have had the second largest gross income among Richmond galleries. Judging from lists published at the time, Minnis & Cowell produced the largest number of wartime cartes de visite of the Richmond galleries. In August 1863 the *Southern Illustrated News* stated that "at the gallery of Messrs. Minnis & Cowell of this city have been preserved life-like pictures of all the prominent officers in the Confederate army."[67]

Not everything went well during the war for Minnis. On 4 July 1862 policeman Kelly "impressed the horse and wagon of G. W. Minnis" to "convey the wounded to the City" after the Seven Days' battle. "From the effects of the drive said horse died," stated an officer. Minnis sought compensation and was required to submit a sheaf of documents about the incident and to certify that the horse was "fully worth three hundred dollars." In April 1864 Minnis advertised for "A good Photographer, who is exempt from military service." In May 1864 appeared: "Notice—The Photograph Gallery of G. W. Minnis, 217 Main St., will be closed until further notice." One possible explanation is that Cowell, whether drafted or called away, had left.[68]

MILITARY APPLICATIONS

Early in the war neither army had a photographic program. In time military photographic units were set up within both the Union and Confederate armies. Although not as well known nor as extensive as the Union engineers' use of photography, Confederate army engineers also employed it.

Much of the early use of photography fell under the general category of intelligence. Alexander Gardner was a friend to James Pinkerton, a fellow Scot and head of the federal protective agency, who is reported to have pored over Gardner's group photographs looking for spies. In another case from July 1861, the crew of a Union ship in the Potomac River below Washington noticed floating toward them an "infernal machine," a buoyant bomb with a burning fuse. The device was defused and hauled to Alexandria "for scientific investigation. It was hoisted out this morning, and taken to the front of the shell house opposite the ordnance shop, where it was fastened up in a convenient position to be photographed." James F. Gibson of Brady's Washington gallery captured the image of

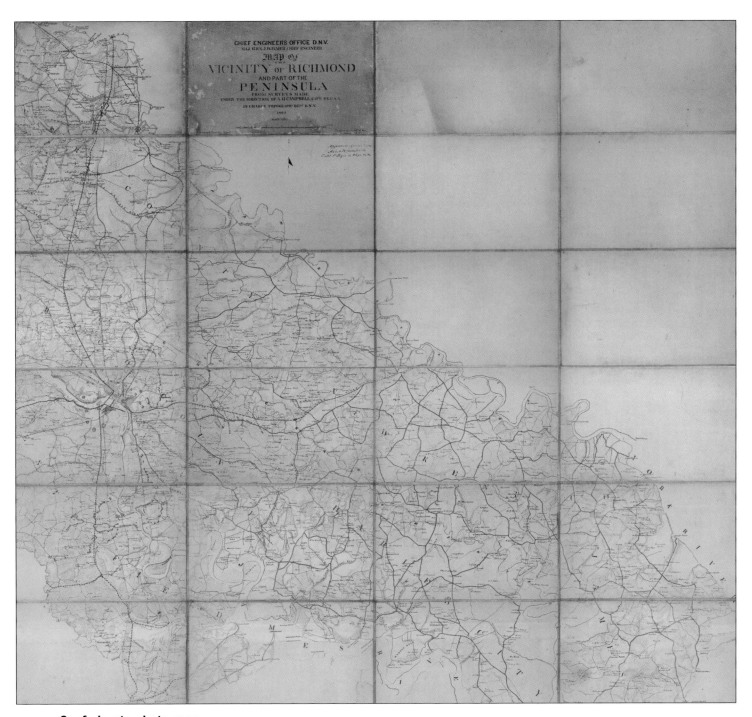

Confederate photo-map

Map of 24 sun-prints, each 6.25 x 9.87 in., mounted together on cloth backing

The original "Map of the vicinity of Richmond and part of the Peninsula" was prepared under the direction of Capt. Albert H. Campbell, and dated 26 April 1864. This photographic copy was made under "Sanzay [sic] & Gomert's patent." The good condition of the photo-map suggests it was not used in the field. *Library of Virginia, Map Collection*

A. J. Russell's team

Probably at their Alexandria office, Andrew J. Russell stands on the porch, Egbert Guy Fowx stands at rear, and seated are two assistants, possibly J. C. Fuller and M. B. Fuller. *Courtesy Ross Johnson*

the device, and a sketch by Alfred Waud from the photograph was reproduced in the *New York Illustrated News*.[69]

The first photographer to attain official military status was Alexander Gardner, who for the 1862 Peninsula campaign was attached to Gen. McClellan's command with an honorary rank of captain. Gardner's primary function was probably to copy maps, which were being redrawn and distributed on an accelerated basis. A July 1864 article explained, "Wherever we go, a number of Engineers are in the advance, who get the topography, roads, &c—all the materials for a complete and accurate map of the country. The Draughtsman soon have this produced in tracing paper, ready for the photographer, who by the transfer process, as it is called, can supply every general officer in the army with a copy in the course of the day." Eventually the Union army developed methods of rapid reproduction using lithography and needed photography for copying maps less.[70]

The Confederate army was a step behind in developing a topographic corps. A "plan for procuring accurate maps" was instituted once Robert E. Lee took command in June 1862, under the direction of Captain Albert H. Campbell.

Campbell sent surveying parties throughout central Virginia to prepare maps of each county. "So great was the demand for maps," wrote Campbell, "that it became impossible by the usual method of tracings to supply them." Campbell "conceived the plan of doing this work by photography." Apparently at that point a search was instituted for qualified photographers to conduct the work, and Richard S. Sanxay and Adolph Gomert were selected. Sanxay's background is known, but Gomert's is not.[71]

Richard S. Sanxay purchased Pratt's Gallery in Richmond in 1856 after serving as the principal operator for several years. He and a partner sustained the business through at least late 1857. By 1860 Sanxay was working as a clerk in a Main Street store. His father, Richard D. Sanxay, was a senior alderman on

Test results
Albumen print, by A. J. Russell, c. 1862–63
Russell's group documented structural tests for the military railroad. This image, titled "Second experiment with board trusses," shows the experimental method in process, before the breaking weight of 95 tons was reached. *Library of Congress, Prints and Photographs Division, LC-DIG-ppmsca-10353*

the Richmond city council and during the war served as Richmond's coroner.[72] As his father had been, Sanxay was a member of the Richmond Light Infantry Blues, one of the units sent to Harpers Ferry in 1859. When the Blues were called into service on 13 June 1861, Sanxay was elected second lieutenant. In February 1862 the Blues took casualties in the defense of Roanoke Island, N.C. One of those killed was their captain, O. Jennings Wise, editor of the *Richmond Enquirer* and son of the former governor, and Sanxay "accompanied the remains" to Richmond. In late February Sanxay served as recruiting officer to fill the Blues' depleted ranks. By August 1862 he was stationed at Chaffin's Farm, on the Richmond defenses east of the city. Later in November 1863 Lt. Sanxay was back in Richmond on furlough from South Carolina, collecting "shoes, socks, and blankets for his fellow members."[73]

Campbell had the idea for copying maps, and the recruited photographers worked out the specifics. In February 1864 Sanxay and Gomert were awarded a patent by the Confederate Patent Office for a method of reproducing maps by contact printing. According to Campbell, "traced copies were prepared on com-

mon tracing paper in very black India ink, and from these sharp negatives by sun-printing were obtained." The negatives were contact printed. "The several sections, properly toned, were pasted together in their order, and formed the general map."[74]

During 1864 Sanxay and Gomert each held the position of "Photographer Engineering Bureau," drawing both monthly pay and payment for production of prints. A dozen invoices for prints submitted by Sanxay and Gomert are found in the records, from April 1864 to December 1864. Almost all the prints cited in the invoices are copies of maps, and a number state "Use of Patent for pho-

CITY POINT AND
TRESTLE BRIDGE over ARTHUR'S SW
Built by Construction Corp
February
Length 1240 F

Russell panorama

Three albumen prints on mount, by Andrew J. Russell, 1865, 11¾ x 28 in. Inscribed title on mount: "City Point and Army Line, Trestle Bridge over Arthur's Swamp near Hatcher's Run. Built by Construction Corps, USMRRds, February, 1865. Length 1240 feet." *Virginia Historical Society*

tographing maps." One from 30 June 1864 includes 317 prints of "Vicinity of Petersburg"; 90 prints of "Gen. Map Eastern Va."; and 478 prints "Vicinity of Richmond." Another map title on 1 June was "East Tenn." An invoice dated 20 August 1864 lists prints for "Report of A. J. Riddle, Chief Photographer Dept. of Tennessee."[75]

The one print title on the invoices that is not a map is "Photograph Copies Dahlgren's letter." Colonel Ulric Dahlgren was a Union officer killed attempting a bold raid on Richmond. On his body was found a dispatch with instructions to assassinate President Davis in Richmond, or so the Confederates, for their purposes, interpreted it. As reported in the newspapers, Gen. Lee sent a copy to Gen. Meade "asking whether [the instructions] had received the sanction of Col. Dahlgren's superior officers." Sanxay and Gomert's 16 April invoice billed for 138 copies of the letter, and that of 1 June included another 85 copies.[76]

Overall the Union army's use of photography was the more extensive and varied. In a number of cases a photographer was contracted for a specific assignment. One such case led to the army creating a position for a full-time photographer. In

early 1863 Gen. Herman Haupt, head of U.S. Military Railroads, was preparing a manual on military bridges and wanted to include photographic documentation. Haupt saw the usefulness of having a photographer on staff, and Capt. Andrew J. Russell was brought on in 1863. Russell was a painter and journalist serving in an upstate New York regiment until reassigned to photography. He was a capable artist but needed to learn the wet-plate process, and for that purpose in February 1863 the Baltimore photographer Egbert Guy Fowx became his instructor.[77]

Over the spring and summer of 1863, working out of an office in Alexandria, Russell photographed for Haupt around northern Virginia, covering such subjects as construction techniques, rebuilt railroad bridges, and structural tests

MY LINE.
r HATCHER'S RUN,
Rds..

conducted by army engineers on the load capacity of wooden bridge components. In May 1863 Russell went to Fredericksburg and photographed Confederate dead at Marye's Heights one day after the battle. He made many prints for Haupt for distribution, including large sets in April and in July 1863, and twenty-nine copies of a volume of eighty-two photographs, completed in February 1864. In his first year as photographer, Russell produced some six thousand prints. After Gen. Haupt resigned in September 1863, Russell worked for both the military railroad under Gen. Daniel C. McCallum and for the army quartermaster under Gen. Montgomery Meigs, providing "visual evidence that the funds for the railroad and quartermaster's department were being well spent."[78]

PHOTOGRAPHERS ALL FOR THE UNION

By 1864 a number of Union military leaders had come to appreciate the value of the view-makers' photographic coverage of the war. Cooperation with proven independents seems to have been standard policy. People in the army enabled photographers by commissioning pictures, supplying permission for access, and probably by facilitating ship and rail transportation and feed for horses.

The Union encampment at Brandy Station from November 1863 to April 1864 was well attended by photographers, many of them portraitists. When the army broke camp at the beginning of May 1864, however, only one cameraman, Timothy O'Sullivan, moved out with the troops. O'Sullivan's work over the next month was as close to the action as any photographer's in the war. He photographed crossings on the North Anna River, Confederate dead at Spotsylvania, Grant and his generals from a second-story window at Massaponax Church, and pontoon bridges over the Pamunkey and James rivers. Once the Petersburg front settled into trench warfare in June 1864, O'Sullivan's war coverage in Virginia (and that of the Gardner group as a whole) became more occasional.[79]

While O'Sullivan was at the front, in May 1864 a number of photographers converged at Belle Plain, a supply base on Potomac Creek. They included Andrew J. Russell of the army, James Gardner of Gardner's gallery, and at least one photographer working for Brady, probably Thomas J. Roche or Egbert Fowx or both. Roche and Fowx were independents who had each worked for Brady and for the government. By the end of the war, Roche was working for Anthony but in this period was still with Brady. Fowx, sometime referred to as Guy Fox,

Negative by T. H. O'SULLIVAN.   Entered according to act of Congress, in the year 1866, by A. Gardner, in the Clerk's Office of the District Court of the District of Columbia.   Positive by A. GARDNER, 511 7th st., Washington.

CHESTERFIELD BRIDGE, NORTH ANNA, VIRGINIA.

[Telegraph Bridge?]

No. 66.

See Evans Military History
vol. 3, North Anna
Campaign.

May, 1864.

On campaign
Albumen print, by Timothy O'Sullivan, from *Photographic Sketchbook of the Civil War*
O'Sullivan was the only photographer to accompany the Union Army of the Potomac when it broke
winter camp and began the 1864 campaign. Chesterfield bridge over the North Anna River was
important to the army's movement at the time of the photograph and therefore under guard.
Virginia Historical Society, Gift of Dr. B. Randolph Wellford

seems to have been Brady's chief photographer for much of the war's final year.

At Belle Plain the main subjects were the wharfs and Confederate prisoners. Regarding the latter, several of the photographers seem to have shot not only at the same time, but even from the same camera position, and perhaps on the same tripod. The parallel recording of a subject by photographers working side by side was an occurrence repeated numerous times in the last year of the war. Photographers not only traveled together but sometimes also took virtually identical views—a practice that has long caused confusion in determining photographer credits. Even though the photographers were supplying different organizations, their working relationships became very close. In certain situations the competitive, individual attitude of being the one to get the best shot had been superceded by a common cause in the struggle to preserve the Union.[80]

After Belle Plain, the photographers proceeded to Fredericksburg, recording sites of the 1862 and 1863 battles and portraying soldiers wounded in the 1864 fighting. As a group Russell, Roche, and Fowx gathered to cover the burial of casualties from the Spotsylvania battles. Their access was provided through Gen. Meigs, Russell's superior officer. Fowx and Roche next covered the new supply base at White House landing, and in June 1864 they traveled with Brady to the main Union army camp at Cold Harbor. There the two recorded twenty views, mostly groups of officers, with Brady slipping into at least one frame. The famous portrait at the Cold Harbor camp of Grant leaning against a tree was shot by Roche and Fowx separately (and identically), so there are two originals.

Since the outset of the war, Brady had been a collector of group portraits of the command staff of the federal forces. Now he aimed to record all the divisions of Grant's forces, including the Armies of the Potomac and the James. On that mission he and his artists moved with the army on Petersburg and to City Point. Several times in this period Brady posed with artillery units, which the visual evidence suggests was also a favorite subject. For the purpose of staff portraits, Brady's artists—presumably Fowx and Roche—in July proceeded to Gen. Sheridan's headquarters above City Point and then to Gen. Butler's at Bermuda Hundred.[81]

Russell went to Alexandria in June and returned to City Point in July. He documented the railroad that was built from the port at City Point to the federal lines, including a three-plate panorama of a long trestle. In October 1864 Russell photographed the Weldon Railroad, south of Petersburg. In November he was accompanied to Broadway Landing on the Appomattox River by Roche, who began to work for Anthony by winter 1864. In fall and winter 1864–65, sometimes together, Russell, Fowx, and Roche photographed along the James River above City Point, at Deep Bottom, Aikens Landing, Fort Burnham, Fort Brady, and Dutch Gap. They all documented the Union ships on river duty.[82]

On 2 April 1865 Union forces broke the Confederate lines at Petersburg, and Lee's forces abandoned the city. Russell in 1882 recalled Roche's words at City Point the night before:

> 'Cap., I am in for repairs and want to get things ready for the grand move, for the army is sure to move tonight. . . . [I must] prepare my glass and chemicals; in fact, get everything ready.' . . . I sat up with Mr. Roche until the 'wee sma' hours; he had everything in A No. 1 order for the morrow. We sat smoking and talking of adventures, etc., etc. . . . The heavy boom of cannons

Photographers' repast
Glass negative, c. 1864
Guy Fowx, on left, holds a cup, and Thomas Roche appears to hold meat on a bone. A box on the photographic wagon is labeled "Brady," for whom Fowx worked in 1864–65. Fowx had also worked with Russell, and Roche and Russell were also comrades. *Library of Congress, Prints and Photographs Division, LC-B8184-B-5077 (detail)*

Wagon drivers
Stereograph, published by E. & H. T. Anthony & Co.
The printed caption states "Colored Army Teamsters, Cobb Hill, Va." The photographer may have been Thomas Roche, who worked for Anthony in 1864–65. The series title suggests that this is a postwar reissue. *Virginia Historical Society*

12 December 1864, I

Stereograph, by Thomas Roche, 1864

This is the second of three views made by two photographers working together. First Andrew J. Russell made a stereo; then Roche made this stereo view, published by E. & T. H. Anthony & Co., and identified by Susan E. Williams as from a negative at the Library of Congress, LC-B811-2540 [3.5 x 7 in.]. The label identifies the scene as "View on the James River, looking east; the double turreted monitor Omdagua [Onondaga] in the River." *Virginia Historical Society*

12 December 1864, II

Albumen print, by A. J. Russell, 1864

This is the third of three views made by two photographers working together. Andrew J. Russell made this print, in the VHS album, page 90b, labeled as "Looking down James River, From Dutch Gap Canal, December 12, 1864," and identified by Susan E. Williams as from a negative at the National Archives, NA-CP, RG-111-B-467 [8 x 11 in.]. *Virginia Historical Society*

were heard in the direction of Petersburg. Roche jumped to his feet, and rushing to the door said, 'Cap., the ball has opened; I must be off,' calling to his assistant. In the next quarter of an hour two horses were harnessed, everything snugly packed, and shaking my hand with a 'we will meet to-morrow at the front,' said 'good-bye,' and the wagon rattled off into the darkness.

On the morning of 3 April, Roche was early to the lines and photographed Confederate dead at Fort Mahone. Russell joined him there and photographed an exact duplicate of one of Roche's most widely distributed images.[83]

Once Petersburg was lost, the Confederate army and government withdrew from Richmond and headed southwest. Early on 3 April, the last elements of the Confederate army departing the city left warehouses and bridges burning. A high wind spread the flames into an out-of-control conflagration, the Evacuation Fire. None of the Richmond photographers recorded the event; by the time the sun rose, the flames threatened or were consuming several galleries and everybody was probably busy.

Much was lost in that fire. A week or so afterward, a Mr. Wright advertised a reward for two trunks and a basket, lost at the American Hotel and "probably taken by mistake," including "Photographs of Rev. P. Courtney and myself, in gilt frames about 8 x 10." Among the losses were many such photographs, in frames, in albums, in bureaus, consumed in offices, hotels, homes, and galleries.[84]

The first Union photographer to enter Richmond after the fire was Alexander Gardner, down from Washington, on 6 April. By Frassanito's count, within two weeks of the fall of the city some 250 photographs were made: 100 by the Gardner group, 60 by the Brady group, and nearly 100 Anthony views. Subjects included the Burnt District, landmarks like the Capitol and Libby Prison, and freedmen. In April and May, Russell made at least 50 views of those subjects and of bridges and trains. Photographers who had not previously been in the field also came to Richmond. "Two enterprising young men" of Philadelphia, Levy & Cohen, returned from the Rebel capital with "mostly excellent photographs," reported the *Philadelphia Photographer* in September 1865, embracing "all the points of historical interest in and about the city."[85]

As familiar as any photographs made then were the portraits of Robert E. Lee made in April 1865. The *Richmond Whig* reported on 21 April that "General Lee and staff . . . were yesterday photographed in a group by Mr. Brady of New York. Six different sittings were taken." Williams states that "Brady and Fowx went to Lee's rented house on Franklin Street and photographed the general standing on the back porch."[86]

Photographic panoramas constitute another significant group of 1865 Richmond images. Several by Gardner have become well known, but most are not. Previously Gardner had produced photographic panoramas with Gibson in 1862 and for George Barnard in 1864 of Tennessee and Atlanta. In all these cases, a camera at a suitable overlook was rotated to take a series of views that could be fit together to make a very wide landscape. For a photographer seeking to convey the expanse of the Burnt District, which was both a powerful war view and a potent symbol of destroyed Confederate hopes, the panorama was an effective way to interpret the subject. William A. Pratt the daguerreotyper had built his castle on the crest of Gambles Hill where the prospect from the tower took in the

Burnt District

Stereograph, 1865

The stereograph has no labels or other printed information. Probably the maker (one guess would be Gardner's Gallery, a user of yellow card stock) was in a hurry to get images of the fallen Confederate capital to market. *Virginia Historical Society*

Entered, according to Act of Congress, in the year 1865, by LEVY & COHEN, in the Clerk's Office of the District Court for the Eastern District of Pennsylvania.

Burnt District

Carte de visite, by Levy & Cohen, 1865

The photographers traveled from Philadelphia to capture the rebel capital. The view is across the canal basin toward the imposing ruins of Gallego mills. *Virginia Historical Society*

Burnt District
Albumen print, by A. J. Russell, 1865
Russell carried his large-plate camera to the top of the Bell Tower in Capitol Square to take this view looking toward the canal basin and the Burnt District.
Virginia Historical Society

sweep of Richmond, its industry along the river, and its notable public buildings on Shockoe Hill. In April 1865 that same prospect gave the most comprehensive view of the ruins. Gardner made a five-plate panorama in 8 x 10 from the tower of Pratt's Castle. Wood engravings from this panorama appeared in *Harper's Weekly* in May 1865 and in the *Illustrated London News* in June.[87]

At least ten other photographic panoramas were shot around the city at this time, but few assembled presentations of any of them exist. The format was not a mass-market item. With the notable exception of Gardner, few galleries had cultivated high-end customers for pricier photography. If the photographs that were shot to make up the panoramas were issued at all, it was as single prints. Among the panoramas were views that looked from Church Hill across to the Capitol, down the James River from Libby Hill, at the Burnt District from across the river, toward Manchester south of the river, from Spring Hill to Belle Isle, and across the canal basin toward ruins.[88]

A final round of war coverage in spring 1865 reached sites that had not been previously accessible to Union photographers. For Gardner, John Reekie documented places east of Richmond where events occurred in 1862 and 1864, and

it was likely Reekie who recorded a large number of views of the batteries that had guarded approaches along the James River. In late April Timothy O'Sullivan went to Appomattox and photographed the key buildings. In May he shot the mills along the Appomattox River in Petersburg. In one view his wagon appears with the identification "Photographer's Wagon Engineering Depart," indicating that at least some of that work may have been a government commission. That month too O'Sullivan took 40 views on the Petersburg front. A photographer working for Brady, possibly Fowx, also made views of Petersburg fortifications. Public interest was fast moving on from the war, however, especially after the jarring news of the assassination of Lincoln. The great wave of field photography in Virginia that came with the war ended soon after the battles stopped.

Petersburg mills
Albumen print, by Timothy O'Sullivan, from *Photographic Sketchbook of the Civil War*
O'Sullivan's final Virginia swing took in Appomattox and then a series of views on the
Appomattox River, including this view, described in the Sketchbook as "Johnson's Mill,
Petersburg, Va., May 1865." *Virginia Historical Society*

Christiansburg
Cabinet card, by W. H. Jewel, Elite Studio, c. 1885–1905
Virginia Historical Society

CHAPTER THREE

THE COMMUNITY PHOTOGRAPHER

Photography in Virginia after Appomattox faced pluses and minuses. To the good were the near-universal acceptance of the photographic portrait and ever-expanding uses for the medium. Less positive was the state's devastated economy. A great deal of prewar wealth was gone, including all investment in slaves and in Confederate bonds. The men who led the state previously had been largely removed from positions of authority, and the abolition of slavery altered social relations for everybody. If racial prejudice was not much abated, a new system was nonetheless in place.

As a consequence, business conditions were rather unsettled in postwar Virginia. Reflecting the times, photography was a changeable trade. Few operators opened a gallery and then stayed for a whole career in one community—only a dozen or so photographers in the state fit that formula in the nineteenth century. More the norm were a different location, a new partner, and a fresh start every few years.

Except for the ambrotype, which disappeared, for about twenty years photography stayed with the formats that had served the North during the war: the carte de visite, stereograph, photographic print, and tintype. Also things of the past were the cases for portraits with glass and fancy mats that had originated in the daguerreotype era. With money short, inexpensive packaging was the rule. The carte de visite with its simple presentation was the primary article of the portrait trade in the 1860s and 1870s, and albums to collect them became popular. Tintypes were sold in paper folders.

Pocahontas
Cabinet card, by P. W. Poff, c. 1880–1900
Unidentified man and woman. *Virginia Historical Society*

For two decades after the war, photographic activity remained centered at galleries, because the wet-plate process required chemical processing at the time of exposing the negative. (An exception was the itinerant photographer, who adopted the war photographers' system of a wagon-darkroom.) At the same time, the price for a photograph dropped because of cheaper materials and competition. Around the state galleries arose in each town, run by a photographer who took in every kind of work. This was the height of the cottage industry period in photography. There was an ever-flowing demand for portraits from maturing young people and just-marrieds, which the war had temporarily dammed up. Between that trade and taking pictures for new practical applications, a community that might previously have been served only by itinerants became able to support a full-time photographer. Although portraits remained the bread and butter of photography, other commissions came to include groups, events, architecture, and copying older pictures. In some towns the emergence of a major customer like a college brought sufficient business to sustain a local gallery or a second one.

Technological improvements that would bring major change to photography began in the 1880s and continued at a steady pace. Symbolizing the new practices, about the turn of the century the general name for a photography business switched from "gallery" to "studio." In a few places, a community photographer who was a "jack-of-all-pictures" generalist stayed in business until the mid-twentieth century. For the most part, however, by the early twentieth century the field of photography was dividing into segments in which specialists reigned.

SKETCHES OF THE PHOTO TRADE

On 7 April 1865, four days after the Evacuation Fire, when Lee's army was still in the field, Union photographers were already relocating to Richmond. John H. Pein, previously at Bermuda Hundred with the Army of the James, opened his new gallery on Broad Street well away from the Burnt District. Another former Bermuda Hundred operator, James Coleman, advertised for "Two Photographists," asking them to call at the Spotswood Hotel. Later in April, Jackson & Harris opened a "Gallery of Art" at 163 Broad Street. One partner was probably the photographer W. B. Jackson, who held a permit for a tent at Bermuda Hundred, and the other could have been either the Charles Harris who worked the Point of Rocks naval station or the Harris formerly of Harris & King at Camp Hamilton. By July 1865, the partners at 163 Broad were Harris & Bancroft.[1]

In Petersburg, the partnership of Lazelle & McMullin, active in town before May 1866, also had Union roots. Henry H. Lazelle had been issued a license to work at City Point in February 1865. It is likely that other parts of the state were served by photographers who became itinerants when the army camps closed, such as the one who set up at Second and Broad streets in Richmond in June 1865: "Get your Likeness Taken! A Good Chance! For One Week Only! You can get good pictures."[2]

James H. Van Ness was a Confederate veteran who settled in Lynchburg soon after the war and learned photography as a partner in Tanner & Van Ness. (Minnis & Tanner, who offered "vitrotypes" to skirt P. E. Gibbs's ambrotype patent, had in 1856 become Tanner's Heliographic Portrait Gallery.) Beginning about 1867 Van Ness became a part-time itinerant, traveling through the Carolinas and Virginia. From 1870 to 1875 he alternated between Lynchburg and Charlotte, N.C., finally settling at the latter.

After his release from a northern prison in 1865, former Confederate Michael Miley (1841–1918) went to Staunton where he apprenticed under

Photographic tent
Half of stereograph negative, 1865
Richmond's Ballard House, at 14th and Franklin streets, was distinctive for its second-story bridge to the Exchange Hotel. An advertisement in the *Richmond Times,* 25 Apr. 1865, stated: "For Sale—The Photographic Tent situated on the northwest corner of Franklin and 14th Streets.— Price $100. Apply on the premises." *Library of Congress, Prints and Photographs Division, LC-DIG-cwpb-00476*

Traveling gallery
Tintype, ninth-plate, in paper mat, 1866
The subject is an unidentified V.M.I. cadet. Stamped on the back is the credit "A. H. Plecker's Traveling Gallery, Oct. 20, 1866." This date and the likely location of Lexington suggests that the portrait was created in the period that Plecker and Michael Miley worked together. *Virginia Historical Society*

James H. Burdette. Miley moved to the Lexington area in 1866 where he worked for another Confederate veteran, Adam Plecker (1840–1929). Plecker was a photographer before enlisting in 1861. After his service, which included the siege of Vicksburg, he returned to the Valley of Virgina and to the trade. Plecker worked as an itinerant ferrotypist (or tintyper), traveling with a wagon set up to be a darkroom and sitting room. Miley taught Plecker the wet-plate process, and the pair famously photographed Robert E. Lee several times on horseback. Miley settled in Lexington, and Plecker kept on the move. He entered the partnership Wheeler & Plecker, "Travelling Artists" based in Wytheville, and in 1873 he was running Plecker's Mammoth Photograph Gallery in Salem. By 1877 Plecker had established himself in Lynchburg, where he remained for some fifty years until retiring in 1926.[3]

William Roads (1824–1890) from Shenandoah County was associated with Osborne's in Richmond in 1855. Later that year Roads opened a gallery in Fredericksburg that he ran until 1858, and he was an ambrotypist in Charlottesville during the Civil War. In September 1865 his staff included James R. Singrey, "late of Hays' Louisiana Brigade," and in 1869 Roads brought on A. F. Smith as a photographer and colorist (who later opened A. F. Smith's Temple of Art). About 1873 Roads moved his business from Charlottesville to Gordonsville in Orange County, where he had family ties.

Nathaniel Routzahn (c. 1828–1908) from Frederick, Maryland, settled in Winchester in 1855 and opened a gallery. In 1859 he won a prize at the Winchester Agricultural Fair, and his autumn 1862 portrait of Stonewall Jackson is well-known. Routzahn operated a gallery in the Masonic Temple building until 1888.

Charles H. Erambert was the son of a Prince Edward County tailor. At age twenty in 1852 he apprenticed to daguerreotypist J. M. Wood in Farmville. Erambert opened his own gallery in Farmville with a partner whom he bought out within a year. After serving in the war, mostly in Richmond, he returned to Farmville where he operated a gallery until 1894.[4]

Charles R. Rees had been the busiest photographer in Richmond until his gallery burned in April 1865. By September 1866 he had reopened as C. R. Rees & Brother, in partnership with sibling Edwin J. Rees. In 1867 Rees & Bro. occupied a new storefront in the Burnt District at 913 E. Main Street, shown in their carte de visite imprint. By 1869 the brothers had been joined by Walter G. R. Frayser as C. R. Rees & Co. The firm split in 1871 when Frayser opened his own shop, and Edwin moved to Petersburg. Charles R. Rees had a new partner during 1873–75, Daniel Stephens, but by 1877 Stephens departed and Rees was joined by his son, Conway J. H. Rees. That year Rees moved a block up Main Street where he stayed until about 1880. At that time Marcellus J. Powers purchased or leased the Rees gallery name for Richmond (which Powers maintained until about 1887).[5]

In Petersburg, meanwhile, Edwin J. Rees first opened on his own. Then in 1873 he became the partner of George W. Minnis, the wartime Richmond photographer who had moved back to his original Petersburg gallery about 1867. E. J. Rees appeared in the 1875 listings but not in 1876. About 1880 Charles R.

Burnt barracks
Carte de visite, by A. H. Plecker, Traveling Gallery, c. 1866–70
The Virginia Military Institute barracks were burnt in 1864 and rebuilt beginning in 1870. Michael Miley later said that he taught Plecker, then a tintypist, the wet-plate process, and that he had made several of the early negatives with which Plecker is credited. This view is likely a product of their 1866 collaboration. *Virginia Historical Society*

Baseball team
Carte de visite, c. 1865–75
Inscribed on reverse: "Creigton BBC [Creighton Base Ball Club] Norfolk 1867, Champions of Virginia." *Virginia Historical Society*

1860s Cartes de visite
Boy, by Joseph Hobday, Portsmouth, c. 1865–69
Girl, by D. H. Maxwell, Lynchburg, c. 1865–69
The visual style of the carte de visite changed over its twenty-year run as the most popular portrait format. Those made right after the Civil War looked much like wartime issues, with the subject commonly shown in full-figure and not very close-up, and on the reverse, a simple letterpress imprint.
Both Virginia Historical Society

Late 1860s vignette
Carte de visite, by Rees & Minnis, Petersburg, c. 1867–70
The bust vignette was a common style of the mid- to late 1860s, with the head rather small in the picture, surrounded by blank space and often delicately hand-tinted. The front of the card was typically printed with a ruled frame. The young woman is unidentified.
Virginia Historical Society

Mid-1870s ovals
Carte de visite, by J. B. Wortham, Winchester, 1878
In the mid- to late 1870s the oval image returned to favor, but with the head larger than before. Inscribed beneath the young woman is "Mle. Randolph," and on the reverse "Jan 1st 1878."
Virginia Historical Society

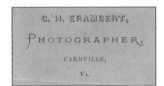

1870s Full figure with props
Carte de visite, by E. N. Medernach, Danville, c. 1870–75
Carte de visite, by A. H. Erambert, Farmville, c. 1870–75
In the early 1870s, settings and props became more elaborate, including painted backdrops and seats made of branches. Another trend was to fancier gallery imprints (although not in evidence here).
Both Virginia Historical Society

Bigger heads
Carte de visite, hand-colored, by Stone's Art Gallery, Alexandria, c. 1875–85
Carte de visite, by J. T. Wampler, Charlottesville, c. 1875–85
Beginning in the mid-1870s, portrait subjects began to fill more of the frame—the heads became larger—as seen in both male and female subjects. Improvements in lens optics may have been a factor. Neither the woman nor the man is identified. *Both Virginia Historical Society*

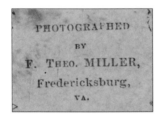

Fredericksburg
Carte de viste, by Theo Miller, c. 1865–69
Unidentified man. *Virginia Historical Society*

Petersburg
Carte de visite, by J. R. Rockwell, c. 1865–69
Inscribed on reverse, "Rose Belle Scott, 3 years old," with her mother, unidentified.
Virginia Historical Society

Danville
Carte de visite, by A. H. Blunt, c. 1870–90
Unidentified girl *Virginia Historical Society*

Rees moved from Richmond to Petersburg and initially was the photographer for the Rockwell gallery, a Petersburg war-era survivor. (For a year or two after the war, James R. Rockwell's partner was Daniel T. Cowell, the wartime photographer for Minnis in Richmond. On at least one project, Rockwell had also collaborated with N. S. Tanner of Lynchburg, also a former partner of Minnis.) By 1888 C. R. Rees had taken over the Rockwell gallery and brought in family members to work there: Charles R. Rees, Jr., James C. Rees, and by 1901, James L. Rees. In 1898 the senior Rees was the only photographer in the Petersburg telephone directory.[6]

F. Theodore "Theo" Miller was from a family that settled in Spotsylvania County in 1853. Miller opened a gallery by 1868 in Fredericksburg and also worked as an itinerant out of a wagon on the Northern Neck. Sometime in the mid-1880s Miller moved to the Northern Neck (his second wife was from Heathsville). He is said to have owned the "first auto in Mathews County," where he moved in the early twentieth century.[7]

David H. Anderson established his business in Richmond by September 1866. Born in New York City, he had worked at various locations in the South and West since 1854. In Richmond Anderson became a pre-eminent photographer of groups, employed a sizable staff, and made fine salt prints. He also did work in Norfolk and eventually opened a branch gallery there. An 1874 advertisement boasted that Anderson "has taken the premium for the Best Photographs at every State Fair since the war." In 1877 Anderson moved to 913 E. Main Street, vacated

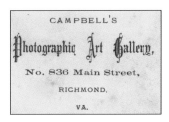

Broadway
Carte de visite, by Aldhizer & Eutsler, c. 1880–85
The unidentified boy leans on a fringed seat commonly
seen in portraits taken in city galleries a decade
earlier. Most card blanks were obtained through
photographic suppliers in places like New York, but
this handsome card was printed in the Shenandoah
Valley by Henkel & Co. *Virginia Historical Society*

Richmond
Carte de visite, by Campbell's Art Gallery, c.
1870–80
Unidentified woman. *Virginia Historical Society*

Richmond
Carte de visite, hand-colored, by Walter G. R.
Frayser, c. 1874–78
Unidentified child. *Virginia Historical Society*

by Charles Rees. Then in 1880 Anderson sold the gallery to George S. Cook and relocated to Norfolk. Anderson "in a few brief years of photographic work in Richmond and the Tidewater region, had made some twenty thousand plate negatives, which he transferred to Cook along with his fully equipped studio." Cook (1819–1902) daguerreotyped in New Orleans in the early 1840s, in the 1850s managed Mathew Brady's New York gallery, and from the '50s through the '70s ran a leading Charleston, S.C. gallery. From the time of his arrival, he was the pre-eminent photographer in the state. Cook settled in Bon Air and commuted to the city by train. He was succeeded by his son Huestis Cook (1868–1951).[8]

The partnership of Aldhizer & Eutsler, "Travelling Artists," was based in Broadway, in Shenandoah Valley, from 1880 to 1884, and then William E.

Eutsler worked on his own as an itinerant from 1884 to 1888. He established galleries in Roanoke (1888–91), Danville (1891–1905), and Greensboro, N.C. (1905–13), before going to work for Holsinger's in Charlottesville (1914–33).

During the 1880s Wise Hoover (1859–1948) of Bath County worked in the photo tent at a circus in Clifton Forge to learn more about photography. About 1888 Hoover returned to Clifton Forge to study with photographer S. S. Griffith and from him purchased a tent for field work. The "first project of my photo work was in Millboro," wrote Hoover. At Warm Springs that season "we made a success in a small way," but at Hot Springs Captain August "would not allow us any room," so he set up at his father's place "to do a little finishing." Hoover returned to Hot Springs and Warm Springs during the 1892 season, and

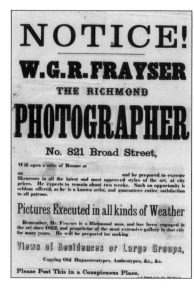

Scene at a Photographic Studio
Pen and ink sketch, by George W. Bagby, c. 1865–80
The sitter says, "Oh! Mr. Delany is that you?" and "Howd'ye do Mr. Wise?" The text reads: "Scene: A Photographic Studio in Leesburg. The very unsatisfactory result of a young Lady's attempting to sit for her picture, and 'make eyes' at two beaux in opposite directions, all at the same time." *Virginia Historical Society*

Harrisonburg
Carte de visite, by Dean, c. 1870–90
Unidentified woman.
Virginia Historical Society

Itinerant's handbill
Printed sheet, 11 x 15.75 in., c. 1881–85
Richmond's Walter G. R. Frayser probably occupied 821 Broad St. after he left his Main St. location about 1880. Frayser is known to have also worked in Charlottesville, Staunton, and Danville.
Virginia Historical Society

Suffolk
Carte de visite, by Parker & Harrell, c. 1880–95
Unidentified man.
Virginia Historical Society

to Warm Springs in 1895, but by 1899 photography became for him "a sideline of effort."[9]

Joseph H. Faber (c. 1858–1922) was a native of Charleston, S.C., and moved to Fredericksburg with his family as a young man. He and his brother were partners in a photography business there in 1880. Soon after Faber moved to Norfolk, where by 1886 he had joined a Baltimore photographer in a partnership, Faber & Friese, that lasted through at least 1889. Faber's younger brother Joannis, who in 1883 had operated a gallery in Warrenton, opened a Norfolk gallery in 1886 called J. J. Faber, which remained listed through 1889. By 1891 Joseph H. Faber was operating under his own name, and eventually he expanded with galleries in Newport News (1900) and Suffolk (1900). The firm became J. H. Faber & Son in 1910 when son George L. Faber (1886–1925) joined. At his father's death in 1922, George Faber took over the business, but it closed when he died in 1925.[10]

Walter W. Foster (1857–1935) opened his first, short-lived gallery on Richmond's Church Hill in 1876. He worked for D. H. Anderson for two

years and in 1879 joined the Davis gallery. By 1883 he was a partner in Foster, Campbell, & Co., in 1888 was back with Davis, and in 1890 opened Foster's Photographic Gallery at 112 N. Ninth Street, facing Capitol Square. Arthur W. Orpin (1879–1966) joined the business and in 1907 married Foster's daughter Nellie Virginia. In 1921 Orpin moved to Homier & Clark and his position at Foster's was taken by Anthony "Tony" L. Dementi, who had started with Foster in 1916. When Dementi moved on in 1924 to open his own studio, Orpin returned to Foster's, and at the death of Foster in 1935 became his successor. Eventually Orpin's son, W. Foster Orpin (1910–1998), took over the business, which merged in 1972 to become Dementi–Foster Studio.[11]

T. R. Phelps (1872–1952) was from Washington County in southwest Virginia and lived his whole life near the north fork of the Holston River. Because he suffered from an affliction to his legs and could not farm, "Tommy" Phelps operated a grist mill, repaired clocks and watches, had a stallion that he bred, and about 1897 became a photographer. In his buggy he plied a circuit offering his

Manchester
Carte de visite, by J. R. Cole, c. 1875–88
Two unidentified boys.
Virginia Historical Society

Charlottesville
Carte de visite, by Wampler, c. 1875–90
Two unidentified women.
Virginia Historical Society

Ashland
Carte de visite, by A. Delemos, 1890
On the reverse the card is dated: "Mar. 22, 1890," and bears the imprint: "Ashland Portrait Gallery, Branch of Vernon Gallery, Richmond, Va." The boy is unidentified. *Virginia Historical Society*

Petersburg view
Carte de visite, c. 1865–80
The staff of Henry Miller & Co., a Petersburg wine merchant, lines up in front of the building, and a cart loaded with barrels stands in the street. Likely the unidentified photographer's gallery was located nearby.
Virginia Historical Society

varied services around Washington and Russell counties. A stroke curtailed his photographing in 1939.[12]

Rufus W. Holsinger was a teacher from Pennsylvania who became an itinerant photographer. In the 1880s by way of Manassas he settled in Charlottesville, where he purchased City Studio in 1887 and Wampler's in 1889 and had great success. Holsinger's view of Monticello was used for the original $2 bill. His University Studio at its peak employed some twenty people. Holsinger was a member of city council, president of the chamber of commerce, and president of the Photographic Association of Virginia and the Carolinas. After an injury from a fall in 1925 ended his career, his son Ralph Holsinger took over the studio and operated until 1969.[13]

Christopher E. Cheyne (1867–1943) was born in Canada and studied art in Cincinnati, where he also learned photography. In 1894 he established a studio in downtown Hampton, eventually operating a music store on the first floor with the photography business on the second. The studio's work was varied, from portraits and hotels to the seafood industry and Buckroe Beach. His son William "Happy" Cheyne (1896–1976) took over the business in 1928 and operated the studio into the 1960s.[14]

A number of women worked in photography, but not many women ran a gallery. Women came to predominate in the areas of negative retouching and print finishing. This included the fine detail work, often using magnification, of removing blemishes that showed up in a print, either from the subject or caused by the process. An early female photographer, Emeline Turner of Portsmouth, may have worked her way up from the production end of the trade. The photographer Augustus M. Turner had a studio at 204 High Street in Portsmouth from 1883 to 1886. Augustus was a close relative to Emeline but not her husband, because when she was a widow they lived at the same address. When Augustus Turner opened a gallery in Norfolk in 1888, Emeline Turner took over the Portsmouth studio and was listed as a photographer from 1891 to 1896 at 208 High Street.

Lynchburg
Carte de visite, by The Lynchburg Photographic Co., c. 1875–90
Five unidentified young men. *Virginia Historical Society*

The mobile photographer
Salt print, c. 1880–90
A Virginia photographer is about to set off for location work. The three cases beside him probably contain a camera, negative plates, and personal provisions, and a tripod would be on the buggy floor under his feet. No doubt he uses dry plates, providing an earliest date of 1880; but the print is an old-fashioned format, suggesting not long after 1880. *Virginia Historical Society, Gift of Frederick Bell*

Large wet-plate view
Salt print, by David H. Anderson, 11 x 14 in., c. 1870–77
Few large-plate landscapes of Virginia subjects are known from 1865 until the advent of dry plates in 1880. Anderson might have been the only Virginia photographer who regularly produced such work. This view probably recorded the completion of the fourth Wren building at the College of William and Mary. *Virginia Historical Society*

Washington's tomb
Carte de visite, c. 1865–1880
Exterior views of Virginia in the carte de visite format are not common. In the wet-plate period, photography in the field remained a technical challenge, and most views appeared as stereographs. Perhaps the photographer operated at Mount Vernon for the visitor season and had a facility on the grounds. *Virginia Historical Society*

Mary W. Tennant was a photographer in Newport News in 1900. At that time she was thirty-seven years old and lived with her parents, the Fitzsimmons. A seventeen-year-old niece who lived with the family worked as a clerk at the photography gallery. (Tennant's husband was not at the home, but whether he was a sailor or gone is not known.) Mary Tennant may have worked at the Newport News branch of Joseph H. Faber's operation.[15]

CABINET CARD, STEREOGRAPH, LIFE-SIZE PORTRAIT

The carte de visite was supplanted by the larger, dressier cabinet card, which came into wide use during the 1880s and 1890s. The image on the cabinet card was twice as big as on the carte de visite and the card stock was of higher quality. There was room for both a gallery imprint on the front and a larger design, often elaborate, on the reverse.

With the larger size of the cabinet card, the character of portraits changed. The poses that had been used for carte de visite portraits looked different in a cabinet card. Because clothing was more evident, details of garments became more visible and fashion gained significance. Knowing this, a subject typically dressed up to sit for a portrait, at times with an almost theatrical air. Blemishes might show better too and thus the photographer's retouching pencil came into greater use. Props and backgrounds were utilized perhaps half the time and also became more visible in the cabinet card.

By the first decade of the 1900s, the cabinet card in turn was succeeded, this time by a variety of portrait formats. No one of the new century's formats was as widely adopted as the earlier ones had been. There were various designs of folders in which the photograph was tucked behind a mat, and card mounts, typically on bleached white stock with embossed decoration, that held images of 3¼ x 4¼ inches, 4 x 5 inches, and other sizes. By the 1910s the thin albumen paper used previously for photographic prints had been almost entirely replaced by gelatin-emulsion papers. The new paper was thicker and did not require mounting on board, which fell out of practice.

The carte de visite and the cabinet card were the most common kinds of photographs from 1860 to 1900, but they were not the only formats in use. The stereograph, first introduced to Virginia just before the Civil War, initially aimed for the armchair traveler. Combining realism with 3-D effect, stereographs were a window to the scenic highlights of the world, a visual Grand Tour for the home-bound. The Civil War views that soon supplemented this fare did not at that time reach the South. Neither as world views nor as war views did the format make significant inroads into Virginia.

In Europe, the stereograph was a phenomenon of the 1860s but then fell off until the late 1890s, when it had a revival said to have been promulgated from the U.S. In Virginia, once postwar economic straits began to improve in the 1870s, the stereograph gained a presence and remained in favor. D. H. Anderson in the 1870s and George S. Cook and Adam Plecker in the 1880s issued a series of topical lines of images. Nationally the 1890s revival was promoted by companies such as Underwood and Underwood. Four different companies issued stereographs of the Jamestown Exposition in 1907. Stereographs were among the old-fashioned things superceded by the new in the 1920s.

Cabinet card at actual size
Cabinet card, 6.5 x 4.25 in. by Wright, Luray, c. 1880–1900
The card is inscribed on reverse: "Bessie 8 years," but her full name is not known. *Virginia Historical Society*

Newport News
Cabinet card, by Rusk & Shaw, c. 1885–1900
Unidentified man. The edges of the mount are
trimmed, probably to fit the card into an album
or frame. *Virginia Historical Society*

Petersburg
Cabinet card, by Charles R. Rees, 1890
Unidentified young man. *Virginia Historical
Society*

Chase City
Cabinet card, by E. D. MacFee, c. 1890–1905
Here the vignette style is used on a cabinet card,
for an unidentified family of father, mother, and
son. *Virginia Historical Society*

Norfolk
Cabinet card, by Charles A. Himmelwright,
c. 1889–92
Two unidentified boys. *Virginia Historical Society*

Front Royal
Cabinet card, by J. M. Hemming,
c. 1885–1905
Unidentified baby. *Virginia Historical Society*

Richmond
Cabinet card, by George S. Cook,
c. 1885–1902
Unidentified woman. *Virginia Historical Society*

Norfolk
Cabinet card, by J. H. Faber, c. 1891–1905
Unidentified man. *Virginia Historical Society*

Winchester
Cabinet card, by Barr, c. 1880–1900
Unidentified family. *Virginia Historical Society*

Hampton
Cabinet card, by Christopher E. Cheyne, 1899
Against a nautical backdrop, an unidentified man poses in the uniform of a captain or pilot (holding a case that is likely trade-related). On reverse is inscribed: "Take yourself, Govan and the <u>kids</u> down sometime & get me a picture. July 4th, 1899."
Virginia Historical Society

Staunton
Cabinet card, by A. L. Hook, c. 1885–1905
Unidentified family group of father, mother, and child. *Virginia Historical Society*

Buena Vista
Albumen print on fancy mount, by J. W. S. Bowling, c. 1900–15
Three unidentified children. *Virginia Historical Society*

Orange
Cabinet card, by A. W. Maxwell, c. 1900–10
Unidentified child, inscribed on the reverse "for Hattie." *Virginia Historical Society*

Picturesque scene
Stereograph, by Kilburn Brothers, c. 1865–85
The Kilburn Brothers of Littleton, N.H., were for several decades the largest American publishers of stereographs. Benjamin Kilburn is known to have photographed in Virginia and may have made this genre view, titled "Cabin House Va." *Virginia Historical Society*

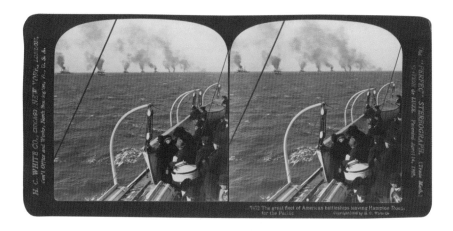

Great White Fleet departs
Stereograph, by H. C. White Co., 1908
Later stereographs, such as this one from a Vermont publisher, were issued on curved mounts that fit the optic characteristics of stereo viewers and made a more vivid visual impression. U. S. Navy ships that had gathered at Hampton Roads for the Jamestown Exposition in 1907 were sent by President Theodore Roosevelt on a muscle-flexing, round-the-world tour. *Virginia Historical Society*

Great White Fleet returns
Stereograph, by Keystone View Co., 1909
Keystone, based in Pennsylvania, was one of the major publishers of stereographs. *Virginia Historical Society*

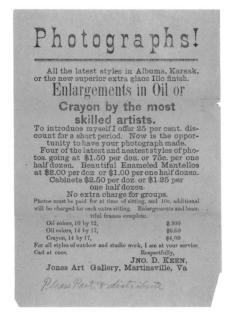

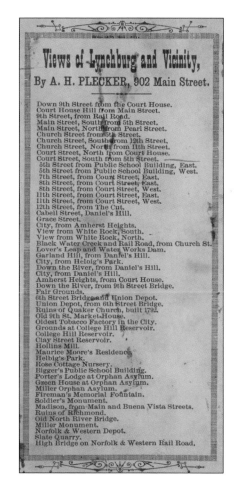

Turn-of-the-century handbill
Although this advertisement for the photographer John Keen is not dated, that he continues to offer cabinet cards—but at the bottom of his list—suggests a date near the end of the cabinet card period, about 1900. *Virginia Historical Society*

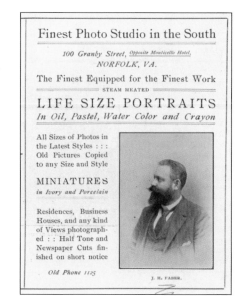

Lynchburg
Stereograph, by A. H. Plecker, c. 1880–1895
On reverse is the title list for Plecker's stereo series, "Views of Lynchburg and Vicinity." A mark on the list identifies this view as "Court Street, South from 5th Street." *Virginia Historical Society*

Advertisement
From *Travel, Entertainment and Enterprise,* by Norfolk, Portsmouth & Newport News Company (Norfolk, 1903)
J. H. Faber placed this notice in a 1903 promotional booklet for Hampton Roads. *Virginia Historical Society*

Life-size portrait

Photograph with hand-coloring on mount, 17.5 x 14.3 in., c. 1890–1910

These large prints were also known as "crayon portraits." An enlargement of a glass negative was made on photographic paper, which because of the materials and equipment of the day was inevitably somewhat faint. The print was mounted on board, then enhanced using charcoal or pastel, and matted and framed. (Today most of these mount boards have become quite brittle.) The words at upper left, which would have been covered by the window mat, are finishing notes: "[illegible—possibly a frame or mat type]/ Carbonette / Pd .50 Due $1.00 50." The subject is Charles Edward Bolling (1852–1929). *Virginia Historical Society*

Life-size portrait
Photograph with hand-coloring on mount, 20 x 15.9 in., c. 1890–1920
The subject is unidentified. The print came from a house near Claremont, Surry County. *Virginia Historical Society, Gift of Mr. & Mrs. James R. Pennington*

Life-size portraits on display
Photographic print, by Frances Benjamin Johnston, c. 1930–40
Portrait enlargements as typically framed and displayed are seen in a room at Bellmont, near Dillwyn, Buckingham County. *Library of Congress, Prints and Photographs Division, LC-J7-VA-1416*

Fincastle
Tintype in paper mat, by W. R. Hayth, one-ninth plate, hand-colored, c. 1865–1900
Inscribed on reverse: "Harry Moore." *Virginia Historical Society*

Possibly Ashland
Tintype, one-ninth plate, c. 1865–1900
Inscribed on reverse: "Ashland Quartette." *Collection of Richard L. Bland*

Winchester
Tintype in paper mat, by Jas. N. McKericher, one-ninth plate, hand-colored, c. 1865–1890
Unidentified woman with hat. *Virginia Historical Society*

The "life-size portrait" was a kind of mixed format that came to Virginia by the 1870s and lasted, particularly in more rural areas, to the early twentieth century. It was a photographic enlargement improved by an artist. Enlarging from negatives began in the 1860s. A sun enlarger was available by about 1868 that projected the image from the negative through a lens into a dark chamber and onto light-sensitive photographic paper. Enlargements made by the sun were, compared to contact prints, rather faint and not as crisp. Therefore the image, typically a head-and-shoulders portrait, was enhanced with a varying mix of charcoal, chalk, pencil, and watercolor wash. The prints were mounted on board and framed. (Today, because of the high-acid content of the board used, these life-size portraits are often quite brittle, with easily chipped edges.) Photographs of room interiors of the late nineteenth century show these portraits displayed in the manner of paintings.

TINTYPE

The tintype was the only format of the 1850s that remained in use until the twentieth century. The durable tintype was well-suited for photographers who were itinerant or otherwise in temporary locations, because they could be developed on the spot and presented to the customer. As a one-step process they were also less expensive. Photographers at fairs, resorts, and amusement parks stayed with the tintype the longest.

Possibly Lynchburg
Tintype in paper mat, one-sixteenth plate, hand-colored, c. 1865–1900
Inscribed onto mat are the words: "John R. Campbell of Lynchburg, Va." The tintype image is reversed, so the sitter's left hand is on the neck of the banjo, and his right is playing the strings.
Virginia Historical Society

West Point
Tintype in paper mat, by Sylvia, one-ninth plate, c. 1900–10
This unidentified portrait of a young man bears a stamp on reverse: "Made by D. W. Sylvia at Beach Park, West Point, Va." The Beach Park development on the York River opened in 1900 and was destroyed by fire in 1910.
Virginia Historical Society

Possibly Richmond
Tintype, one-ninth plate, c. 1890–1905
The subjects are Albert H. Hill (1866–1933), Byrd Lee Hill, and an unidentified woman. Albert Hill was superintendent of Richmond Public Schools from 1919 to 1933.
Virginia Historical Society

WAR PHOTOGRAPHY REVISITED

The Civil War remains a presence in American culture, and a big factor in its quasi-radioactive half-life is the photographic record. The images in their often mundane representations make the people and places seem very real. A problematical aspect is that not all of the photographs that circulate as Civil War images have the same historical relationship to the event. Given the continuing relevance of the topic, there is value in sorting the images linked to it. A good portion of Civil War photographs are discussed in chapter two, those that were taken during the war and distributed then. A second portion, which may include a larger number, is based on photographs taken during the war but issued postwar in the medium of another era—in the forms of reprintings, copies, published reproductions, and today in digital files. Finally, another set of Civil War-related photographs were taken later, of veterans, reunions, parades, and dedications.

The public's attention during the war to battles and leaders could hardly have been expected to survive with the same intensity following the end of the Confederacy. Especially after the climactic events of April 1865, interest dipped on both sides. Enough war-time sentiment remained while events were relatively recent that a good portion of the vintage images that circulate today were produced. But by about 1867, except for subjects like Lee and Grant, the sale of views and portraits of the war was reduced to a smaller specialty trade, serving collectors, veterans, and diehards.

Just as with prints issued during the war, the first wave of re-issue photographs came from two sources: original negatives and copy negatives. Despite copyright claims, it remained standard practice for a photographer to copy a portrait made by another and then issue the copy himself. Even the photographer of an original portrait would often copy his own print to convert it to carte de visite size. The only advantage the original photographer held in this situation was being able to copy a first-generation print in good condition, producing a better-quality result. A photographer who had only a fuzzy, multiple-generation-removed print of a particular individual to work from, yet wished to issue a sharper portrait, would sometimes employ an artist to improve the print on hand (which also served to disguise which original had been copied). Thus one key to value in postwar production is how many generations removed the photograph is from the original negative.

As it had during the war, postwar production of Union and Confederate images followed different paths. The Union's entrepreneurs in the field had created a broader documentary coverage. With one of the largest and most accomplished negative archives, Alexander Gardner, from his Washington, D.C., gallery, issued panoramas, stereocards, and photographs. His most comprehensive production was in album format, the two volumes of Gardner's *Sketch Book of the Civil War,* issued January 1866, which remain today the standard of comparison for Civil War photography. The set was costly at $150,

Photographic History
Stereograph, by Timothy O'Sullivan, 1863, reissue by the War Photograph & Exhibition Company, c. 1885–95
The quality of the photographic prints made from original Civil War negatives and issued in the late nineteenth century is generally superior to the prints issued during the war. The caption states: "Non-commissioned Officers' Mess, Co. 'D' 93d New York Infantry. This view was taken at Bealton, Va., in August, 1863, and if any of the members of this Company are now living they will doubtless appreciate the scene." *Virginia Historical Society*

Russell album
The bound volume containing 132 photographic prints was prepared by Andrew J. Russell and his staff, probably in 1865 after the end of the Civil War. The album was presented to James J. Moore, who worked for the United States Military Rail Roads starting in 1862. In November 1864 Moore became chief engineer and general superintendent of the military railroads of Virginia, a position that made him Russell's supervisor. In turn, Moore presented the album to the Virginia Historical Society in 1931. *Virginia Historical Society*

but as Keith Davis states, "the postwar public disinterest in war photographs had no impact on the reception of these volumes, which were priced far beyond the means of the average citizen."[16]

Another producer of albums was Andrew J. Russell, the Union army captain who had photographed for the engineer and quartermaster departments, mostly in Virginia. Russell's albums were custom-produced for politicians of influence or for higher-ups in the army departments that he served under. For an army official, the album was a memento of appreciation with contents keyed to the interests or responsibilities of that individual. One such album was presented to James J. Moore who had served as chief engineer and general superintendent of the military railroads of Virginia. In that position he was a direct supervisor of Russell. Most of the photographs in Moore's album were Virginia subjects. Likely that was a reason he chose in 1931 to donate the album to the Virginia Historical Society.[17]

In addition to the negatives that Gardner and Russell accumulated, even larger collections were held by Brady and by Anthony & Anthony. One measure of the postwar lack of interest in war pictures is the fate of these glass negatives. Though some were always recognized as having value, not all were, and a portion were lost. The individual who best kept alive a vision of the value of the negatives was Mathew Brady, who pursued their preservation for years. That he had a financial interest in the outcome does not diminish his efforts. Brady had come out of the war burdened by debt, and his plan to pay it off was to sell his negative collection to the government. At a time when Gardner and Russell, for example, had moved on to new projects, Brady continued to be an advocate for the historical value of the images.[18]

The several collections of Civil War photographs took varying paths. When Brady's Washington gallery failed in 1867, he regained his footing by selling his house and other assets. In 1871 he almost had Congressional approval for a government purchase of a large group of portraits, but bankruptcy in 1873 cost him both his New York and Washington galleries. A consequence was that the Department of War in 1874 purchased some 2,200 Brady negatives at auction. Then in 1875, on a motion by Rep. Benjamin Butler of Massachusetts, Congress approved a $25,000 payment to Brady for another 3,400 negatives. In the late nineteenth century these negatives were intermixed with negatives from the Army Corps of Engineers, probably including those of Russell. The Department of War's roughly 6,000 negatives of the Civil War were transferred in 1940 to the National Archives.[19]

In 1865, Anthony & Anthony held two large groups of Brady negatives, provided to the firm under the publishing agreement worked out by Gardner early in the war. The Anthony firm kept the negatives after the war to apply toward Brady's debts. One group was about 7,000 stereograph negatives, some of which Anthony continued to issue. In 1879 former officers Albert Ordway and Arnold Rand purchased the stereo negatives from Anthony & Anthony, which they mixed with about 2,000 negatives they had acquired from Gardner's Gallery. In 1884 Rand and Ordway sold the combined lot of negatives to John C. Taylor of Hartford, Conn., who inaugurated a new line of stereographs in the late 1880s and 1890s. Taylor in turn sold the collection in 1907 to Edward Eaton, who used them for several books that culminated in Frances T. Miller's

Lee Gallery imprint
For about two decades, including a long period before the Lost Cause gained critical mass, the Lee Gallery was a main purveyor of Confederate photographic images. *Virginia Historical Society*

Soldier with flag
Carte de visite, hand-colored, by Edward S. Lumpkin, c. 1866–70
The unidentified subject was a former soldier when he posed, because Lumpkin did not open his gallery on Richmond's Main Street until after the war. *Virginia Historical Society*

Original portrait
Carte de visite, by Julian Vannerson, c. 1861–65 Vannerson photographed Fitzhugh Lee (1835–1905) during the Civil War and at that time produced this card. *Virginia Historical Society*

Copied portrait
Carte de visite, after Vannerson by E & H. T. Anthony, c. 1861–70
The New York publisher Anthony copied Vannerson's portrait of Fitzhugh Lee and issued its own version. The copy is rendered with higher contrast than the original: detail is lost in the hair and beard, and the texture in the coat is emphasized. *Virginia Historical Society*

Copied and improved portrait
Carte de visite, after Vannerson by E & H. T. Anthony, c. 1861–70
This Anthony reissue of Vannerson's portrait of Fitzhugh Lee has more detail than the original, especially in the beard and eyes. An artist enhanced a less-detailed photographic copy, and that hand-improved portrait was copied for this carte de visite. *Virginia Historical Society*

1911, ten-volume *Photographic History of the Civil War.* The Library of Congress acquired these stereo negatives for the storage fees in 1943. The second group held by Anthony & Anthony in 1865 was about 5,400 negatives used for cartes de visite. This set was sold to collector Frederick Meserve in 1902 and in 1981 was acquired from his daughter by the National Portrait Gallery.[20]

The Confederate archives were smaller and less complete. There was interest after the end of the war in portraits of leaders whose pictures had not been easily obtained before. Photographers had been unable to meet the full demand for portraits of Confederate leaders during the war for a number of reasons. In 1865–66 there was a wave of production of cartes de visite of leaders, especially in Richmond and also in Lynchburg, Baltimore, and New York. In addition, at this time a number of Confederate soldiers posed for photographs of themselves in uniform. However there was not enough to sustain much business for very long.[21]

Many if not most of the re-issued war portraits were copies from prints. Of the Richmond galleries, only Minnis and Vannerson had original negatives. Minnis reopened in Richmond after the war, appearing in the 1866 directory, with an imprint on cartes de visite as "George W. Minnis." Vannerson also reopened after the war with a partner named Charles E. Jones. Vannerson & Jones (on some cards, "Jones & Vannerson") was the most active firm in reprinting Confederate leaders immediately after the war. The possibility that Jones was from the North is suggested by the firm's June 1865 offering of "Lincoln Mourning Badges, Photographs of President Lincoln, and all the Prominent Confederate Generals." By September 1866, however, Jones had departed. A new partnership, short-lived and likely a product of hard times, was "Vannerson & Minnis." Not long after, Minnis returned to Petersburg. By September 1867 "Vannerson & Levy" had opened, and after that Vannerson & Co. was briefly at 920 East Main.[22]

Union veteran gathering
Albumen print on mount, by Charles R. Rees, 1887
A typed caption glued to the mount states: "The 57th [Massachusetts regiment] & guests at Crater, May 3, 1887. Man in front center white whiskers & cane is Gen. Billy Mahone, who commanded the Georgia Brigade, who captured the 57th after the Explosion." *Virginia Historical Society*

Confederate memorial
Silver gelatin print, c. 1980–90, from glass negative by Michael Miley, c. 1880–90
Gathered at Gen. Thomas J. "Stonewall" Jackson's gravesite in Lexington, Va., are female students from Anne Smith Academy. *Virginia Historical Society*

At least several of the Confederates whose portraits during wartime had been credited to Minnis & Cowell appeared on cartes de visite issued by Vannerson & Jones. In some way, whether by purchase, trade, or borrowing, Vannerson obtained Minnis images; that the two were subsequently briefly in partnership implies that Minnis had no hard feelings about it. Other Richmond galleries were in the Confederate trade—Lumpkin & Co. advertised in 1866 "Card Photographs of the Confederate Generals for Sale"—but Vannerson seems to have had the largest pool of original negatives and prints to work from, including his originals and those of Minnis.

The gallery Vannerson took at 920 East Main was over the Richmond Musical Exchange, operated by John W. Davies and his sons, George L. and William W. Davies. The Davieses sold sheet music, which also made them dealers in images, because the title pages of musical scores were often illustrated. One room in the store was a gallery where paintings were exhibited, often (if not always) with a patriotic Confederate theme. By 1869 Vannerson departed Richmond and sold to the Davies family, who took over the photograph gallery above their shop, complete with Vannerson's archive of Confederate images. The Davieses named their establishment the Lee Gallery and became a primary source for Confederate portraits. By 1885 the son William W. Davies had taken over. He kept the operation going until 1891, when he sold the collection to George S. Cook, whose studio was across the street at 913 East Main.[23]

Cook's timing was good, because interest in the Civil War had rebounded in the 1880s. In both North and South, reprints of war images became marketable again. New subjects for photographs emerged. Northern veterans came to Virginia to tour the battlefields and had their visits recorded. In the imagery of the Lost Cause, southerners stayed true to their wartime iconography of heroic leaders, represented in monuments, statues, cemeteries, and their dedications with parades and finery.

AFRICAN AMERICAN GALLERIES

The earliest known African American photographer in Virginia was John B. Bailey, from Boston, who was working at White Sulphur Springs in 1845. There Bailey taught Virginia-born James P. Ball to daguerreotype, and subsequently Ball operated a gallery in Richmond for a short time. Later in 1864–65, black photographers were making portraits at Union camps at Bermuda Hundred.[24]

After the Civil War, African Americans entered photography in several cities around the state, generally starting in the darkroom and in some cases moving forward to become an operator who took portraits. From 1869 through the 1880s, Thomas H. Hill of Richmond was employed continuously as either a photographic printer or a photographer. (The job of "photo-printer," as listed in city directories, could have included such duties as preparing chemicals and plates, loading plateholders, developing negatives, retouching negatives with

Pointer of Petersburg
Cabinet card, by Arthur Pointer
Unidentified woman. *Virginia Historical Society*

Pointer of Petersburg
Cabinet card, by New York Gallery, 1892
The reverse has the imprint, "A. Pointer, Artist." The man is unidentified.
Virginia Historical Society

Richmond's Broad Street
Cabinet card, by Vernon Gallery, 107 E. Broad St., c. 1886–97
Unidentified woman. *Virginia Historical Society*

pencil, shooting copy negatives, and of course making prints.) In 1882 Hill was a printer for George S. Cook. Thereafter he sometimes worked as a waiter and sometimes as a photo-printer, the latter as late as 1909. Another darkroom man in Richmond was George O. Brown (1852–1910), first recorded as a printer in 1871. Brown's family came to Richmond from Orange County when he was young. By 1895 Brown had been the "head printer at the Davis' Gallery for nineteen years" with a good reputation for his darkroom skills.[25]

Arthur Pointer was a photograph printer in Petersburg in 1870, when he was twenty-seven years old, working at the gallery of George W. Minnis. By 1876 he was listed as a photographer, one of at least two at the Minnis gallery. By 1888 Pointer had taken over the Minnis gallery location, and one imagines the business too. In 1888 the Lynchburg directory listed Louis Edley as a photographer, but no more is known of him.[26]

At the 1907 Jamestown Ter-centennial Exposition, blacks exhibited separately from whites in the Negro Building. In the judging, also done separately, Arthur L. Macbeth of Charleston, S.C., won a silver medal for his photographs. A report on the fair also noted that the agriculture "display was very attractively arranged by Mr. A. L. Macbeth." During his time in Norfolk, Macbeth must have liked what he saw, for by 1909 he had moved there and was operating a gallery. A year

later he had become the manager of the Mt. Vernon Moving Picture Theatre on Church Street. Subsequently he moved on to Baltimore.[27]

In Richmond, by the 1880s the central locus for galleries was shifting from old-fashioned Main Street to modern Broad Street. From 7th to 9th streets, where the streetcar lines converged, Broad became Richmond at its most fast-paced, with theaters, hotels, and electric lights. Photography galleries occupied upper floors on these busy blocks, generally on the south side of the street to take advantage of the north-light though their front windows. The Davis Gallery opened in 1875, and in 1877 it was still the only one on Broad, although there were seven on Main. By 1888 there were six galleries on Broad and only two on Main.[28]

Broad Street in the last quarter of the nineteenth century had a different ambience than Main and in particular had a greater African American presence. Before Jim Crow restrictions that after 1900 aimed to push blacks off Broad, numerous retail businesses on that street catered to African American or mixed patronage. Among them were photograph galleries. The Vernon Portrait Gallery opened about 1886 on Broad near First. Extant cabinet cards show that the clientele was mixed. The Vernon was taken over in 1891 by Benjamin Bloomberg, who renamed it the Carbon Studio in 1898–1902 (carbon prints were a current

Broad Street
Carte de visite, by George W. Davis, 821 Broad St., c. 1877–81
Unidentified woman. *Virginia Historical Society*

Broad Street
Carte de visite, by Richmond Photograph Co., 827½ Broad St., c. 1882–95
Unidentified woman; the photographer was probably James C. Farley. *Virginia Historical Society*

Broad Street
Cabinet card, by Richmond Photograph Co., 827½ Broad St., c. 1882–95
Unidentified man; the photographer was probably James C. Farley. *Virginia Historical Society*

fancy format). The earliest gallery to be noted as black-owned in the city directory was Jerome & Co. in 1898 and 1899, at 34 W. Leigh Street, with photographers O'Hagan Jerome and Horace S. Davis.[29]

The first African American to be employed on a regular basis as a photographer worked for the Davis Gallery. James C. Farley was born in 1854 in Prince Edward County and moved to Richmond in 1861 with his slave mother, where she worked at the Columbia Hotel. Farley attended school for three years and in 1872 went to work "in the chemical department" for Charles R. Rees & Co. In May 1875, "having become thoroughly acquainted with the business," Farley "became an operator for G. W. Davis." Davis opened his first Richmond gallery that year.[30] Very soon in Farley's career at the Davis Gallery came a signal incident:

> There were four white men in the gallery, Mr. Farley being the only colored operator, and they all objected to his being employed. On Saturday night they stated that they would not work if Mr. Farley was employed any longer. . . . Mr. Davis, the proprietor, met them on a Sunday morning. . . . They were injured, so they said, by Mr. Farley putting on a disagreeable air. . . . They never explained what it was that he had done

that was so disagreeable, and it was left to be judged that it was simply his color. . . . The following Monday morning the proprietor handed Mr. Farley the document containing their statement, with their names signed. Mr. Farley at once told him to keep the white men and let him go, as he did not desire to do any harm. . . . But Mr. Davis informed him that he had already discharged all four of them. His orders were "pull off your coat and go to work and fill their places." He ever remembers Mr. Davis' treatment in this matter, and was thankful that he had an opportunity to show what he could do, and eventually developed into a first class operator.

Mr. Davis and Mr. Farley then went to work and filled the other men's places. The business continued to improve, and Mr. Davis established a cheaper priced gallery and employed several white men to take the position Mr. Farley formerly held (that of operator), paying them enormous salaries, while he went to the business of "retouching." One of the white men remained a week; another only a few days. Mr. Farley was again in 1879, put in the position of operator of the gallery.[31]

Broad Street
Cabinet card, by Richmond Photograph Co., 827½
Broad St., c. 1882–95
Unidentified woman; the photographer was probably
James C. Farley. *Virginia Historical Society*

James C. Farley
Book reproduction, from G. F. Richings, *Evidences
of Progress among Colored People* (Philadelphia,
1900), p. 495.
From his appearance, Farley seems to have been
of mixed racial ancestry.

Farley & Brown
Cabinet card, by Jefferson Art Gallery, 523 Broad
St., c. 1897–1902
Unidentified woman. *Virginia Historical Society*

Brown & Churchill
Fancy Cabinet card, by Old Dominion Gallery, 111 E.
Broad St., c. 1899–1904
Unidentified man and boy. *Virginia Historical Society*

Broad Street
Photograph on decorative mount, by Davis
Gallery, c. 1902–10
Unidentified woman. *Virginia Historical Society*

Brown
Photo-postcard, by George W. Brown, 603 N. 2nd
St., c. 1906–10
Unidentified woman. *Virginia Historical Society*

In 1881 Davis opened a branch gallery, the Richmond Photographing Co., at 827 East Broad a few doors away from the first, and James C. Farley became the operator, who as the photographer took the lead role in a gallery. The *Richmond Planet* called Farley "our colored photographer" in 1885. "He has shown remarkable ability for the work and ranks among the best photographers in the city, he having few equals and no superiors." At that time Farley was supplying photographs to the *Planet,* largely studio portraits that were sent to New York to be copied into wood engravings for reproduction in the newspaper. Farley also traveled out of town to photograph on occasion, such as the Virginia Baptist Convention at Hampton in May 1893. An 1895 article noted that "Mr. Farley has been for twenty-one years connected with the Davis Gallery, being the chief operator."[32]

In August 1895 the *Richmond Planet* announced "The New Gallery": "Mr J C Farley and Mr George O Brown have opened a high-class photograph gallery at 523 E Broad St. . . . Their palatial establishment is known as the 'Jefferson.'" The name echoed that of the grand new hotel that opened the same year in Richmond. Though Brown and Farley were the main figures, and featured by name in the advertisement in the *Richmond Planet,* the manager for the first two directory listings in 1897 and 1898 was a white photographer named Churchill Webster. The gallery had both white and black clientele, so whether Webster represented white ownership of the gallery or was hired to make white customers feel comfortable is not clear.[33]

In 1899 Brown and Webster left the business. Farley stayed at the Jefferson where he was listed as the manager beginning that year. In 1901 the Jefferson Photograph Co. was listed as "colored," and one assumes that Farley had finalized his purchase of the business. Through 1906 the Jefferson was listed at 523 East Broad with Farley as the manager, until that location was taken over by the construction of the Miller & Rhoads department store. Farley moved the gallery a block east

Brown
Photo-postcard, by George W. Brown, c. 1906–10
Two unidentified men. *Virginia Historical Society*

to 627 East Broad where it was listed through 1908. By 1909 the Jefferson was no longer listed, and in 1910 Farley himself was absent from the directory.[34]

Churchill Webster, the white man connected to the Jefferson Gallery, was born in Massachusetts about 1859 and moved to Richmond by 1880 with his twin sisters and their Virginia-born, widowed mother. Webster worked as a photographer in Richmond from 1889. His financial link to the Jefferson Photograph Co.—whether a founder, an added partner, or uninvolved—is not clear. After splitting from the Jefferson, he opened the Old Dominion Gallery at 111 East Broad St. in 1899. Joining Webster there as photo-printer was George O. Brown from the Jefferson. Based on that fact alone, Old Dominion likely had considerable black patronage. The gallery was owned by C. Webster & Co., comprising Churchill Webster and his sisters who were a year older. By 1901 Churchill Webster was absent from the directory, but Old Dominion Gallery was still owned by C. Webster & Co., which by 1902 was composed of the two sisters only, Laura (Mrs. Wilbur C. Root) and Jennie W. Wyant. The sisters operated the gallery through 1904, apparently the first women to own a photographic gallery in Richmond.[35]

The other principal at the Jefferson Gallery, George O. Brown, worked as photo-printer to the Old Dominion Gallery into 1904 but departed soon after the Webster sisters sold it. By 1906 Brown had his own establishment at 603 North Second St. His son George W. Brown and daughter Bessie Gwendola Brown worked at the gallery, and when father Brown died in 1910, the two children took over the business and ran it as "The Browns." The studio was a mainstay of African American photography in Richmond for much of the twentieth century. The son died in 1946, and his widow and his sister kept it open until 1969.[36]

Out the gallery window
Albumen print on mount, by Jefferson Art Gallery, 523 Broad St., c. 1897–1902
As Confederate veterans gathered on Broad Street., the photographer at the Jefferson Gallery, probably James C. Farley, across the street and a story up, photographed them. *Virginia Historical Society*

State Fair tintypist
Silver gelatin print, by W. Edwin Booth, 18 x 16.5 in., c. 1930–40
Tintype folders cover the portraitist's camera, and a sign above the
lens says "Keep smiling." *Virginia Historical Society*

CHAPTER FOUR

Techniques, Process, Method

The technical improvements of the late nineteenth century extended photographic capability. Photographers could range farther and capture a wider variety of situations. Their images reached viewers in more ways with advances in reproduction for published works and for projection to audiences. Enough different pieces came together in the 1890s to put in place the essentials of modern photographic practice. The picture system that was silver-based, chemical, negative/positive, and recorded on light-sensitive emulsion would dominate for over a century, until the rise of electronic/digital systems in the late 1990s and early 2000s.

A major technological improvement that came to Virginia in the 1880s was the dry plate, named in contrast to the wet plate. The wet plate required sensitization immediately before exposure and development right after. With the dry plate, the preparation was at the factory. The photographer was able to load negative holders in advance, photograph in one or more locations, and process later. A key effect of the dry plate was to unlink the exposing of the negative from the necessity of immediate preparation and developing. Picture-taking as a discrete activity is characteristic of modern

Stop Action

Gelatin silver print on page, 5.3 x 3.1 in., Nancy Astor album, 1910
Ralph Johnstone demonstrated flight at the Virginia State Fair in Richmond in October 1910. *Virginia Historical Society*

Stop Action

Gelatin silver print on album page, by Jamestown Official Photograph Corp., 4.7 x 6.6 in., 1907
As negatives became more sensitive to light, exposure times became shorter. A brief exposure could freeze movement, producing a new look at a subject in motion. Among the activities at the Jamestown Tri-Centennial Exposition in Norfolk was track and field, including the pole vault. *Virginia Historical Society*

practice. Once dry plates became widely available in the early 1880s, adoption by photographers was nearly universal.

Photographic emulsions had always been overly sensitive to blue light. During the 1870s, the German chemist Hermann Wilhelm Vogel had discovered that dyes could be used to extend sensitivity to other colors and reduce the blue bias. By the 1880s, manufacturers were producing negative emulsions that were much better at recording all the colors of visible light, and the first fully panchromatic film appeared about 1906. The Lexington photographer Henry Miley said of an 1895 landscape that "the picture was one of the first around that time to retard the blue light and get cloud effects." As well as properly balancing visible frequencies, emulsions were becoming more sensitive, requiring less light to make an exposure. A photographer would say that films were becoming faster. Combined with lenses that contained a built-in shutter mechanism—enabling shorter, more accurate shutter speeds—quick exposure times of a fraction of a second became possible. The new faster emulsions used with these "instantaneous" shutter speeds could create images that stopped action, freezing subjects in poses that usually escaped the eye. Related developments were methods of artificial illumination that permitted photography without sunlight, either by electrical lights or by flash powder or flashbulbs.[1]

The early 1880s saw the first introduction of film, a clear flexible material, as a support for negatives instead of glass. Film had its own deficiencies, including questions of stability and transparency, but it eliminated breakage and weighed less than glass. A great advantage was that the flexibility of film allowed it to be rolled up on a spool. When George Eastman's roll-film camera was introduced in 1885, it was not the only one of its type on the market, but it was the first big success. In 1888 Eastman introduced the Kodak roll-film camera with the slogan, "You press the button and we do the rest." The company was both a manufacturer and a photofinisher. The Kodak came loaded with a roll of 100 exposures. For processing, the customer sent the camera back to the company, and it was returned with negatives, prints, and reloaded with film.[2]

With electric light bulbs for illumination, photographic enlarging became a more exact procedure and results much more successful. Photographic papers were introduced that, rather than being "printed out" by the sun in a contact frame, in which the image appeared during an exposure of hours, were "developed out" in a chemical bath in minutes. Before this period, photographic processing plants had been few in number and were always labor-intensive. The 1880s saw the beginning of big growth in the photofinishing industry with the introduction of mechanization. Machines exposed frames on long rolls of photographic paper that were cut into many single prints. Finally, the late 1880s and 1890s marked the introduction to Virginia of methods for reproducing photographs in continuous tone for publication. One of those methods, the halftone, brought photographs into news reporting and advertising.

Numerous strains of photography find a beginning in the late nineteenth century, made possible by the new capabilities of the medium. The breadth of practice, although not comparable to the late twentieth century, increased enough that the framework for the modern way of photography was established. Looking at the long century from 1890 to perhaps 2005, there was much technological improvement, but even the big steps were incremental, not a fundamentally different way of image-making. The difference between photographing the departure of a steamship in 1905 with an 8 x 10 view camera, and having the black and white print reproduced in half-tone in a newspaper, and in 1990 using an automatic 35mm single lens reflex camera with a zoom lens to shoot high-speed slide film of a rocket launch, which is printed four-color in a magazine, is one of degree, not of kind. Whereas, on the other hand, capturing an image on a phone and sending it as an attachment to be posted on a website that can be accessed anywhere on earth—literally in seconds—is a fundamentally different system.

Depth of field: Shallow
Silver gelatin print, by Earl Palmer, 8 x 10 in., c. 1970–80
The opening where light passes through the lens is called the aperture. One of the ways to control exposure is to vary the size of the aperture. The aperture setting also affects depth of field: how far in front and beyond the plane of focus will be sharp. With a wide opening that passes more light, an aperture setting such as f/2, depth of field is shallow. In this view, the moonshiner crossing the creek is in focus, but his comrades beyond, and the foliage in front, are not. *Blue Ridge Institute, Ferrum College*

Depth of field: Deep
Silver gelatin print, by Earl Palmer, 8 x 10 in., c. 1970–80
To make this view of a "mountain coffeepot," a type of moonshine still, a small aperture was used, such as f/16 or f/22. Objects in the foreground, mid-ground, and background are in focus. *Blue Ridge Institute, Ferrum College*

EXPOSING THE NEGATIVE

Although it is similar to the human eye is many respects, the camera cannot handle as wide a range of conditions. The subjects that photographs are able to capture have always been limited for technical reasons. Early methods required a great deal of light to record an image. Pictures were usually made in bright light to shorten the long exposure time as much as possible. Because daguerreotypes and wet plate processes also needed to be convenient to processing facilities, most early images were made in galleries well illuminated by windows and/or a skylight. The exposure times required were typically several seconds up to a minute.

In time the sensitivity (or speed) of photographic materials improved to the point that exposures in bright light could be measured in seconds or even fractions of a second. New materials also permitted photographs to be taken in low-light conditions with long exposures. The general principle is that the amount of light that needs to strike the sensitized plate to make a satisfactory negative—a correct exposure—can be achieved either by a large quantity of light in a short period of time or by a smaller flow of light accumulating over a longer period of time. The latter possibility of extended exposures in low light seems to have become more feasible with the improvements in emulsions at the time of the dry plate, for that is when such images first appear in any number.[3]

The use of artificial light for illumination created new potential subjects for photography. The earliest such images in Virginia were created in 1882 at Luray Caverns, which had just opened as a tourist attraction. The steam engine that was installed at the Luray Inn to pump water to the hotel and to the nearby railroad station also ran a generator to power electric lights in the cave over a mile away. Operating as a direct current system, the single wire carrying the current extended three and a half miles, very long for that date. The lamps were arc lights, in which electric current produced a luminous bridge over the gap between carbon poles. Using "carbons" that lasted "for about an hour and a half," the lamps would be switched on "for any party of more than four." Photographer C. H. James of Philadelphia utilized the lamps in February 1882 to make more than sixty views within the Luray Caverns, in both stereo and 8 x 10 inch format.[4]

Few places were supplied with electricity in that way for the next several decades. A more portable kind of artificial lighting was "flash" in its various forms. A flash provided a lot of light in a short period of time to make a correct exposure. As early as the 1860s, the intense bright flare derived from the combustion of very thin magnesium ribbon (along with gobs of smoke) was used as illumination for photography. In the late 1880s an improved method, magnesium flash powder, was introduced and became the main way of illuminating interiors through the 1920s. As early as the 1890s, an inventor had replicated this bright burning inside a glass bulb, but it was not until about 1930 that the flashbulb became a product that was generally available. A flashbulb typically contained thin aluminum strands in an oxygen atmosphere that would be set off by a tiny spark. Flashbulbs were a very effective light source and a primary tool for photographers through the 1960s.[5]

The inventor Harold Edgerton developed a stroboscopic light source in the 1920s that produced a very bright and very short flash. Edgerton famously used his strobes to make photographs of milk splashes and bullets passing through light bulbs. In a strobe, electricity is temporarily accumulated in a capacitor and then on signal from the camera (or some other switch) releases to the lamp,

Exposure by moonlight
Gelatin silver print on page, Whitley Album, 1912
O. Gaines Whitley was a member of a railroad survey team for the Norfolk & Western that spent Christmas 1912 in the mountains. On Christmas eve at Squirrel Camp, near the Kentucky line in Millard, Wise County, Whitley made a number of photographs that he described as "Taken by Moonlight."
Special Collections, Virginia Tech

Carbon arc lights
Stereograph, by C. H. James, card 4.2 x 7 in., each image 4 x 3 in., 1882
James, from Philadelphia, photographed Luray Caverns using electric lights in 1882, the earliest known application of artificial lighting in Virginia. Jones shot both stereo and 8 x 10 inch negatives, producing a series of seventy views, each available as "stereoscopic" or "7x9 Views." This view is titled "Double Columns, Caverns of Luray." *Virginia Historical Society*

Electric light bulbs
Silver gelatin print, by Jamestown Official Photograph Corp., 7 x 9.2 in., 1907
For this photograph, a waterfront bridge at the Jamestown Tri-Centennial Exposition, the subject provided its own illumination. *Virginia Historical Society*

Flash powder
Silver gelatin print, by Jamestown Official Photograph Corp., 10.2 x 13.3 in., 1907
To illuminate the whole banquet hall, two units were fired, one in front and another in back, hidden from the camera and set off by an assistant. People were not yet accustomed to flashes and tended to close their eyes, "corrected" in this print by dark pupils drawn on the eyelids of some subjects. *Virginia Historical Society*

Flash bulb
Silver gelatin print, by Nate Fine, 8 x 10 in., c. 1955
Flash bulbs were more convenient than flash powder, and the light output was more consistent. By May 1955, as seen at Richmond's Beaux Arts Ball, held at the Jefferson Hotel, people had become habituated to flash, blinking less and posing more casually. *Virginia Historical Society*

Copy of miniature painting
Miniature portrait on parchment, c. 1820–50
Tintype copy of miniature, c. 1858–80
Because most mid-nineteenth century portraits were one-of-a-kind originals, an early application for photography was copying portraits. Like a daguerreotype, a tintype reverses its subject, in this case a portrait of an unidentified member of the Meade family.
Virginia Historical Society

Copy of photograph
Carte de visite, by Tanner & Van Ness, Lynchburg, dated 28 Feb. 1866
Cabinet card, by Wampler, Charlottesville, c. 1880–1905
The negative used to make the carte de visite was not available some years later when a copy was desired. The copy image shows improvements that were likely the result of pencil work on the copy negative, smoothing over the lines on the coat and cravat, and darkening around the outline of the head. The subject is Alexander Brown.
Virginia Historical Society

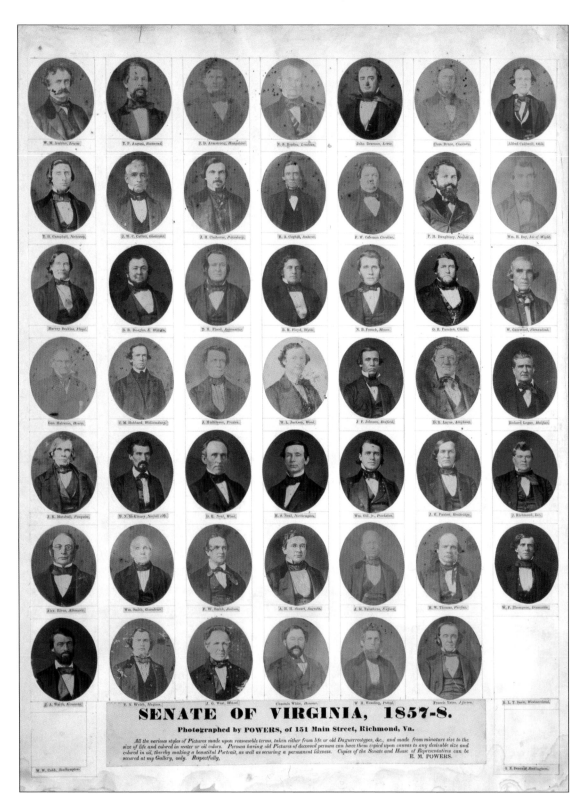

which glows brightly and very briefly. When electronics manufacturers became able to produce affordable capacitors in the 1960s, the strobe made its way into general use in the form of the electronic flash. In the 1970s electronic flash drove flashbulbs out of use with improvements that included more powerful lights, sensors to adjust light level, and remote triggers.

COPYING

The ability of a photograph to reproduce another picture was an important attribute from the beginning. In 1840 the primary medium for copying was the engraving. The limitations of the daguerreotype copy—that it was reversed, in black and white, and small—were similar to the deficiencies that an engraving suffered from, and the daguerreotype was truer to the visual appearance of the original.

Compared to the daguerreotype, negative/positive photography was a better system for copying. The copy could be larger, it was not reversed, and a quantity of prints could be produced. A large proportion of cartes de visite were made from copy negatives, especially those of well-known subjects. Photographic printing in the nineteenth century generally meant contact printing, in which the size of the print was exactly the same as the size of the negative. Therefore, the subject when photographed had to appear at the right size on the plate. A print that was not the right size could be resized by making a copy negative of it at the desired dimensions. Most of the issuers of series, such as Civil War leaders, added to their available titles by copying the best images available.[6]

Another kind of copying was to photograph paste-ups or collages of individual portrait photographs. These image collections were laid out in designs

Art for copying
Forty-eight salt prints, by E. M. Powers, each oval 2.5 x 1.9 in., mounted on board 17.3 x 23.8 in., 1857–58
One advantage of paper photographs was that a number of them could be combined in a collage and photographed to make a new piece. This item is the original art prepared for copying by Richmond photographer Powers, with ruled rows and columns and typeset labels. (No examples of the copied piece have been located.)
Virginia Historical Society

Assembly
Silver gelatin print, by W. W. Foster, 24.4 x 29.9 in., 1907–08
As seen in this presentation of the Virginia Legislature, 1907–08 session, the
basic method for assembling individual portraits into a group remained much
the same in the twentieth century. *Virginia Historical Society*

Jurors

Salt print, by David H. Anderson, 11 x 14 in., 1867
Salt print, by David H. Anderson, 11 x 14 in., 1867
Anderson photographed the jurors gathered for the trial of former Confederate president Jefferson Davis in Richmond in 1867, the first integrated jury pool in the history of the state. Anderson took the pool in two groups, but rather than blacks in one and whites in the other, the two photographs were integrated too. *Both Valentine Richmond History Center*

Assembled jurors
Glass negative, by W. W. Foster, 5 x 7 in., 1911
Because Jefferson Davis did not come to trial, Anderson's jury photographs were probably not as commercially valuable as they might have been. The two jury images were melded into one for a display piece about the trial, supplemented with portraits of Davis, the trial judge John C. Underwood, and Supreme Court Chief Justice Salmon P. Chase. The piece was issued not by Anderson but by the Lee Gallery, perhaps better able to tap the Confederate market, both as a photographic copy and as a large original.
Virginia Historical Society

Assembled True Reformers
Silver gelatin print, by Jefferson Fine Art gallery, 16 x 20 in., c. 1900–05
Photographer James C. Farley incorporated 113 photographs and images of the
United Order of True Reformers, made over several years, into the sort of display
that might hang in a lobby, or might represent an organization at a public event
like a fair. The display itself was then photographed. *Virginia Historical Society*

Collage of Ministers
Silver gelatin print, copy of oval
collage with 231 numbered heads,
1873
The key providing the names for the
numbered portraits bears the heading:
"Ministers attending Baptist General Associa-
tion and Professors of Richmond College, 'June
Meeting'–1873, Semi-centennial of Richmond College."
Virginia Historical Society

Collage of children
Glass negative, by Michael Miley, 11 x 14 in., c. 1875–95
Miley probably prepared this collage of child portraits to advertise his experience and success in this branch of work. *Virginia Historical Society*

that included neat grids of rows and columns, circular "medallions," and irregular conglomerations. Most designs incorporated some means for identifying the portraits. By the 1850s these assembled group portraits had already taken the forms that are familiar today in school yearbooks and other organization pictures.

MAKING PRINTS

Of the two parts to the negative/positive process, the first, creating the negative, is generally the more significant—selecting the subject, choosing lighting and exposure, and then developing properly. It is common darkroom-technician wisdom that "a good negative will print itself." Thus in many operations the photographer would produce the negative, and an assistant would make the prints.

Although producing the negative might require the more crucial decisions, producing a positive print is clearly also essential to photography. In it there is craft, and there are choices. A first step is deciding which negatives to print. At the time of glass negatives and a limited number of exposures, a higher percentage of negatives were routinely printed. In a later period, a photographer using roll film would often make contact sheets of negatives and then examine the results to decide which frames to print. In commercial or editorial situations it might not be the photographer who decided which images to print but rather an art director or an editor. In portrait studios, it is typical for proof sets from a sitting to be forwarded to the customer for selection.

Once negatives have been identified for printing, new choices arise. In the nineteenth century, same-size contact printing was standard. Sun enlargers were introduced in the 1860s, but the enlarger's role as a key tool in the darkroom emerged with electricity. Precision machines with high-quality optics made good results possible even from miniature negatives, as 35mm film was first known. Enlargers create new options: the size of a print, the cropping, and the degree of enlargement. Other choices were among the many varieties of photographic papers that once were available, affecting the

Fine prints

Four platinum prints, 4.7 x 6.7 in., c. 1895–1905

Platinum prints are particularly expressive in the middle range of the black and white tonal scale. These views of the grounds at the University of Virginia, Charlottesville, are from a larger set that was produced over a period of years. (One was published in 1900, others depict buildings completed in 1902.) The initials "G.W.M." appear on the reverse of several, possibly the photographer, who was likely a member of the university community. The images here include a view on the Lawn, a snow scene, "The New Driveway (East of East Range)," and "The road to Monticello." *All Virginia Historical Society*

Making choices

Two photographic prints, one cyanotype, by Frances Benjamin Johnston, c. 1900–01

Johnston operated a studio in Washington, D.C. As a project she traveled to the Shenandoah Valley to photograph along the route of Sheridan's Ride. (In October 1864, Union General Philip Sheridan had ridden twenty miles rallying his forces—a heroic tale, but not one taught in Virginia schools.) From two similar negatives made at Snickers Gap, Johnston experimented with different printing effects: one darker with cool tone, one lighter with warm tone, one in blue. One of the prints is titled on reverse, "Watching the stage go by." *All Library of Congress, Prints and Photographs Division, Frances B. Johnston Collection*

Making changes

Four silver gelatin prints, by Harry Bagby, three 8 x 10 in., one 6.5 x 9.5 in., c. 1935–50

Bagby wished to produce an overview of the lake and swimming area at Fairy Stone State Park, in Patrick County. He shot two 8 x 10 negatives that fit side-by-side to produce a view with both the width and the detail that he was after (the upper two images). Not satisfied with the sky on his right-hand image, however, Bagby printed that negative without its sky (as seen to the left), and then substituted the sky from the left-hand image. He put the two prints together and made a copy negative of the whole image (below: notice that the clouds repeat themselves). *All Virginia Historical Society*

Single-negative panorama, 1911
Silver gelatin print, by W. W. Foster, 9.5 x 22.8 in., 1911
Cameras that could capture a wide view in a single exposure were introduced in the late 1890s. Panoramic views were popular into the 1920s. The caption in the image states "Richmond, Va., Annual Meeting of the United Daughters of the Confederacy, Richmond, Va.. Nov. 7–11–1911, Photo by Foster." The group poses on Franklin St. on the steps of Second Baptist Church. *Virginia Historical Society*

tonality of the paper (warm or cold), surface (glossy or matte), and contrast (adapted to the varying contrast of the negatives). In exposing the image on the paper, choices include the relative darkness or lightness of the prints and the application of techniques such as "burning" and "dodging" that alter relative values within an image.

THE PANORAMA

Big and wide landscapes were a main strain of nineteenth-century art. Bird's-eye views, prospects, and panoramas appeared as oil paintings, murals, aquatints, and lithographs. Popular theatrical exhibitions of the 1830s–1840s that featured big views included the original "Panorama" (a huge 360-degree painting), Daguerre's "Diorama," and moving panoramas like Banvard's 1846 "three-mile-long" Panorama of the Mississippi River.

In photography, the panoramic tendency began with the daguerreotype, despite the fact that the medium was not well suited. The cases and glass that protected the plates made it difficult to group them, and anyway the daguerreo-type was more about precision than breadth. By 1860 the wet plate had made the photographic panorama significantly more feasible. The negatives were a scale larger, and the paper positives were more readily assembled into a single view. During the Civil War quite a few photographers were thinking panoramically, and many negatives were shot to be parts of panoramas that were never assembled.

Another avenue toward panoramas followed later in the nineteenth century. With advances in optics, a camera lens could be designed to capture a wide angle of view. However, beyond a certain angle of coverage, the image seen in the camera becomes distorted. (For 35mm cameras, a 24mm lens would usually produce evident distortion, whereas a 35mm wide-angle lens would not.) When distortion is minor (and it is present in every camera image) the eye adapts and overlooks it. Distortion in the image beyond a certain point cannot be overlooked or normalized by the eye.

To be able to photograph a wide view yet avoid distortion, scanning cameras were developed that used clockwork-like mechanisms to coordinate

a movement of lens, shutter, and film. These cameras produced panoramic photographs that were printed from a single long negative rather than multiple negatives. In one kind called a circuit camera, as the lens rotated in one direction and scanned across a scene from right to left, the film slowly moved in the opposite direction and was exposed through an open slot in the shutter curtain. The entire negative was not exposed simultaneously; instead the exposure began at one end and proceeded to the other as the film gradually advanced by the open slot.

The great era for the single-negative panorama was from about 1900 into the 1920s. In that period a number of photographers specialized in these kinds of pictures. Some of them traveled widely, photographing scenes. Besides the resulting commercial overproduction, it may be that the popularity of the format fell off because more photography was being seen in publications, and panoramas did not fit well in their pages. One application for wide pictures that continued into the 1960s was group portraits for schools and other organizations. An anecdote

Single-negative panorama, 1919–20
Silver gelatin print, 7.4 x 25.9 in., 1919–20
Gathered on the portico of the Second Baptist Church, Richmond, in 1919 or 1920 are members of the Equal Suffrage League. *Virginia Historical Society*

Single-negative panorama, 1918

Silver gelatin print, by F. J. Conway, 7.9 x 55.1 in., c. 1918 (above)

Different types of panoramic cameras produced varying sizes of negatives. In extremely long-negative cameras, the lens rotated and the film moved during the exposure. In this view by a Norfolk photographer, the women appear to be exercising. The location is either the Navy Yard in Norfolk or the Naval Supply Station in Hampton. *Virginia Historical Society*

Single-negative panorama, 1921
Silver gelatin print, 7.1 x 36.4 in., 1921 (below)
After attending services at a historic church, the recently inaugurated President Harding and his wife pause in their departure to allow the photographers to take their shots. The D.C.-based panoramic photographer (whose logo cannot be deciphered) captures the whole of the scene, from the individuals in the crowd, the soldiers along the drive, the girls in white dresses, the automobiles parked to the sides. Printed in the image are the words: "The President and Mrs. Harding, after the Pohick, Virginia church services, May, 29, 1921." *Virginia Historical Society*

Assembled panorama: factory

Four silver gelatin prints, glued together, 2.38 x 11.75 in., c. 1910–20 (above)

One way of making a wide photographic view is to assemble together a number of normal views. This panorama shows the Sparrow & Graveley plant, at High and Fayette streets, in Martinsville, Henry County. It was probably made for a property agent, because on the reverse are the building dimensions—from left, 164 x 110 ft., 75 x 33 ft., and 98 x 50 ft.—and information about street frontages. *Virginia Historical Society*

Assembled panorama: German village
Three silver gelatin prints, taped together, probably by C. M. Best, 3.88 x 19.25 in., c. 1916 (below)
The even horizon line indicates that this panoramic view was carefully prepared. Two German ships that were commerce raiders sought refuge at Hampton Roads in 1915. The U.S., which had not yet entered the World War, held the ships and crews at the naval shipyard in Portsmouth. There the sailors built a German village that became an attraction for visitors until taken down in 1917. Beyond are the ships, the *Prinz Eitel Friedrich* and *Kronprinz Wilhelm. Virginia Historical Society*

W. T. WATSON, Onancock and Chincoteague Island, Va.

W. T. WATSON, Onancock and Chincoteague Island, Va.

Assembled panorama: ordnance works
Five silver gelatin prints, mounted together on cloth, 7.3 x 41 in., 1940
The comprehensive view served as a record of construction progress. As a working document, the harm of taping labels to the picture surface was not a concern. The label on the reverse states: "Radford Ordnance Works 462, Hercules Powder Company Project 7700, Nov. 28, 1940, Monthly Progress Photo No. 3. General view taken from Point A, Station 2 baseline 800' south. Left: Acid and shops area, Left center: N.C. [nitro-cotton] area, Center: Smokeless powder "A" line, Right center: Temporary employment office, Right: Barracks area." *Virginia Historical Society*

Panoramic effect: Cape Charles Venture
Three albumen prints, No. 3, No. 4, No. 5, by W. T. Watson, each 7.1 x 9 in. mounted on 10 x 12 in. board, c. 1880–1910
The three photographs, although mounted separately, fit together as a panoramic view. Watson, a photographer based in Onancock and Chincoteague Island, produced the images for an Eastern Shore land development project, the "Cape Charles Venture." Inscribed on the mounts are: "No 3– North West Corner of farm– Looking east"; "No 4– North-west corner of farm– Looking south on driveway along bluff"; and "No 5– North-west Corner of farm– Looking South along Bay Shore." *Virginia Historical Society, John S. Wise Collection*

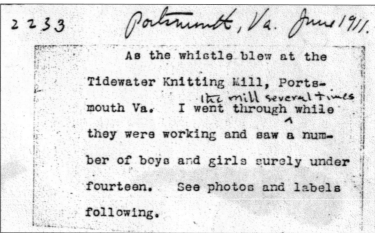

Documentary caption

Gelatin silver print, by Lewis Hine, 4.5 x 6.63 in., 1911

Having made the photograph to document child labor, Hine's caption—on an index card—includes information that enhances the image's evidence: "Portsmouth, Va. June 1911. As the whistle blew at the Tidewater Knitting Mill, Portsmouth. I went through the mill several times while they were working and saw a number of boys and girls surely under fourteen." *Virginia Historical Society*

from the Petersburg area, perhaps apocryphal, tells of an old photographer who made class pictures of students seated on the stadium bleachers. He used a circuit camera with very slow movement—so slow that a student posed at one end of the stands, waited for the lens to pass by, and then ran around the back to the other end of the class and posed again.

WORDS & PICTURES

Sometimes a photograph seems obvious upon first glance. The reason it was taken is evident from the image—for example a beautiful sunset, or a portrait, or a famous sculpture. Another photograph might not be so obvious and withhold its meaning at first. A viewer might well need some words of explanation to understand it. In still another circumstance, the meaning of a photograph that appears evident might change a good bit once explained verbally.

Most photographs are accompanied by words. Published images have captions and credits. A photograph prepared for exhibition may have a title or label. A print in an album typically has written identification. A loose photograph may have writing on the reverse. The title may be chosen by the photographer and be incorporated into the presentation of the image, for instance written on the mat or mount. Other titles are attached by an editor in the context of a larger whole, or by a cataloger as a way to refer to the picture. The standard meaning of "caption" would be edited text that accompanies a published image. In many cases only a few words need to accompany a photograph to create a complete package—the name of the sitter, for example, to go with a portrait—while in other cases more explanation is necessary to convey what is going on.

Captions work in many and varying ways. Some provide data about the making of the photograph. Some are all about the subject, discussing who, what, when, and where. Some captions may also address why, or they draw lessons or recommendations from what the photograph shows. Some captions provide

Fictionalized narrative
Four tintypes, about 1 x .75 in. each, held by corners on card, c. 1870–1900
A series of four images of a young woman is linked to attendance at church by titles inscribed beneath each image. The subject smiles a little more each time as the sequence progresses: "During church," "Last hymn," "Benediction," and finally broadly smiling, "Church is out." In reality, the subject's expression was probably unrelated to her church attendance; the words have created an amusing but untrue context for the images. *Virginia Historical Society*

Explanatory inscription
Albumen print on mount, by J. T. Wampler, 4 x 7 in., on mount 5.2 x 8.5 in., 1888
University of Virginia students are identified by the Greek letters of their respective fraternities, inscribed directly on the print: from left to right, ΦΔΘ, ΣΝ, ΠΚΑ, ΣΧ, ΦΚΣ, ΧΦ, ΔΨ (John Hampden Chamberlayne Bagby, 1867–1934), ΔΚΕ, ΑΤΩ, ΦΚΨ, ΦΘΑ, ΚΑ, ΣΑΕ, and ΚΣ. *Virginia Historical Society*

Circumstantial evidence

Photographic postcard, 5.5 x 3.4 in., c. 1926–27

Words on the reverse of the postcard are pieces of a story, beginning with the typeset caption: "Made by J. Sidna Allen while in prison. This table contains more than 75,000 pieces, finished in natural wood finish, no paint, no stain. The different kinds of wood make the color." Allen (1866–1941) was involved in the Hillsville courthouse shootings in March 1912 that left the judge and four others dead. Upon his release from incarceration in 1926, Allen toured for several years displaying handcrafted wood items that he had made in prison. The pencil inscription "Price 10 cts" was likely the cost of the postcard at his exhibition. And the ink inscription "J. Sidna Allen, Hillsville, Va." was noted in pencil by the original collector: "4/28/27 autographed photo." *Virginia Historical Society*

2829   A view probably unique in the annals of American sailing vessels in
showing five schooners of three, four, five, six, and seven masts.
September 12, 1906.

Schooner SALLIE I'ON   (3 masts)   In Dry Dock 2
    "   MALCOLM BAXTER, Jr.   (4 masts)   "   "   " 2
    "   See note   (5 masts)   Anchored in stream
    "   ELEANOR A. PERCY   (6 masts)   Near head of Pier 4
    "   THOMAS W. LAWSON   (7 masts)   South side of Pier 5

This picture was made from roof of the office building and shows the
blacksmith and galvanizing shops in the foreground.

In the right background may be seen excavation under way for building a
third dry dock.

It may be noted further that when this scene was first observed there
was also a two-masted fishing schooner in the view but, with the flood
tide, that had sailed out of range on the right before the photographer
could get his camera in position on top of the office building.

Note.   The white five-masted schooner at anchor in the background of
the picture must have been one of the Palmer fleet, several of which
were in the harbor at the time.

        The negative of this picture is dated September 12, 1906.
The actual exposure must have been made in the forenoon of
September 11, before the two schooners were removed from the
dry dock at 9.30 a.m. on that day.   This hour agrees with
known circumstance to the effect that the scene was first
observed soon after the arrival of the engine drafting force
at the office at 8 a.m.   It may be noted that the flooding
of the dock had not been commenced.

        Scene first observed by E.W.Sniffen
        *Photographer C.J.Dorr_*

SPECIAL RECORD PRINT A
Return to E. O. Smith

A unique event explained
Silver gelatin print, 8 x 10 in., by
C. J. Dorr, with written description on reverse, 1906
The special circumstance documented in the photograph is
fully explained by the attached
sheet. It tells of the observation
of the scene, the photographing
of it, and what happened after
the exposure, and provides the
names of the ships and information about the shipyard.
Mariners Museum

Sale in front of "Grand Centr

Group of Buyers

The original owner

THE OLDEST INHABITANT

THE JUDGE

The Plunger

Narrative commentary

Twelve albumen prints, round images 2.5 in. diameter, on mounts 5.3 x 4.3 in., c. 1890

The photographer shot these images using one of the original Kodaks, then sent the camera containing the exposed film to the Eastman Company, which produced the prints. The pictures document a land auction at Big Stone Gap, near Virginia's western tip. In the late nineteenth century a number of areas in southwestern Virginia experienced land speculation related to industrial development. The inscribed comments below the images help describe the auction and its atmosphere: "Sale in front of "Grand Centr[al Hotel]"; "Group of Buyers" (with Big Stone Gap visible beyond); "The original owner"; "The oldest inhabitant"; "The Judge"; "The Plunger"; and next page: "Fixed to be took"; "'That was my bid'"; "'Whose bid was that?'"; "The Association buyer"; "A Boomer"; and "'Five more.'" *Virginia Historical Society*

Fixed to be took

"That was my bid"

"Whose bid was that?"

THE ASSOCIATION BUYER

A BOOMER

"FIVE MORE"

layers of meaning, describing for example the event depicted but also speaking to the setting for the event. Some are superfluous: in a newspapers, a photograph for which a caption is unnecessary will often get one anyway. Captions that are attached to a photograph long after its making may attempt to re-interpret the image from an original intention or to correct previous misidentification.

REPRODUCTIONS IN INK

Even the most popular photographs of the 1860s and 1870s never approached the circulation numbers of the wood engravings published in top periodicals. When copied by artists and engravers, photographs played an ever bigger role as a source for illustrations in print, but it was not until the twentieth century that photographs took the central place as pictures in the popular press. By 1910 photographic reproductions were produced in numbers that well surpassed the earlier era's wood engravings.

The first publications that presented photographs directly were books. Books had the advantage that pages printed on different presses and on different types of paper could be bound together for the final work. (Indeed, books with plate sections have been produced into the twenty-first century.) The technique of running a page through two different presses, the one to print an image and the other words in type, was long-established, utilized for instance by Theodor de Bry in his 1590 edition of Thomas Hariot's report on Virginia. In the nineteenth century, books were illustrated with steel engravings, etchings, and lithographs, none of which could be printed simultaneously with type on a press.[7]

In the late nineteenth century, a time of remarkable innovation in printing technology, a number of image systems appeared that incorporated photographic processes. In the 1880s Wittemann Brothers of New York issued a series of small books of views starting with *Centennial Album of Yorktown and of Richmond, Va.* (1881). The format presents an illustration on each of twelve leaves that fold out to make one long sheet. The images are "photo-views," described as "reproduced from photographs by [German lithographer] Louis Glaser's process." Printed on yellow-tan paper in white and black, the glossy images look like they are derived from photographs, but

Albertype

Collotype, from *Richmond Illustrated in Albertype,* by A. Wittemann, 1888

The collotype was a reproduction process that did not require an artist as intermediary. The image was translated directly from the continuous tone of the photograph. The Albertype was a variety of collotype that instead of a stone plate used a glass plate. "Electric Railway" shows a streetcar from the Richmond line that was the first successful electric system in the world in 1888.
Virginia Historical Society

Lithograph after photo

Photo-lithograph, from *The Shenandoah Valley,* by Wittemann Bros., 2.4 x 3.8 in., c. 1882

For Glaser's process, seen here, an artist used a photograph as the source for an image that is reproduced by lithography. This image, "Rope ferry over the Shenandoah River, at Riverton," is one of sixteen prints mounted together on a single, long folded strip. Riverton is on the west bank of the Shenandoah River, opposite Front Royal.
Virginia Historical Society

all the rendering has passed through the hand of an artist.[8]

The next step was the collotype, a type of photolithograph that reproduced a photograph more directly, without the artist's hand. The collotype originated in France in the 1850s as a continuous-tone image printed from a lithographic stone. The method was refined by Joseph Albert of Munich to print from glass plates. The Albertype Company of Brooklyn, N.Y., used this process to print a subsequent series of Virginia picture books. Beginning in 1888 with *Richmond Illustrated in Albertype,* titles included *James towne Island* and *Souvenir of Old Point Comfort and Environs* (1890).[9]

In these publications, the reproductions produced by photolithography were 5 x 7 inches or smaller, with most about 3 x 5 inches. A high-quality reproduction in a larger size was introduced with photogravure. Photogravure is not a lithographic method but comes from the engraving family of prints, in which the plate is inked and wiped and the ink left in the crevices makes the image. A photogravure has a fine grain like

Photogravure
Photogravure, in *Art Work of Norfolk and vicinity,* Pt. 6, 1895
An intaglio process like engraving, photogravure is capable of high quality reproduction—it was not until the 1930s or later that the halftone reached equivalence—but it has the disadvantage of being incompatible on the press with type. "McCullough's Docks" is a view on the Elizabeth River in Norfolk.
Virginia Historical Society

aquatint and a subtle tonal range that is similar to a platinum print. Following the publications of Virginia views in collotype that began in the 1880s, similar collections were issued in the 1890s in photogravure. In 1891 an Indianapolis publisher offered *Richmond, Virginia Illustrated,* and in 1895 Anderson Brothers in Charlottesville issued *University of Virginia; Photo-gravures.* The first of a series of publications with similar titles and formats also appeared in 1895, *Art Work of Norfolk and Vicinity.* Published in Chicago, and issued in twelve parts, the photogravures are large, about 7 x 10 inches, mostly exterior but with some interior views of architecture and places. Other titles in the photogravure series, issued in from nine to twelve parts, include: *Art Work of Scenes in the Valley of Virginia* (1897); *Art Work of Richmond* (1897); *Art Work of Lynchburg and Danville, Virginia* (1903); *Art Work of Danville* (1903); and *Art Work of Petersburg, Virginia* (1903).[10]

As methods, both the collotype and the photogravure created high-quality reproductions of photographs in ink. To print either, however, required a specialized facility, and neither could be quickly produced. The method that became the standard for reproduction was the halftone, introduced in the 1880s. In its

early forms the halftone was inferior to the collotype or the photogravure. Perhaps its key advantage was that it could be produced locally. A halftone is a photographic copy of an original made through a dot-screen that translates the continuous tones of the original into a graduated dot pattern. For printing on a press side-by-side with type, the halftone negative would be used to expose a metal plate. Although the earliest halftones were not great reproductions, it was the rise of the halftone that in time made engraving by hand a lost art.[11]

The halftone made its way into Virginia commerce first in books, then in weekly papers, and finally in daily newspapers. In *Shadows in Silver,* the Richmond photographer Huestis Cook reported that his first assignment in the field, as a young man of 20, was to photograph Westover in Charles City County. "One day in 1888, Marion Harland . . . proposed that he take the pictures for her forthcoming work, *His Great Self,* a life of William Byrd II." Marion Harland was the pen-name of Mary Haws Terhune, a prolific Virginia author in the late nineteenth century. Cook "was to visit and photograph Westover . . . as well as nearby Shirley and others of the plantation houses . . . she would make the necessary arrangements with their owners for his reception. Cook accepted the proposition, journeyed to these plantations and took exterior and interior views of the mansions for Miss Harland."[12] Cook later told the story that "as he landed at the wharf" at Westover "on his first plantation assignment," the proprietor Major Drewry greeted him and said "Come right up and we'll have a mint julep."[13]

Harland's book about Byrd did not appear until 1892 and was not illustrated. She did, however, utilize Cook's photographs in the November 1888 issue of *The Home-Maker.* Harland had just become editor of the New York-based women's magazine and utilized Cook's work at Westover to illustrate an installment of her series "Some Old Virginia Homesteads."[14] In the article, most of Cook's photographs served as source material for line art illustrations. One view of the house, however, appeared in halftone as a photographic reproduction. By his account "Westover—River Front" was Cook's first published photograph. The views at Westover were "just the beginning of his work in this field," reports *Shadows in Silver.* "As it happened, Huestis Cook was the first photographer ever to be admitted to many of these houses." In succeeding issues of *The Home-Maker,* Harland used Cook views of Shirley plantation and the John Marshall house in Richmond. Harland used the photographs again when she assembled the articles into a book in 1897 called *Some Colonial Homesteads.* The authors of *Shadows in Silver* state that "once [Cook's] photographs began to appear in Marion Harland's books and become known, other writers of Virginia history and commentators on the Virginia scene, such as John Fiske and Mary Newton Stanard, commissioned him to take plantation pictures to be used as illustrations."[15]

Young Cook was not the only photographer of historic estates. For the 1893 *Gloucester* by Sally Nelson Robins, "the photographs were taken by Miss Blanche Dimmock, of Sherwood." The publisher was West, Johnston, & Co. of Richmond. Each of the half-dozen halftone reproductions is a small (2¾ x 3½ in.) image placed by itself on the page. It is one of the earliest Virginia-printed books with halftones, but the quality is fair at best. The halftones are significantly better in an 1897 Virginia production, Anna Venable Koiner's *Echoes from the Land of the Golden Horseshoe,* printed by Henkel & Company of New Market.[16]

A kind of halftone reproduction that was very familiar to Virginians during the twentieth century was newspaper photography. Halftones are made at different levels of quality, measured at lines to the inch that correspond to dot size. A book might use a fine 135-line screen, and newspapers have typically used a less-fine 65-line screen. In the early period, halftones were produced by specialists like engraving companies and were tricky to print. Their utilization fit better into the production schedules of weekly or monthly, rather than daily, periodicals.[17]

In Virginia, it was not the bigger daily newspapers but a weekly newspaper that was the first to use halftones on a regular basis: the *Richmond Planet,* edited by John Mitchell, Jr. Like other newspapers, the *Planet* regularly used photographs as the source for line art that could be printed on a newspaper press. As early as 1885, the paper noted that "the photographs from which the 'cuts' are made that appear in this journal are finely executed by Mr. J. C. Farley." Most of the photographs were portraits (usually uncredited). The initial change that the *Planet* effected in January 1895 was not to alter the style of picture from the bust portrait but to replace the line-art version with the halftone head-shot. The *Richmond Planet* of 9 February 1895, for example, printed halftone portraits of eight candidates for city council. Almost all Virginia newspapers moved into halftones similarly: images of the same kind as before, reproduced by a different method.[18]

But if the *Planet* followed a pattern that would become typical for its first halftones, editor Mitchell's next step was not. Mitchell himself began to take photographs of newsworthy subjects in the field. He seems to have been the first press photographer in Virginia. On 9 March 1895, the *Planet* ran a photograph of the interior of the Richmond police court. This was not a head-shot and in fact was a difficult subject that a more experienced photographer might not have attempted.

Photo-illustration: line art
Albumen print, by Huestis Cook, 4.5 x 7.4 in., c. 1888
Line illustration, in *The Home-Maker,* Nov. 1888
The artist for *The Home Maker* used Cook's photograph of the stairs at Westover as the basis for the illustration. Other than the figure descending the stairs, added by the artist, the drawing is reasonably true to the photograph.
Both Virginia Historical Society

STAIRCASE AT WESTOVER.

Photo-illustration: halftone

Albumen print, by Huestis Cook, 4.4 x 6.3 in., on mount 5 x 7.5 in., c. 1888

Photograph in halftone, in *The Home-Maker,* Nov. 1888

The print is from the same negative but is not the one that *The Home-Maker* used. Huestis Cook was only twenty years old when he took the steamer to Westover to make the photograph, but he knew how to make the line of the chimney vertical. At the time, the east dependency of Westover had not yet been replaced (on the foreground side). *Both Virginia Historical Society*

SIDE VIEW IN BALL ROOM.

Virginia-printed halftone
Photograph in halftone, from Anna Venable Koiner, *Echoes from the Land of the Golden Horseshoe,* Henkel & Company, Printers, 1897.
An early example of a book-quality halftone printed in the state is "Side view in ball room," a Luray Caverns view, from the well-known Henkel press of New Market. *Virginia Historical Society*

RICHMOND, VA., POLICE COURT.

Newspaper halftone I
Photograph in halftone, by John Mitchell, Jr., *Richmond Planet,* 9 March 1895
Not one Mitchell photograph used to make a halftone for the *Planet* is known to survive. Even copies of the images as printed in the newspaper are rare. "Richmond, Va., Police Court" shows the room in old Odd Fellows Hall used for two decades to try misdemeanors. Justice John J. Crutchfield sits at center in front of the window. Seen in profile, lawyer Giles B. Jackson sits at the bar in center; next left at the bar, also seen in profile, is Commonwealth's Attorney Col. M. L. Spottswood. In front of the foreground railing are the witnesses; to the left is the "pen" for prisoners; at right around the stove are the spectators. *Library of Virginia*

(The image came out too murky to be seen clearly in the newspaper.) Mitchell probably began taking his own photographs for two reasons: first, because he did not have to pay someone else to do it, and second, he had powerful stories that photographs could help to tell, and he had a great desire to tell these stories.

Mitchell's courageous campaign to expose the miscarriages of justice in rural courtrooms around Virginia is an important tale from the late 1880s and 1890s. He traveled to county seats where African Americans were in jail, facing trials for crimes that only prejudice, and not evidence, could link them to. At times Mitchell traveled equipped with a camera and was able to convince jailors to allow him to photograph the defendants in the jail yard or corridor. On his return to Richmond, Mitchell had someone develop the plates and print them, and then an engraving company make halftones to run in the newspaper. The first photograph credited to Mitchell, a portrait of Solomon Marable in jail, appeared in the *Planet* on 12 October 1895. No extant photographs identified as by Mitchell are known; even

copies of the halftone reproductions as they appeared in the *Planet* are rare.[19]

Virginia newspapers tended to be conservative and were not early adapters of new features like halftones. When the *Richmond News* began publication in October 1899 as an afternoon penny paper, it may have been the first daily in the state to print halftone reproductions on the front page. Most of the illustrations in the paper remained line-art, although a good proportion were noted as based on photographs. A passing comment in the *News* from this period suggests that likenesses from artists were not always great: "The newspaper artists seem to be working more havoc with Gen. Otis than the insurgent forces are doing." At first the halftones in the *News* were not of timely events but of subjects that could be prepared in advance, such as portraits of politicians or of "a reigning belle." In mid-1900 the *News* started a weekly picture section that came on Saturday. The section displayed a large number of photographs, but still the images were not of news events but rather illustrated features on fashion, neighborhood history, and the social whirl.[20]

Newspaper halftone II
Photograph in halftone, credited "From photograph taken by Editor Mitchell," *Richmond Planet,* 12 Oct. 1895
John Mitchell, Jr., became known for going to rural Virginia counties to cover cases of injustice to African Americans. One of his most famous rescues was of Mary Abernathy and Pokey Barnes, of Lunenburg County, charged with murder. "Solomon Marable, in the Richmond City Jail" depicts the man whose untrue testimony initially imperiled the women but who changed his story and helped free them. Marable was hanged. *Library of Virginia*

Same-day newspaper halftone
Photograph in halftone, *Richmond News,* 2 Jan. 1900
The view of the fire at the Richmond offices of the Chesapeake & Ohio Railway, at Eighth and Main streets, appeared on the newspaper's front page with the caption: "Early Morning Scene at the Fire. The First Half-tone picture of a fire ever taken and printed on the same day in Richmond." *Virginia Historical Society*

Nevertheless, by the time the Saturday section debuted, the *Richmond News* had already proven it could produce a timely photograph. On the morning of 2 January 1900, fire struck the offices of the Chesapeake & Ohio Railway at Eighth and Main streets. The first alarm was called at 6:10 a.m., and despite difficulties caused by the cold and ice, the fire was under control by 9:50 a.m. In that pre-radio era, newspapers would cover important breaking events by issuing quickly produced reports called extras, and the *News* issued an extra about the fire by 10 a.m. That afternoon, the regular edition ran a photograph of the ruins captioned "Early Morning Scene at the Fire." The caption claimed, "The First Half-tone picture of a fire ever taken and printed on the same day in Richmond." Timely photographs like that did not become a regular feature of Virginia newspapers for a few more years.[21]

COLOR

In his writings Joseph Nicéphore Niépce, the early inventor of photography, is said to have expressed some surprise that his pictures were black and white and not color. We see the world in color, of course (though perhaps not all of us the same), and a sense took hold early that the development of photography would not be complete until it could record color.[22]

With daguerreotypes the lack of color was addressed in two ways. First, experimenters continued to push the daguerreotype to record in color. They modified the process, varying formulas and coating the plates with dyes. Indeed some claimed success. No doubt in certain cases people simply looked hard into plates and became convinced they were seeing colors, an understandable illusion because daguerreotypes survive today with a luminosity that seems to shimmer in color. On the other hand, some folks may have seen something: modern researchers have repeated certain experiments undertaken by early investigators and produced plates with noticeable colors (which however fade under light).

The second way that color was incorporated into daguerreotypes was by adding it, by painting or tinting the image, in the manner of engravings and aquatints. Because the daguerreotype image is essentially a flaky surface deposit and can be easily wiped off, adding color required careful technique. A raft of effects was developed for daguerreotypes, primarily for putting warmth in faces and gilding jewels and buttons. In many cases the coloring was performed with great skill, for with occupations such as portraitist or miniaturist displaced by the daguerreotyper, numerous painters found positions in photographic retouching. The first patent for photography issued to a Virginian was for a daguerreotype coloring process.[23]

The two approaches to putting color into the daguerreotype—to record it directly, or to add it later—represent the main paths to color in photographic images generally. Adding color to an image that is recorded in black and white, because the hues are the choice of the maker, can be called "selected" color. Examples from the nineteenth and early twentieth centuries would include not only the varieties of hand-tinted photographs but also photolithographs and other color prints made on a press. The other approach, to photograph color directly, might be called "recorded" color, because it primarily relies on an optical and chemical process to produce the colors of the image. Not until the mid-1930s did recorded color fully arrive, in the form of the Kodachrome transparency.[24]

Two decades into photography, about 1860, the general public had become accustomed to the black-and-white photograph. Compared to previous years, the percentage of portraits that were hand-colored seems to have diminished (as seen for example, in the collection at the VHS). While there are a fair number of examples of tinted cartes de visite from the 1860s, there are almost none from the 1870s or among cabinet cards from the 1880s or 1890s. No doubt the expense of coloring encouraged the trend: often stronger than the desire for color was the wish to save money. Yet sometimes taste is weightier than parsimony. A good portion of late-nineteenth century photographs that were improved by an artist's hand were finished in gray-scale rather than in color.[25]

Colored daguerreotype
Daguerreotype, one-sixth plate, hand-colored, c. 1845–55
Early photography did not show color, and the absence was felt. A first corrective step was to apply color by hand. The subject is Eliza Cocke, daughter of Elizabeth Ruffin Cocke and Captain H. H. Cocke. *Virginia Historical Society*

A non-photographic kind of mid-nineteenth century color imagery that became a popular standard was the chromolithograph. These prints first appeared substantially in Virginia in the 1850s and became familiar as views for parlor display, labels for tobacco and other products, show posters, and Christmas cards. The topographic view produced in "chromo" was capable of a comprehensive sense of place that photography strove to equal. Each chromolithograph sheet was printed with two, three, four or five ink colors, with a typical view's palette black, yellow-tan, brick-red, sky-blue, and green. While a well-made chromolithograph gave an impression of full color, the exact hues and their implementation in the image were selected by the lithographer.

In the 1860s, methods that used photographs as the art for lithographs were under development, and by the end of the century photolithography had entered into wide use. The chromo palette was adopted to produce photographic images in color by companies such as the Detroit Publishing Company, a leading maker of views in color that were printed on a press. Photolithographic products included postcards, 8 x 10 inch prints, and souvenir booklets. Color photolithographic images of this type shared the common feature that, while there was a printing plate for each ink color, all the plates derived from one black-and-white photograph, and thus from a single black-and-white negative.

Another route taken by experimenters was the use of multiple black-and-white negatives to photograph a scene in color. By the 1860s the many new discoveries about light were indicating that color was not a single thing but a sum of things. Experimenters realized they would not find a process that could record color all at once. One measure of the complexity of color is that it can be described on both a linear scale and as a circular pie-chart. Newton and others discovered that white light can be split into the spectrum using a prism, a procedure that expresses the character of light in a linear form. The spectrum of visible light rises from invisible low-frequency infrared, with each color appearing in sequence, red, orange, yellow, green, blue, to violet, beyond which is invisible high-frequency ultraviolet. The most familiar expression of the spectrum in this form is a rainbow.[26]

Yet color can also be described as the color wheel, with three primary colors and, each the opposite of a primary, three complementary (or secondary) colors. The theory of the color wheel is that any tone of color can be produced through a combination of primary colors. The second part of color-wheel theory is that there are two variations of the color wheel, one for transmitted light (such as from the sun or a light bulb) and another for substances (such as paint pigments or hard surfaces). For transmitted light, the primary colors are red, blue, and green. They are called additive colors because when combined, such as two theater lights

with gels aimed at the same spot, the colors add together to create a new color. Combining all three of the primary colors in light adds up to white light. The second color wheel, for substances, has been simplified in paints to red, blue, and yellow, but it is actually composed of the complementary colors magenta, cyan, and yellow. Called subtractive colors, all three combine to produce (in theory) black (and using real substances, dark mud).[27]

An important discovery of the 1860s was that a subject could be recorded in color by photographing it with three black-and-white negatives. Each separation negative was exposed through a filter of a different primary color. Then, based on the theory of the color wheel, the separation negatives could be reassembled to

Colored photograph
Albumen print, hand-colored and mounted, by Foster, image 8 x 5.8 in., c. 1892
Larger than a cabinet card, the board is labeled a "Paris Panel," a name to imply art and sophistication. Not only are the faces and skin colored, the girls' dresses are highlighted in white. The subjects, said to be descendents of Thomas Jefferson, include Thomas Jefferson Moore (b. 1880), Mary Irwin Moore (b. 1884), and Julia Grant Moore (b. 1887). *Virginia Historical Society, Gift of Mary Agnes Grant*

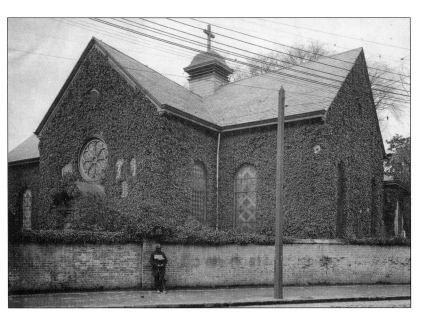

A. Silver gelatin print, by Henry C. Mann, 7.4 x 9.6 in., on mount 8 x 11 in., c. 1907–10
View on Granby Street, Norfolk

B. Platinum print, 5.5 x 7.5 in., on mount 11 x 13 in., c. 1895–1910
St. Paul's Church, Norfolk (with indigent blind man)

C. Color Postcard, 3.4 x 5.4 in., printed by Louis Kaufmann & Sons, Baltimore, c. 1910–15
Mann's Granby St. view, with color added

Color photo-lithographs

New techniques for printing photographs in color appeared in the first decade of the twentieth century. These processes began with a black-and-white photograph and used selected colors and lithography to create a colored version of the black-and-white image. Here are two black and white photographs, **(A)** Harry Mann's view of Granby St., and **(B)** a view of St. Paul's Church, both in Norfolk. Different colored versions of the Granby St. view appear in **(C)** the postcard and **(D)** the folding brochure; note the different colors selected for the awnings, street, and sky. The same image of St. Paul's Church with the blind man standing by the wall appears in the brochure, with selected color added, but with the pole and wires removed. A different black-and-white photograph served the Detroit Photographic Co., a major image publisher at the turn of the century, as the basis for its color view **(E)** of St. Paul's. The firm printed using a color lithographic process called "Photochrom." In its version the wires have vanished but the pole remains.

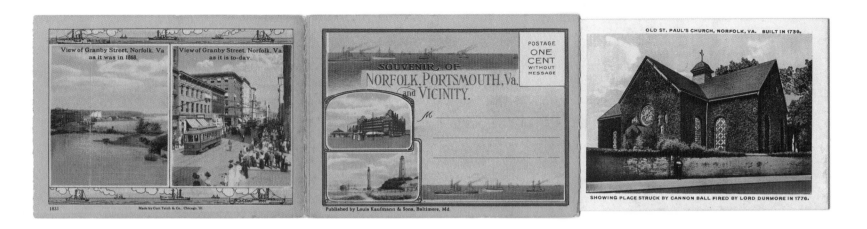

D. Color brochure, *Souvenir of Norfolk, Portsmouth, Va. and Vicinity,* accordion-fold with cover,
3.2 x 4.3 in. closed, published by Louis Kaufmann & Sons, 1910
Included among the brochure's twenty images are Mann's Granby Street view (2.2 x 1.9 in.),
and the view of St. Paul's Church with the man in front (2.5 x 3.5 in.), both with color added.

E. Color photo-lithograph, 7 x 9 in., by Detroit Photographic Co., 1902
St. Paul's Church, Norfolk

Color blending

Carbon print, by Henry Miley, 3.7 x 5.3 in., on mount 5.5 x 6.8 in., 1897
Henry Miley recalled that in 1897, he and some friends posed for "a bust picture of us seated in a row. I thought that I would try printing these three heads in different carbon colors, on one piece of paper, from the negative. I proceeded to print myself in green carbon, blending out to the next head in red-chalk and then blending out to the next head in black. I finally succeeded and it made a peculiar looking picture." The print is marked on the reverse, "1st experiment in color blending," and "Henry Miley on left and friends." *Virginia Historical Society*

create a full-color image. Accomplishing the reassembly, however, was the harder part of the scheme. The first attempt was by the Scottish physicist James Maxwell in 1861. Maxwell used a magic lantern with three lenses, the images of each color superimposed on the projection surface, to display a tartan ribbon. The result would necessarily have been temporary and quite imperfect. Even today with modern equipment, to superimpose and align three projected images is not a simple task.[28]

Much of the early color experimentation took place in France. A color print that utilized the three-color process, a view toward the town of Angoulême, survives from 1877, made by the French inventor Louis Ducos du Hauron. It was a signal accomplishment, but the method had too many steps for practical adoption. Among the difficulties Ducos faced was compensating for the extreme blue sensitivity of the negatives. He reported his exposures as 25–30 minutes for the red filter, 2–3 minutes for the green filter, and 1–2 seconds for the blue-violet filter. Ducos printed each negative individually on pigmented gelatin, a photosensitive material that could be obtained in various colors, matching each filtered negative to an appropriate color. Next, for each he separated the image layer from the base, and then on a single sheet superimposed all three color image layers.[29]

The 1877 Ducos color print was a step toward *recorded* color. Both the Ducos print and a chromolithograph were similar in the way that the color layers when superimposed formed new colors. Although Ducos *selected* the colors for printing—from the varieties of pigmented gelatin available—his method had a key difference from a chromolithograph. In a lithograph the artist decided not only the hue of each color but also the distribution of the color in the image. In the

Ducos print, while he may have selected the hues of the colors, he did not arrange their distribution in the image. Instead the distribution of color was determined by the separation negatives, and thus it was derived from the light that passed through the lens.[30]

The improvement brought by the dry plate in the 1880s included not only convenience but also steadily bettered sensitivity across the spectrum (panchromatic plates appeared in 1906). This meant emulsions were not so blue-biased and could record more accurately all the spectrum of visible light. One benefit was to facilitate the making of separation negatives. Among the first Americans to take advantage of the dry plate's improved sensitivity to color was Frederick Ives, an important innovator in graphic arts who contributed as much as anyone to making the halftone practical. Ives experimented with a three-color system in the late 1880s and during the 1890s introduced a series of color devices. Ives's 1893 Photochromoscope was probably the first successful American color system. The camera took three separation negatives in succession, and then the color images were presented as three-layer transparencies in a special viewer. Yet even for Ives, the color photographic print remained an elusive target.[31]

The first Virginia photographer to work in color photography was Michael Miley of Lexington. Miley had long experimented with chemicals and processes, at one point making his own dry-plate emulsion when commercial-issue plates had halation problems. In 1894, when Miley was fifty-three, his son Henry graduated from Washington and Lee College and joined the business. In early 1895 his father made him a partner. With Henry assuming much of the daily work, Miley had more time to experiment and in autumn 1895 taught himself the carbon process. Carbon prints were handsome and would not fade, but in Henry Miley's words, "we soon found out that the carbon printing was no easy process." The procedure utilized photosensitive bichromated gelatin, colored with a pigment that the Mileys ordered from the Autotype Company in England. It was supplied in rolls, "like a printed wall paper," and came with "20 x 24 inch sheets of white celluloid" that were used to make the transfers. [32]

In Henry Miley's account, "the first suggestion of the making of color photography" came from him. "During the summer of 1897 I spent several weeks at

Photographed color
Three-layer carbon print, by Michael and Henry Miley, 5.9 x 4 in., c. 1900
Henry Miley said that this print of flowers in a vase was the Mileys' first success in the tri-color process. Narrow reddish lines on several edges are imperfections where an underlayer shows through. Michael Miley was an avid and accomplished horticulturalist, and it is likely that the selection of zinnias and decorative plants came from his garden.
Virginia Historical Society

Henry Miley seems to have had the idea, but his father took the lead in pursuing it. Miley's approach was methodical and empirical. He had probably heard about the color experiments of others from the photographic conferences he attended and from trade publications. It is not known whether the Mileys knew that pigmented gelatin was the material Ducos had used for his 1877 color print or simply arrived at the same solution. Henry Miley "asked father what he thought of the idea, and he said that I would not get much, going about it that haphazard way. He thought we should experiment with the three color filters and see if the Autotype Company could make some colored paper in red, yellow, and blue, the three primary colors, that we were taught, in certain combinations, would make all the colors that we generally encountered. Then we would try to produce photo-

the Alum Springs with two friends, and when we returned to Lexington, we had a photograph taken. It was a bust picture of us seated in a row. I thought that I would try printing these three heads in different carbon colors, on one piece of paper, from the negative. I proceeded to print myself in green carbon, blending out to the next head in red-chalk and then blending out to the next head in black. I finally succeeded and it made a peculiar looking picture." In the photographic journals at that time were reports of experiments "with color filters to separate the red, blue and green lights from daylight." Henry Miley "thought of getting some colored glass—orange, green and blue for filters and making a colored picture of some kind. . . . I intended to make colored carbon prints on glass in sea-green, red-chalk, and sepia; as near as I could to the primary colors, red, yellow and blue, and superimpose them, one over the other, on the same sheet of paper."[33]

graphs in natural colors. This was the beginning of our color photography."[34]

They wrote "to the Autotype Company stating just how we would like the tri-colored paper prepared." However the company was "not willing to undertake it at first as it was very expensive and there was no demand for it. We tried to make our own paper but were not successful. The Autotype Company must have gotten interested finally for the summer of 1900 they sent us one roll of each color, red, yellow, and blue." Michael Miley "finally became so interested in this work that he gave most of his attention to it, and finally gave up everything else for experimenting with the tri-color process." Henry found that he had to devote his own time to running the regular photographic business. Miley did produce results. "It was due to father's experiments and work that the color photography gained the success that it did."[35]

Grapes
Three-layer carbon print, by Michael and Henry Miley, 7.2 x 9.4 in., on mount 12 x 14.5 in., c. 1900–16
In this still life, Michael Miley the gardener was likely showing off his grape varieties. *Virginia Historical Society*

They eventually worked up a method that was painstaking but worked well with immobile subjects like still lifes and paintings. The Mileys photographed each subject three times in black and white, without moving the subject or the camera between shots. For each shot, the negative was prepared a particular way, and a different color filter was used. An "orthochromatic plate flowed with cyanin solution" was exposed behind the red filter; an orthochromatic plate with the green filter; and for the violet filter "a plain gelatino-silver-bromid plate" was used. After development, the negatives were printed to "bichromated gelatin-pigment paper (carbon tissue)," each to a different color: the red filtered negative to blue-pigment paper, the green-filtered to red paper, and the violet-filtered to yellow paper. In turn, each carbon paper was exposed, the image layer transferred to an intermediate support for processing, and then the developed image layer transferred to "a piece of gelatin-coated paper, which forms the final support." The Mileys stated in their patent that "if desired, the red may be superposed on the yellow instead of the yellow on the red; but we find that to obtain the best results it is always desirable to superpose the blue last of all."[36]

Henry Miley recalled that in 1901 and 1902 a wealthy New Yorker named Ben Cable "saw some of the pictures somewhere and came down here to see us,

with his lawyer. He wanted us to form a company with him financing it and patent it all over the world. He said we would be made equal partners, so father and I agreed. I went to Washington where he had his own good patent lawyer and stayed there about a week giving information about the process." The Mileys were awarded a patent in October 1902. Henry Miley could not "remember just when these patents were given, but they were issued to us from every important European country except Germany—England, France, Spain etc. as well as Canada and the United States. Mr. Cable's idea was to promote the company after we got it on a working basis and sell stock at $100. a share to the public."[37]

Perhaps with a boost from Cable and his associates, in 1903 an article appeared in a scientific journal about their process, and in May 1905 the Mileys were awarded a Medal of Merit from the Franklin Institute. The Miley Color

Peaches (red and yellow)
Three-layer carbon print, by Michael and Henry Miley, 7.2 x 9.2 in., c. 1900–16
The Mileys produced two photographs of peaches—probably from the senior Miley's trees—that represent the acme of their achievement in color printing. *Virginia Historical Society*

Photograph Company was incorporated in 1904. However in the end Miley was disinclined to be ambitious. "When the time came to promote the company," Henry Miley said, "father balked. He said that he thought that the process could not be used commercially for it was too difficult and he did not care to have anyone invest money that might not bring returns." When Miley "wasn't willing to promote the company, Mr. Cable didn't press him." The company was dissolved in 1907. From the venture, Henry Miley was left with an image, anyway: he "had to go to New York and Washington several times on the patents and the last time I went to the New York office, I came to a door with 'Miley Color Photograph Company' on the outside in black."[38]

Henry Miley reported that they "photographed in color as many as 100 different kinds of subjects. . . . In all we made about 500 prints, from 5 x 7 to 14 x 17 sizes." They sold 8 x 10 inch prints for $3.50 and eventually for $5.00, but at those rates "the materials were so expensive and the time it took to make them so long that there was no profit." Probably their best sellers were the copies of paintings, including portraits of Lee and Washington. A setback to the Mileys came on 13 October 1907 when a fire heavily damaged their studio. The front room was entirely lost, and "all the registered negatives from 1894 to 1905 were destroyed," including many of the separation negatives for the color work. Later, color became impossible because by 1915–1916, "most of the best English workmen were called to arms and the carbon paper got so inferior in color value that practically all the work that we did for about 2 or 3 years was a complete loss." Miley died in 1918. Henry Miley recalled that "the years from '17 to the depression in '31, were the busiest of my life," and he was apparently too occupied to return to color.[39]

The color photography of Michael and Henry Miley was, in the end, not a step in the evolution of a modern method. Like many experiments, it was a side branch. The principle of recording each primary color separately through the camera and recombining them in the final product was sound. The drawbacks to the Mileys' method were too great, however, for others to adopt it. By requiring three negatives

Peaches (orange and yellow)
Three-layer carbon print, by Michael and Henry Miley, 7.2 x 9.2 in., c. 1900–16
Virginia Historical Society

St. Fabiola
Three-layer carbon print, by Michael and Henry Miley, 16.1 x 12.9 in., c. 1906–07
One practical application for the Miley color process was to copy paintings. About 1906, according to Henry Miley, a businessman named Ben Cable "sent by express to the Miley studio in Lexington, Va., a large painting that belonged to him and that had hung in a hall at the University Club of New York." Cable, however, "never received a copy" because Michael Miley "did not think any of the ones we made were quite good enough." Not long after the painting was returned, in Oct. 1907 the Miley photography studio burned and the separation negatives were destroyed. Since that time, too, the original painting has disappeared. "The first experimental color photograph of this picture," noted Henry Miley, "is the one I sent to the Virginia Historical Society." *Virginia Historical Society*

Color prints, mid-1940s

Two Kodachrome prints, by Edwin Booth, each 2 x 3.5 in., 1946

Eastman Kodak Company introduced Kodachrome transparency film in the 35mm format in 1937, and then in 1941 a service to make color Kodachrome Prints from the 35mm slides called Kodak Minicolor Prints 2X. The print of the flowers is dated 21 May 1946, and the night-time view of Richmond's Broad St., looking west down the trolley tracks from about Fifth St., 15 June 1946. The prints are deficient in yellow but other than that have aged relatively well.

Both Virginia Historical Society

Color print, early 1950s

Kodacolor print, 3 x 3 in., 1952

Eastman Kodak Company made color prints from negatives under the name Kodacolor from 1946 to 1954. These early Kodacolor prints have not lasted well; today every one is faded and exhibits a deep yellow stain. This print was made by Kodak during the "Week of February 15, 1952." The subjects are identified on reverse: "Left to right, 1. Aunt Donie, 2. Alice K. Kenny–Great Aunt (Aunt Kit), 3. Mary O'Byrne–G. Grandmother (Mother Mattie), 4. No relation, 5. Mary B. Shenk–Grandmother (Mother Shenk)."

Virginia Historical Society

Comparing two color prints
Kodacolor print, 2.9 x 5 in., 1946
Kodachrome print, 2.2 x 3.2, 1946
The two snapshots, which appear to have been taken at the same time, were printed on different materials and have aged unequally. The larger Kodacolor print, left, is dated 6 June 1946, and the Kodachrome print is dated 27 Aug. 1946. Ludwell Kimbrough, Jr., collected both prints and appears in one; the woman is unidentified. *Both Virginia Historical Society.*

Color print, late 1960s
Kodacolor print, 3.5 x 5.25 in., 1969
For the most part color materials continued to improve in both picture quality and in stability. Still, the majority of color prints remain susceptible to image deterioration to a much greater degree than black and white prints. This view at Bugg's Island Lake, dated "Nov 69" on the print, is inscribed on reverse: "Prestwould Shore Line, Mecklenberg County, Va., 1968." *Virginia Historical Society*

Instant color

Polaroid dye diffusion transfer print, 2.9 x 3.8 in., c. 1965–75

In the period of this print, Polaroid film came in a pack of eight or ten shots that slid into the camera. After loading, a tab would stick out of the camera. The photographer pulled the tab until the dark paper that covered the first shot was removed and a new tab emerged. The photographer made the exposure and grasped this new tab to pull the film tightly through two rollers and out of the camera, with a new tab again emerging. The pressure of the rollers began the developing process. After 60 seconds the front and back of the film were separated, one part being the print and the other trash to be discarded. The thin early Polaroids like this were glued to mounts that came with the filmpack. The unidentified man and woman sit in a Richmond backyard.

Virginia Historical Society

for each image, only certain subjects could be captured, and most importantly, their system depended upon a high level of camera and darkroom skills.

Any color method that worked with one exposure would have great advantages. A partly successful single-plate medium was Autochrome. Introduced in 1907 by the Lumiere Brothers in France, Autochromes were magic lantern slides. Between glass layers was a mix of potato starch particles dyed in three colors. The coloring is muted and the results often charming. Autochromes were limited to bigger cameras, and the results were not sharp enough to make prints. The format mainly stayed in Europe. A version that used a film base instead of glass was introduced in the 1930s as "Filmochrome."[40]

The growth of the movie business gave an impetus to new developments in color. Many of the problems to be solved were the same for still or motion picture photography. By the late 1910s and 1920s the potential revenues from a major motion picture made the costs of color production less prohibitive. The Technicolor process was introduced in 1917 and first used for a motion picture in the early 1920s. It worked by splitting the camera image through a prism into different colors, each recorded separately on black-and-white film. In the lab the black-and-white separation films were colored appropriately and then merged again into a final print. The portion of movies shot in color dipped with the onset of the Depression but revived later in the 1930s.

The 1910s and 1920s saw dramatic growth in the number of people who used cameras. Medium-format cameras that used roll films gained in popularity including twin-lens reflex and folding-bellows cameras. With faster films and better shutters, cameras that were carried on straps and tripods were no longer a necessity. In the 1920s, a camera designed to use 35mm movie film, the Leica, was introduced in Germany. Called "miniature" at first, 35mm cameras would become standard in the second half of the century. With more cameras in circu-

lation, photographic companies could see a growing market for new products. Investment in research could pay. In the twentieth century, although such individual inventors as Edwin Land of Polaroid might still make a mark, progress in color photography would come primarily from corporations with formidable R&D departments.

A major landmark in photography came in 1935, when the Eastman Kodak Company introduced Kodachrome, the first single-exposure full-color film, or more precisely, the first successful integral tripack color film. This was the dawn of the age of *recorded* color. A transparency film, Kodachrome was initially released in 1935 as 16mm movie stock, then in 1936 as 35mm still film, and in 1938 as sheet film for large format cameras. The ASA (film-speed) was 10. This early version had some problems; most especially, the yellow dye layer would fade. The version of Kodachrome introduced in 1938 worked out most of the deficiencies and in years since has been a highly successful color material. The main limitation on Kodachrome's use has always been the cost. The processing of Kodachrome is an exacting procedure, requiring multiple developers, precise temperature controls, and re-exposure through filters, and in addition has always remained proprietary.[41]

A number of products were introduced in the decade after Kodachrome but because of World War II did not have an impact until after 1945. The German company Agfa introduced a color transparency film called Agfacolor Neu in 1936 that was easier to process than Kodachrome. Had Germany won the war, it would likely have become the international standard. Instead, with the other photographic manufacturing countries, especially Germany, France, and Britain, all knocked back by the war, Kodak became the preeminent manufacturer and distributor, able to establish standards. In 1946 Kodak introduced Ektachrome, its version of a more simply processed color transparency film. By the early 1950s, Kodak had switched its sheet films from Kodachrome to Ektachrome. It sold

Color print, early 1960s
Kodacolor print, 5 x 7 in., c. 1961–64
In the early 1960s Galeski Photo, which had long operated a photo-lab in downtown Richmond, opened a new photofinishing plant on Leigh Street. To garner press coverage, the Central Richmond Association staged events to mark business openings, as seen here. The print was probably made at the new Galeski facility.
Virginia Historical Society

its processing system for Ektachrome to photofinishers throughout the United States and in most other countries. Other manufacturers were in the position of having either to make their films compatible with Kodak's processing system or to set up their own photofinishing outlets, which several companies tried. Each time Kodak introduced an improved version—the systems known as E-1 (introduced 1946), E-2, E-3 (1959–1976), E-4 (1966–1977), and E-6 (introduced 1977)—photofinishers and other film manufacturers had little choice but to adopt it.[42]

For Kodak in the period 1939–1941, looking to the mass market, Kodachrome had two main deficiencies: good results required accurate exposure, and it was a transparency film. For people unable to calculate exposure settings, and for use in simple box cameras with limited controls, Kodak wanted a film with exposure latitude, meaning it was forgiving of imprecision. The company also wanted a film that made prints. With those inten-

Color print, c. 1970
Color print on Kodak Ektacolor resin-coated paper, 7.6 x 9.8 in., by R. C. Tamburino, c. 1970
On 7 Mar. 1970, Norfolk was on the path where an eclipse of the sun was total. Here the phenomenon is safely viewed by Lieutenant Governor J. Sargeant Reynolds and family. *Virginia Historical Society*

Glass transparency I

Lantern slide, by George Carrington Mason, 3.3 x 4 in., image 2.8 x 3.1 in., c. 1925–43

Mason (1885–1955) published a series of articles on Virginia colonial churches from 1938 to 1948, and in 1945 the book *Colonial Churches of Tidewater Virginia*. From the same negatives that he used to illustrate his publications—this one is Plate 42 of his book—Mason also produced lantern slides for illustrated lectures. The Old Brick Church (1682), in Isle of Wight County, is today known as St. Luke's Church (a renaming that Mason did not countenance). *Virginia Historical Society*

tions, Kodak introduced Kodacolor, a color negative film, in 1942. Kodacolor was printed on color paper to make snapshots and processed by Kodak or by photofinishers using its chemicals and paper. This was the beginning of the postwar photography world, in which color negative materials became the predominant medium. By 1990, a few years before digital photography began to have an effect, more than 80 percent of photography used color negative film.[43]

For color prints, Kodak offered two formats at the beginning. Kodachrome prints were available through Kodak's processing labs from 1941 to 1946 under the Minicolor name and from 1946 to 1955 as Kodachrome prints. These came on a white acetate base and were primarily marketed as prints from transparencies using internegatives. The other print paper was Kodacolor, offered both through Kodak's labs and through independent photofinishers. The original version of Kodacolor paper, in use from 1942 to 1953, was unfortunately flawed. All photographs made with this material have aged poorly and today are faded and stained yellow-orange. Kodachrome prints from the same period show loss of yellow dye but have lasted better.[44]

Kodak's Ektacolor films and papers were introduced in 1947 and permitted photographers to process their own color negatives and prints. Improved versions have been released at intervals; like the early Kodacolor prints, some of these products have proven to have problems with image stability. Other manufacturers have also produced color materials. Polaroid, maker of instant photography cameras and materials, introduced a color material called Polacolor in 1963 and then a new product, SX-70, in 1972. The Swiss company Ciba introduced Cibachrome, for color prints directly from transparencies, in 1963. By the 1970s, international manufacturers began to take a larger place in the American market, especially the Japanese company Fuji for film products and Agfa for photofinishing materials.

TRANSPARENCIES & PROJECTION

For most of the history of photography, transparencies and projected images were a side path to the main avenue of the medium. That has changed in the twenty-first century: illuminated images have become an everyday standard on the computer, camera, and phone.

In contrast to the print, which is seen by reflected light, a transparency is illuminated by light passing through it. Beginning with Talbot's paper negatives in 1839, transparent images have been part of photography all along, if not always as a final product. The first positive photo-transparencies appeared in the 1850s, as a by-product of the wet-plate. By the mid-twentieth century transparencies had become the primary medium for photographs intended to be published in color.

Considering the stained-glass windows of great churches, the translucent image is much older than photography. Also predating photography is the projection of a transparency, using a lamp and lens to enlarge the image on a flat surface. Early projectors of various types were known as the "magic lantern." The

Glass transparency II

Lantern slide, by George Carrington Mason, 3.3 x 4 in., image 2.8 x 3.1 in., c. 1925–48

Yeocomico Church (1706), Westmoreland County. *Virginia Historical Society*

Film transparency I
Kodachrome 35mm slide, by George Carrington Mason, c. 1949–52
After World War II, the glass lantern slide was superseded by the 35mm slide in a 2 x 2 inch cardboard mount. Not only were 35mm slides less prone to damage, they were also in vivid color. Mason revisited all one hundred or so colonial churches to shoot them in color slides. Here is Old Brick Church in color. *Virginia Historical Society*

image was painted on glass, and the glass placed into a wooden frame that would slide into the magic lantern for projection. The action associated with inserting the wooden frame, and thus with bringing the image to view on the screen, came to be the name for the projected image and its mount: the "slide." The source of illumination for a magic lantern evolved over the years, from the early oil lamp, to a mid-nineteenth-century lamp that burned gaseous oxygen and hydrogen to make "lime-light," to the electric light bulb in the 1890s.

Magic lantern exhibitions were a regular feature on the lecture circuit of the late nineteenth century. Common themes included travel, scientific topics, and moral lessons. Another name for the shows was "dissolving views," because fancy theatrical set-ups employed two or three projectors so one image flowed into the next. Because the components of a show were all rather difficult to pull together and to maintain, the magic lantern was chiefly presented by touring or specialist exhibitors. Once projectors with electric bulbs were introduced, "lantern slides" became a much more widely used format for lecturers and clubs. In schools, lantern slides were the beginning of modern "AV," short for Audio-Visual.

By the late-1890s electricity enabled the introduction of motion-picture projection, and the first movie theaters were opened in the 1900s. As a theatrical feature, lantern slides could not compete with motion pictures (although one of their last practical applications was in movie theaters throughout the twentieth century to advertise popcorn and make announcements). Lantern slides found their niche as a medium for illustrated lectures, lasting into the 1950s. One evolution was to the filmstrip presentation, which a number of lantern slide projectors were adapted to present as well. Filmstrips were often prepared on topics for school use with sequential images (printed on 35mm film as horizontal half-frames). The filmstrip was presented in many classrooms from the 1940s to the 1960s. Later presentations were sometimes accompanied by a tape-recorded soundtrack. Many students from that period will recall that at the end of each frame's commentary, a beep signaled the operator to advance to the next frame.

Film transparency II
Kodachrome 35mm slide, by George Carrington Mason, c. 1949–52
Yeocomico Church, Westmoreland County. *Virginia Historical Society*

Modern photography
Albumen print, by Charles W. Hunter, Jr., 3.4 x 3.7 in., 1896
In Hunter's album the image is inscribed, "'Taking your
picture,' Aug/96, LWP." The location is possibly at Tinker Creek.
Virginia Historical Society

CHAPTER FIVE

TWENTIETH-CENTURY SUBJECTS

By the turn of the twenty-first century, photographs had found their way into almost every corner of society. (The odds are good that the reader at this moment has a photographic image in purse or pocket.) The number of photographs made in Virginia during the twentieth century is not known with precision but would certainly be in the billions.

So pervasive has the medium become that it is difficult to think of "photography" as a single field anymore. Like writing, it is divided by category. The present survey, in its description of twentieth-century photography, begins with the recognition that it will not be comprehensive and can only suggest the century's diversity of subjects and specialties. Just to compile a list of Virginia photographers over the period would be a daunting research project. Here, not only will entire branches of practice be left out, other disciplines that themselves could encompass a book will only be mentioned.

From a railroad album
Cyanotype, 4.6 x 6.5 in., c. 1890–1910
The view of a bridge over Occoquan Creek is from an album of 42 cyanotypes that was prepared by the Richmond, Fredericksburg & Potomac Railroad, containing mostly views of bridges from Washington to Richmond. *Virginia Historical Society*

Because the improvements that assembled to make it modern came largely in the 1880s—the dry plate in 1880 and the Kodak camera in 1888—photography's "twentieth" century began before 1900. The round year of 1890 can serve to mark the start, and the conclusion was probably about 2005. Digital photography emerged in the mid-1980s and became a big factor in image-making in the 1990s. In 2002, sales of digital cameras surpassed film cameras. Compared to chemical-based modern photography—or as it is now termed, "analog" photography—electronic digital photography has fundamental technical differences. (How much they differ is not obvious at present because subject matter in digital has been substantially continuous with analog. Eventually deeper changes to content will grow from phone-cameras, the blurring of the line between still and moving images, and post-exposure pixel play.) In 2007 the

For most of the nineteenth century, the development of photography was closely tied to its technical progression. As new inventions were adopted, the medium increased the range of subjects it was capable of recording. Then, late in the century, photography reached a kind of technical threshold when a number of improvements coalesced. The image-making system that came together at that time was essentially what we think of as modern photography. A photographer from 1905 and one from 1975 would have used different cameras and films and just about every other item of equipment and material, but the process and the product would have been fundamentally alike. The two would have captured light in much the same way.

commercial photography lab that was the only remaining processor in Richmond of E-6 sheet film—once the mainstay of professional work—shut down that service. Without aiming to be too precise, one might speak of 1890 to 2005 as modern photography's long century.[1]

Technical development did not stop in 1890, of course. Cameras continued to become smaller and more convenient. Field cameras for photographing without a tripod appeared in the 1890s and press cameras by 1912. The Leica 35mm rangefinder camera appeared in 1925, enabling a mobile, unobtrusive mode of shooting. Influential medium-format cameras included the first Rolleiflex twin lens reflex in 1929 and the Hasselblad in 1948. The 35mm single-lens reflex camera came out in prototype in the 1940s and as a product in the 1950s. Models with through-the-lens light meters were introduced in the early 1960s. By the 1970s the Japanese-made single-lens reflex had become the predominant field camera, displacing the large-format press camera and other big cameras.[2]

Kodak had been a pioneer in introducing photofinishing in the 1890s. By the 1910s services became more widely available, and after World War II spread to every city. Kodachrome transparency film and processing debuted in 1935, and color negative film and prints in 1942. Slides were big in the 1950s and 1960s for amateurs, and for professionals from the 1940s into the 1990s. The Polaroid instant process, introduced in 1948 and for color in 1963, did not change photography as much as it might have because a Polaroid print was a one-of-a-kind. In the mid-1970s plastic-coated photographic paper replaced rag paper for prints. Dramatic gains came in printed reproduction of photography. When people in the nineteenth century viewed photographic images, they looked at originals. By the twentieth century, people mostly viewed photographs in reproduction: in publications of all sorts, embedded in packaging and advertising, and on television.

Yet as much as the machines and materials improved, the change was incremental, not transformational. Photography may have been a better mousetrap at the end of the century, but it still worked on the same principles. The more significant areas of evolution for twentieth-century photography were social and visual.

By the end of the nineteenth century, photography was no longer restricted to a guild of practitioners who alone were capable of producing images. The chemical part became optional, because anyone with sufficient aptitude to operate a camera could make the exposures and then hire out the processing and printing. Useful jobs well-suited to photography that did not justify the expense of a professional photographer could be accomplished by someone already on a payroll. As the field grew, more photographs were produced without thought of monetary returns. Most importantly, the work of new practitioners led to new kinds of subjects that reflected modern societies and ways of investigating those societies.

At the same time, photography was also becoming more comfortable with itself as a visual medium. In the nineteenth century the influence of painting especially was very strong on photographers in suggesting what pictures ought to look like. Gradually effects inherent to photographic images that previously had been suppressed or ignored in trying to be painterly or artistic were recognized and accepted. Photography's contingencies and quirks came to be appreciated: the blur, the accidental cropping, the unintended gesture or passing facial expression frozen. The "candid camera" grew into "the decisive moment." In the way that modernism in all the arts was about each medium finding the means of expression inherent to it, so photography came to be seen and defined on its own terms.

Here, twentieth-century Virginia photography has been grouped under five main headings: practical, pictorial, promotion, documentary, and personal. These subject categories are not the only way that twentieth-century photography might

Construction progress
The construction of Creighton Court, a public housing project in Richmond, was documented by photographs made at intervals from specified viewpoints. The images recorded the progress of the private contractors working for the Richmond Redevelopment and Housing Authority.

Highway engineering
Silver gelatin print, 8 x 10.5 in., 1944
The northern Virginia highway interchange is identified as: "Three-level bridge in the War Department Building network in Virginia." Not only the engineers but also the contractors and the state highway department would have wished to have the image in their files. *Virginia Historical Society*

Silver gelatin print, with label, 1951
The label at lower-left includes the information: "Oct. 23, 1951, Creighton Ct. Richmond, Va., Point 2 looking S., on Kane St."

be sorted. The categories are not separate and distinct, as if slices of a pie; instead, a better comparison might be to a cookie-cutter applied to rolled dough where some of the outlines overlap, because some photographs fit into more than one category. Perhaps rather than categories they might better be called tendencies. The headings are not intended as rigid characterizations, but as a means to discuss the photographs.

PRACTICAL PHOTOGRAPHY

One of the primary tasks assigned to photography is to make a record. A photograph produced for this purpose informs: this is the way this thing looked at this time. Because such photographs perform a defined function, they can be called "practical." Typically a practical photograph would be expected to be as sharp and clear as possible. Many fields of endeavor make use of visual records, from archives and research to commerce and construction. In engineering and the sciences there are condition reports, stages of progression, and test results. Building interiors are photographed for insurance purposes, retail displays to record ideas for later re-use, and all kinds of projects to show "before" and "after." Investigators rely on photography for archaeology, criminal justice, and medical fields. Health and public safety agencies use photographs for identification and to record the scene of an event. Surveillance cameras record intermittent photographs of banks, traffic interchanges, and building entrances. It is practical for the mechanic to head to the auto junkyard carrying an image of the needed part.

Archaeological excavation
Silver gelatin print, by Layton's Studio, c. 1926–29
The image records progress at the site of the Governor's Palace, Williamsburg. *Virginia Historical Society, Ragland papers*

Silver gelatin print, with label, 1952
The label at lower-right includes the information: "Feb. 18, 1952, Creighton Ct. Richmond, Va., Point #2 looking S.S.W., on Kane St."

Silver gelatin print, with label, 1953
The label at lower-right includes the information: "June 22, 1953, Creighton Ct. Richmond, Va., Point #2 looking S.S.W., on Kane St." *All Library of Virginia*

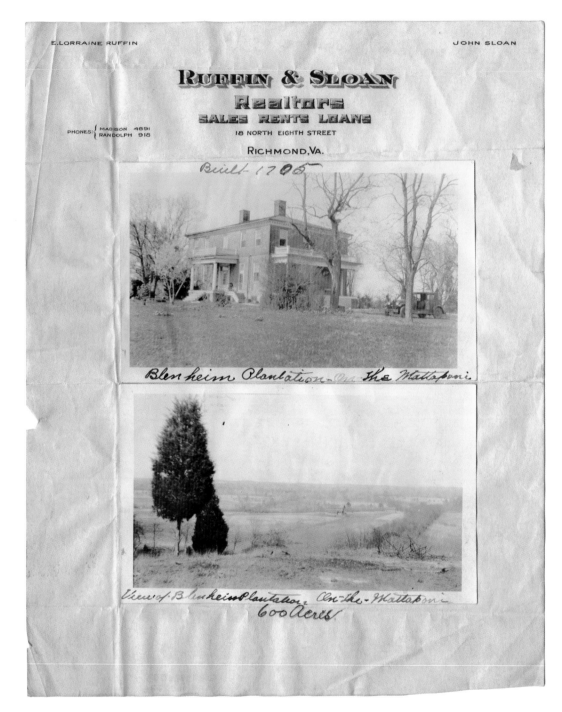

Illustration for realtor

Two silver gelatin prints, each 3.2 x 5.3 in., on stationery, 8.4 x 10.9 in., c. 1920–30

The sheet with two photos was prepared at the Richmond firm Ruffin & Sloan Realtors, for use in selling the Caroline County estate. Comments are written on the upper photograph: "Built 1705, Blenheim Plantation, on the Mattaponi;" and on the lower photograph: "View of Blenheim Plantation, on the Mattaponi, 600 Acres." *Virginia Historical Society*

ENGINEERING & ARCHITECTURE

At engineering schools in the nineteenth century, one topic of study was perspective drawing. Once dry plates came into use, photography was able to appropriate much of the function that perspective drawing served. Probably every large structure in the state was photographed for its builder, designer, owner, and/or occupant. Construction projects were recorded in phases, for many purposes: to document progress for funding, such as draw-downs of accounts keyed to phase completion; as references for the next job of the same kind; as training illustrations for apprentices; to make a record for the contractor that the project was completed as planned; to serve as a reference for inspectors checking later for deterioration or other changes; for insurance documentation.

A photograph of a completed project was also a measure of accomplishment for the builders and all those who had contributed to its construction. While the true meaning of their efforts was expressed in a useful, hopefully handsome structure, a photograph was a way to capture the project whole and also help to convince the next client.

HARRY BAGBY, PHOTOGRAPHER OF NEW ARCHITECTURE

W. Harry Bagby (1883–1965) was a photographer active in Virginia during the 1920s, 1930s, and 1940s. He spent much of his childhood in Richmond and married there before moving to Indiana about 1905, where he worked as a photographer in a South Bend studio. Returning to Richmond in 1921, he set up his own business. In 1930 he was located downtown and advertised as a child, garden, and architectural photographer. Among his clients was the Virginia State Chamber of Commerce. In 1929–30, Bagby photographs appeared in *The Black Swan*, an artsy Richmond magazine. In following years he worked out of his Northside home and as late as 1960 continued to be listed as a commercial photographer there.

Bagby established himself as a photographer who worked statewide, with particular specialties of architecture, both exterior and interior, and of views for travel promotion made for the chamber of commerce and for state agencies. In 1950 he advertised "Individual service for a limited number of clients." His primary medium was black and white 8 x 10 inch negatives. When he shot newly completed buildings, Bagby was probably commissioned by the architect or the general contractor, although the bill was in essence paid by the new owner, usually a large organization. The photographs would have been of value to all the members of the production team, including the engineers, sub-contractors, and suppliers of featured building materials.[3]

Architect's view in brick
Silver gelatin print, imprinted "H. Bagby–Photo/ Richmond, Va.," image 6.5 x 9.3 in., c. 1951
Not only the architect, but probably also the engineer, general contractor, and school would have wanted a copy of Harry Bagby's view of the fine arts complex, built 1951, at Mary Washington College, Fredericksburg. Seen are DuPont Hall to the left and Melchers Hall to the right. *Virginia Historical Society*

Architect's view in stone
Silver gelatin print, by Harry Bagby, image 5.9 x 9.1 in., c. 1945–55
New building at Virginia Polytechnic Institute and State University, Blacksburg. *Virginia Historical Society*

COMMERCE

Photography has served many purposes for manufacturers and merchants besides marketing. Photographs could record the condition of raw materials and commodities, show machinery and parts, and depict inventory. For insurance, photographs documented the state of things. For a maker of complex machines or a distributor of components, photographs could illustrate catalogs for spare parts or manuals for repair technicians, or isolate features for the sales force. Photographs of events and of personnel served as scrapbook material, helping to create a company community or culture that recognized employees for their service and helped to engender long-term loyalty.

An efficient workspace
Silver gelatin print, 7.8 x 10 in., stamped "A. L. Dementi, Richmond, Va.," 1927
The image is dated by the calendar as April 1927. The view is of offices at the James McGraw Co., a machine parts distributor in Richmond. Note that three panoramic photographs are on display in the office. *Virginia Historical Society, Gift of James McGraw Co.*

Catalog illustration I
Silver gelatin print, c. 1912–13
The Kline Car was manufactured in Richmond for about ten years. This view is labeled at lower-left: "Brakes, 1912–13." On the negative, the area surrounding the parts has been painted to be opaque, which in the print makes the parts appear to float in blank space. The image was probably made for use in a catalog or repair manual. *Virginia Historical Society, Kline papers*

Catalog illustration II
Silver gelatin print, c. 1912–13
This view is labeled at lower-left: "Clutch." *Virginia Historical Society, Kline papers*

Sales team seminar
Silver gelatin print, by TV & Motion Picture Productions, Inc., 8.2 x 10 in., c. 1955–65
A salesman demonstrates a new item at the James McGraw Co. in Richmond. *Virginia Historical Society, Gift of James McGraw Co.*

Coal mine supports
Silver gelatin print, by Herman Work, image 3 x 4 in. on 3.7 x 4.7 in. album page, 1923
Work was a wood-products forester who drove his Ford Model T to forests, mills, and transportation sites, and shot and developed his own photographs. His caption for this image is: "Anthracite props, Diascund, Va. 17 June 1923" (in James City County). *Virginia Historical Society*

Pulpwood
Silver gelatin print, by Herman Work, image 3 x 4 in. on 3.7 x 4.7 in. album page, 1923
Work's caption reads: "Newcastle Bridge, Va. Gum pulpwood, 13 June 23" (on the Pamunkey River, between King William and Hanover counties). *Virginia Historical Society*

SCIENCE

Photography has had a place in scientific research since John William Draper's daguerreotypes of the spectrum in 1840. In astronomy, photographs reveal things not visible to the eye, through long exposures and through plates sensitive to invisible wavelengths of light. Microphotography has become able to record individual molecules. Photography in these and other scientific fields would comprise whole studies of their own. A significant portion of scientific researchers have used photography in some way in their experiments or studies, to record a process, to describe a method, or to illustrate results for publication.

Bird photographer's method

Silver gelatin print, by C. F. Stone, mounted on paper, c. 1900–13
Written on the mount is the caption: "Collecting in a swamp, water knee deep. The string that released the camera shutter is shown by the white streak from the man's hand to the lower right corner." The line has been emphasized by ink on the negative, so that it shows up white on the print. *Special Collections, Virginia Tech, Bailey-Law Collection*

Art for publication

Three silver gelatin prints mounted on paper, two on left by H. H. Bailey, one on right by W. O. Emerson, c. 1900–13
These photographs were reproduced in the book *Birds of Virginia*, by Harold H. Bailey, published by J. P. Bell Co. of Lynchburg in 1913. The crop marks and dimensions for the reproductions are marked on the paper. *Special Collections, Virginia Tech, Bailey-Law Collection*

A collection of trees

In 1902 a professor at VPI in Blacksburg named Arthur Ballard Massey photographed the trees on the campus, numbering his images and creating a typewritten index titled "Old Photographs of Campus Trees." Massey's project exemplifies the scientific use of photography as a carefully observed documentation of a precisely limited subject.

Gelatin silver print, by Arthur Ballard Massey, 1902
#44 Birch in bottom by large elms 10 yrs.

Gelatin silver print, by Arthur Ballard Massey, 1902
#46 P. fastigiata – 10 yrs. – 27 paces
Pluchea fastigiata has no common name.

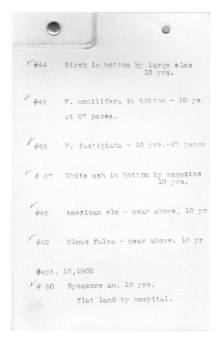

Notebook page, by Arthur Ballard Massey
All Special Collections, Virginia Tech, Arthur Ballard Massey Collection

Gelatin silver print, by Arthur Ballard Massey, 1902
#48 American elm– near above. 10 yr

Gelatin silver print, by Arthur Ballard Massey, 1902
#50 Sycamore am. 10 yrs., Flat land by hospital.

OFFICIAL PORTRAITS

Among the functions of the government are a number that require portraits of individuals for identification. These are made in a straightforward manner that tries to eliminate interpretation. Agencies that produce such portrait photographs include those responsible for law enforcement, criminal justice, security, motor vehicle regulation, and international travel.

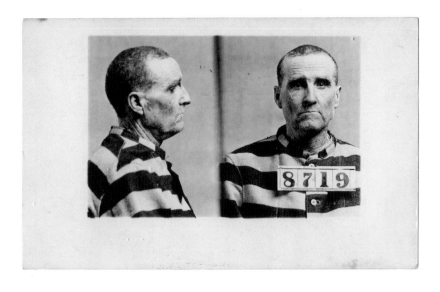

Mug shot for police
Silver gelatin print, on printed form, 1916
The mug shot generally includes two well-lit head shots, one facing front and one in profile. Along with the Bertillon measurement system and fingerprints, the mug shot was one of the new methods for police identification adopted in the late 1800s and early 1900s. The reverse of this Richmond Bureau of Identification card is for fingerprints. The subject, Moses D. Hoge, Jr., son of the famous Presbyterian minister, was a physician. Perhaps his fingerprints were on file in case he were called to a crime scene. *Virginia Historical Society, Hoge papers*

Mug shot of escapee
Silver gelatin print on printed card, 1916
Reverse of printed card, 1916
Escapees were a continuing problem for the Virginia Department of Corrections, especially with the widespread use of prisoners for road crews and other labor out-of-doors. Because an escapee would usually return home, the prison system developed cards that could be sent to the appropriate authority. After his Aug. 1916 escape from a Mecklenburg County road crew, Charles Bowen was expected to return to the vicinity of Chesterfield County or south Richmond. *Library of Virginia, Archives #37432*

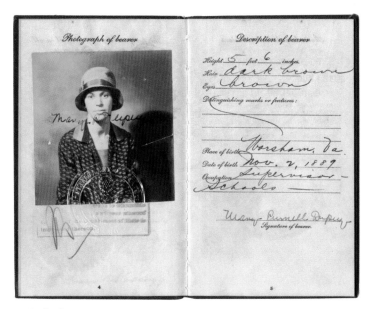

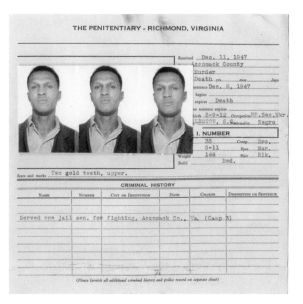

Passport photo
Silver gelatin print, mounted in bound booklet, 1928
In the 1920s passports began to include identification photographs. The authenticity was vouched by the continuity of the embossed seal and by the signature on both photo and page. *Virginia Historical Society, Dupuy papers*

Execution record
Silver gelatin print on printed form, 1948
Attached to a Department of Corrections form are three portraits of Sam Baldwin, exposed one after the other. The thirty-five-year-old man was sentenced to death for an Accomack County murder. In the file is the record of the execution of Baldwin on 23 Jan. 1948. *Library of Virginia, Archives #38103*

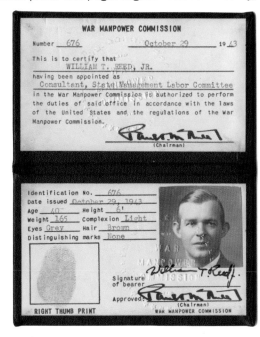

ID card
Silver gelatin print, mounted on printed card, 1943
William T. Reed, Jr. served on the War Manpower Commission during World War II. The card included his portrait, fingerprint, and signature, and was authenticated by an embossed seal. *Virginia Historical Society, Reed papers*

Military ID
Color photograph on plastic card, c. 2005
The manufacturing process makes the ID difficult to replicate. *Virginia Historical Society*

AERIAL

The concept of looking at land from above arose long before the first human flight in a hot air balloon. It was not until balloons came into use, however, that views from above became at all common. Not that many people had actually gone up in balloons, but apparently enough did that the idea was less abstract for everybody else. Lithographic bird's-eye views of a half-dozen Virginia towns were issued in the 1850s by Edward Sachse of Baltimore, and at the beginning of the Civil War John Bachmann produced dramatically high views of the whole state. Near the end of the lithographic view era, a bird's eye of Hampton Roads illustrated a poster for the 1907 Jamestown Exposition.[4]

Given that people had become familiar with views from the air, photography was a logical next step. However some difficulties needed to be overcome. Because early plates required sensitization just before use and development soon after, considerable preparation and a deliberate plan (and good fortune too) would have been necessary to make an exposure in a balloon. In addition the oversensitivity of plates to blue light was particularly troublesome in aerial work, because it caused the mistiness of the atmosphere to be much exaggerated and green things to go dark without gradation. In 1858, Nadar made an aerial view of Paris that does not survive, and in 1860 James W. Black made a view of Boston from a tethered balloon that is the oldest surviving aerial photograph. These were rare exceptions however until dry plates and (an important develop-ment for aerial photography) the first successful airplane flight in 1903.[5]

Wilbur Wright piloted for a photographer in 1909 in Italy, one of the earliest such ventures. The military value of aerial photography during World War I brought concentrated attention to the technical problems, and there were significant advances. Specialized cameras and cockpit mounts were developed, and image clarity was much improved by using plates sensitive only to a particular spectrum of light. Army Air Force photographers flew out of Langley Field, established 1916 at the end of the Peninsula near Hampton, and photographed Virginia sites probably as training exercises. In 1921 Langley fliers documented Gen. Billy Mitchell's demonstration of aerial bombing of ships in the Chesapeake Bay. Richmond photographer Walter W. Foster made photographs on a flight with barnstormers appearing at the Virginia State Fair in 1922. Through the 1920s the firm Underwood & Underwood actively photographed Virginia from the air, supplying a good portion of the plentitude of aerial photography that appeared in Virginia State Chamber of Commerce publications.

Advances that came out of World War II included the use of infrared film, which had value during combat because it could penetrate haze and detect foliage camouflage, and after the war because it could effectively photograph plant life. Comprehensive aerial photography of the state for mapping purposes was first completed in the 1940s and since then has been repeated in cycles that are currently five to seven years long.[6]

A new way of seeing
Silver gelatin print, 7.5 x 9.4 in., c. 1920–30
Attached to the bottom of the print is the caption: "Aeroplane photograph of Jamestown Virginia–Courtesy Virginia Pilots Assn." The pilot group probably distributed the photograph to newspapers and magazines to cultivate new aerial assignments. *Virginia Historical Society*

Aerial camera and crew
Photograph in halftone, in *Virginia, First in the Heart of the Nation*, Winter 1928
The editors at Virginia State Chamber of Commerce publications had great enthusiasm for aerial photography from the mid-1920s into the 1950s. *Virginia Historical Society*

Oblique aerial view
Gelatin silver print, 7.8 x 9.8 in., by Underwood & Underwood Aerial Department, c. 1930
Oblique aerial view of New London, south of Lynchburg in Campbell County. *Virginia Historical Society*

Vertical aerial view
Gelatin silver print, 8 x 10.2 in., by Air Photographics, Inc., 1948
Vertical aerial view of Arlington along the Potomac River. *Virginia Historical Society*

Tyson's Corner
Black and white 4 x 5 in. negative, by Charles Baptie, 1964
Baptie produced a large number of aerial views of northern Virginia for Texaco. The company likely used the views to help it decide where to locate new gas stations in the fast-growing suburbs. The oblique aerial view of Tyson's Corner was taken 10 April 1964. *George Mason University Archives*

Annandale
Black and white 4 x 5 in. negative, by Charles Baptie, 1967
The oblique aerial view of Annandale, another northern Virginia suburb, was taken 11 August 1967. The Baptie index lists the view as "Fort Ward tower, Southern Jarvis." *George Mason University Archives*

PICTORIAL PHOTOGRAPHY

Quality in a practical photograph is measured by success in rendering the subject clearly. In "pictorial" photography, by contrast, clarity is not necessarily foremost. Pictorialism is remembered in art history as a movement among artist-photographers from the 1890s until about 1912, named by some of its adherents as the Photo Secession and led by figures such as Alfred Stieglitz. However, the artist-photographers were only at the crest of a much larger wave that did not stop rolling when these leading figures, influenced by modernist art, turned to other approaches. Regarding pictorialism, about the time of World War I art history and photo history diverge. Despite its middle-brow nature to the eyes of the elite, pictorial photography became probably the twentieth century's most popular kind of photography.[7]

In describing "the aims and aspirations of pictorial photography," George Allen Young in 1937 called it "a romantic approach to subject matter with emphasis on mood and emotion." There have been a series of looks to twentieth-century pictorialism. The first came out of the art movement. Practiced in black and white and more in the early and middle parts of the century, the photographer begins with a negative that is a realist view but "feels free to utilize all methods of modifying the original negative." By employing a variety of techniques, a photographer might well "present a finished print considerably different from what was originally before the camera." These techniques could include "hand work on negative or print," and "so-called 'controlled' printing processes such as the paper negative, bromoil, bromoil transfer, oil, fresson, etc."[8]

A second tendency in pictorial photography goes back to the popular views of historic sites and scenic nature marketed in the late nineteenth century as stereographs, lantern slides, and mounted prints. These are straight black-and-white views in harmonious pictorial designs, though often with clouds added and other darkroom printing effects. This sort of pictorialism gained added prominence in the picture magazine,

Frame house
Silver gelatin print, by Frances Benjamin Johnston, 1927
Fredericksburg. *Library of Congress, Prints and Photographs Division, Frances B. Johnston Collection*

Brick house
Silver gelatin print, by Frances Benjamin Johnston, 1927
Johnston photographed these two Fredericksburg-area dwellings in 1927 as part of a self-assigned project to document vernacular architecture and included the images in her 1929 Fredericksburg exhibition. *Library of Congress, Prints and Photographs Division, Frances B. Johnston Collection*

which showed up in a big way in the 1920s and especially flourished beginning in the late 1930s when *Life* and *Look* magazines appeared.

A third kind of pictorial photography emerged once color was widely adopted. The processing of color materials requires more precision than black and white and does not offer the same possibilities for darkroom interpretation. In color, therefore, pictorial effect must be created at exposure, using lighting, design, and atmosphere. The picturesque in color photography is a scene that the camera can translate into a pictorial image. In recent years, with an automatic camera and shooting in color, an effect such as "pretty" or "beautiful" is so easily captured that such photographs have become common and unremarkable. (Think of the proverbial relative's slide show of travel.) A variant of the pictorial approach has been to revive the "sublime," a favored descriptive term for artists of the nineteenth century, conveying a sense of awe or profundity, but not necessarily beauty in a traditional manner. To cite one branch of modern pictorial photography, a superior nature photograph today is more likely to be sublime than pretty.

VIEWS

Frances Benjamin Johnston. Frances Benjamin Johnston (1864–1952) was a versatile photographer who in her long career produced enough images to appear in any of the categories presented here. She began her career in the early 1890s as a Washington, D.C. –based commercial photographer. Along with views of the Washington elites, she wrote and illustrated articles for magazines. In time her Washington connections led to numerous commissions for portraits and event coverage, much of it marketed through the picture-service agent George Grantham Bain. Some of her best-known work was of schools, including Virginia's Hampton

Enola, Dismal Swamp Canal
Silver gelatin print, by Harry Mann, 6.8 x 9.5 in., c. 1910
A number of vessels have collected in the canal lock. The sloop *Enola* is to the right. The melon hauler on the left is probably a Chesapeake Bay bugeye. *Mariners Museum*

Institute in 1899–1900, the U.S. Indian Industrial School in Carlisle, Pa., and Tuskegee Institute in Alabama.[9]

About 1909 Johnston relocated to New York. In the late 1910s she turned to gardens as subjects and traveled extensively for several years, almost settling in California. Based again in Washington, she made architecture her focus in the late 1920s. In 1927 she began another important group of Virginia images. She photographed Chatham, an estate near Fredericksburg and while in the vicinity took the opportunity to shoot a number of vernacular, less-pedigreed structures. An exhibition of prints from this visit in April 1929 in Fredericksburg attracted considerable local attention. In November 1929 Johnston was photographing in Middleburg. In June 1930 she agreed to provide photographs for the writer Henry Irving Brock's book *Colonial Churches in Virginia*. As she photographed for the project that summer, she was receiving Carnegie Corporation funding, the first of a series of awards of financial support. In the same period she also began to document architecture at the University of Virginia. In January 1933 Johnston received $3,500 from Carnegie to support photography of architecture in Virginia. Bettina Berch notes of Johnston's work that "she took great pains to search out the humbler buildings—the slave quarters of plantations, the sheds covering the cotton presses, the old city water fountains, the warehouses. . . . No building was too insignificant for her attention; the most 'minor' were often the most endangered." By 1936 she was funded to document North Carolina and moved south after that. She eventually retired to New Orleans.[10]

Harry C. Mann. Harry C. Mann (1866–1926) grew up in Petersburg, the son of a court clerk who became a judge. His uncle William Hodges Mann was governor from 1910 to 1914. Little is known of Harry Mann's early career. Between 1902 and 1910 he served as a clerk for the Virginia Senate. In 1907 his brother James arranged a position for him with the Jamestown Official Photograph Corp., his first known connection to photography. In that job Mann found a calling. In 1909 he opened

Truck boats, Norfolk
Silver gelatin print, by Harry Mann, 4.8 x 6.7 in., c. 1909–23
The caption on the reverse reads, "Truck boats ready to transfer their cargo to steamers, Norfolk, Virginia."
Virginia Historical Society

Menchville, James River tongers
Silver gelatin print, by Aubrey Bodine, c. 1950–68
In creating his pictures, Bodine used darkroom techniques simple—like burning and dodging—and complex—such as replacing the sky with one from another negative. For this print, Bodine appears to have substituted a more dramatic sky and darkened the foreground. Menchville is in upper Newport News, below Fort Eustis. *Virginia Historical Society, Gift of Aubrey Bodine*

a studio in Norfolk, for a time at Bank and Main streets, which he operated until 1923. Mann never married and resided at the home of his brother and family in Norfolk. In 1923, "seeking to regain his health," Mann moved to Lynchburg where he died in 1926.[11]

In his relatively short career Mann was very productive. Norfolk photographer Carroll Herbert Walker, Sr. (1904–1990) was an admirer of Mann's work and used it in two pictorial books about Norfolk. Mann "took a lot of pictures," said Walker in a 1980 interview. "He probably took thousands and thousands and thousands of pictures." However by Walker's account some portion of Mann's work was lost, for much early film used a nitrate base that proved unstable. Mann's negatives had gone after his death to the Virginia State Chamber of Commerce. "Towards the latter part of his photographic career," stated Walker, Mann "was using film because I saw some of it in the State Chamber, but unfortunately that had deteriorated to such an extent that you couldn't reproduce anything on the sheets of film. It was all stuck together."[12]

Perhaps because his training came in the context of an outdoors exhibition, and he may not have been as encumbered by conventions as someone who had trained in an indoor studio, he was able to create visual sense from places or situations that were not necessarily as orderly or organized as his views suggest. Much of the work presents its subject so effortlessly and without strain that it almost seems like anyone could have made the picture.

Aubrey Bodine. Aubrey Bodine (1906–1970) was a feature photographer for the *Baltimore Sun* from 1924 until he died of a stroke in his darkroom. His images appeared in the *Sunday Sun* every week for most of that time. Bodine is best known for his views of work and life on the Chesapeake Bay. During his lifetime his photographs were featured in two guide books and four other books, mostly oriented toward Maryland but also including *The Face of Virginia*, published

Weems
Silver gelatin print, by Aubrey Bodine, c. 1950–68
In this print, Bodine appears to have substituted the sky and added the sun and its reflection. Weems is on the Northern Neck near the mouth of the Rappahannock River. *Virginia Historical Society, Gift of Aubrey Bodine*

Solomon's Seal
Silver gelatin resin-coated print, by Earl Palmer, 7.5 x 9.5 in., c. 1955–75
From Palmer's caption: "The roots of this perennial are claimed to possess healing powers." *Blue Ridge Institute, Ferrum College*

in 1963. The book features crisp reproductions in black and white made by a photolithographic process. Bodine noted that it had been over thirty years earlier that "assignments in the Tidewater area began to fall my way. . . . In between I have spent many days and traveled many miles to get the portrait of the great Commonwealth presented in these pages."[13]

Earl Palmer. Earl Palmer (1905–1996) grew up in eastern Kentucky and worked for the A&P grocery chain there. In 1943 he moved to southwestern Virginia and opened a general store in Cambria, today a section of Christiansburg. The store did well, and he became a leader in his community, serving as mayor for a number of years.[14]

Palmer had made photographs beginning in the 1930s and took it up more seriously in the late 1940s. Palmer's great subject was Appalachia and mountain life. He described himself as the "Blue Ridge Mountain's Roamin' Cameraman." He also wrote and in the 1950s and 60s produced illustrated articles for publications such as *Scenic South* and *Dodge News Magazine*. He remained an active photographer until about 1970, producing by his estimate 20–30,000 negatives.

Palmer identified a mountain culture that for him was traditional and unsullied, and this was what he wished his images to portray. According to Jean Haskell Speer, who interviewed him for *The Appalachian Photographs of Earl Palmer* (1990), "Palmer's inner vision of Appalachia is the touchstone by which he made judgments about what to photograph." He came to know a number of older inhabitants of the mountains who were skilled and capable at a life drawn from the land, and in his photographs he tried to illustrate the folk knowledge they used to get by and the independent character such a life expressed. Speer says, "Palmer created a visual metaphor of Appalachia as the embodiment of a harmonious universe."[15]

Green Wade's ginseng
Silver gelatin resin-coated print, by Earl Palmer, 9.5 x 7.5 in., c. 1955–75
From Palmer's caption: "Green Wade shows off a prized wild ginseng root he dug near his home on Shooting Creek Mountain" (located between Floyd and Franklin counties). *Blue Ridge Institute, Ferrum College*

Wild ginseng
Silver gelatin print, by Earl Palmer, 9.5 x 7.5 in., c. 1950–70
From Palmer's caption: "Mountain people use ginseng along with other herbs to concoct a year round remedy for various ails, feelin' poorly's and just tollables, both real and imagined." *Blue Ridge Institute, Ferrum College*

Indian wash weed
Silver gelatin print, by Earl Palmer, 9.5 x 7.6 in., c. 1950–70
From Palmer's caption: "The leaves of this plant, when crushed, produce a deep green, copious lather to alleviate skin infections and bruises." *Blue Ridge Institute, Ferrum College*

THE CAMERA CLUB AT HAMPTON INSTITUTE

One feature of the late nineteenth century was the rise of organizations of photographers. Through their trade groups, professional photographers held conventions and published journals. Amateurs also joined together, most notably in camera clubs.

Perhaps the first camera club in Virginia was organized at Hampton Institute in October 1893. Though the students at the school were largely African American, the club members were primarily white faculty and staff, with a few black members. It was named the Kiquotan Kamera Klub, after the Alquonkian town once located in the vicinity (and likely alliterated as a defiant gesture to the notorious racist organization). In the four extant albums of club members' work, many of the images are of waterfront and sailing scenes, and most of the prints are cyanotype (an iron salt print, also called blueprint).

The range of the Hampton camera club's activities is unmatched by any other Virginia photography group of the period. In 1895 club members began to produce lantern slides for presentation as illustrations of poetry at readings. The poems of Paul Lawrence Dunbar were illustrated for these programs in 1897. Through fortuitous connections, this effort led to the club providing photographic illustrations for a book of Dunbar's poetry, *Poems of Cabin and Field*, published in 1899. The book in turn was successful enough to lead to the publication of two more books of Dunbar's poetry illustrated by the camera club, *Candle-Lightin' Time* in 1901, and *When Malindy Sings* in 1903. For a number of years the club also produced a Hampton calendar. When Frances Benjamin Johnston photographed on the campus in 1899–1900, a meeting with camera club members led to an exhibition of photographs from her collection of her work and that of Gertrude Kasebier, Alfred Stieglitz, and F. Holland Day. In 1905 Day visited Hampton, made photographs there, and met with club members.

The camera club was assigned a cottage on the campus for a darkroom and meeting place and usually also had an exhibition space, which over the years migrated to different buildings. The club remained active until 1926. Later in the early 1940s a new camera club was organized with student members.[16]

Picture room
Cyanotype, by Leigh Richmond Miner, 7.4 x 9.4 in., on mount, 1907
The Hampton Camera Club organized exhibitions of photography at different times and at a number of locations around the campus, featuring work of both members and others. This 1907 gallery wall was in the library. *Hampton University Archives*

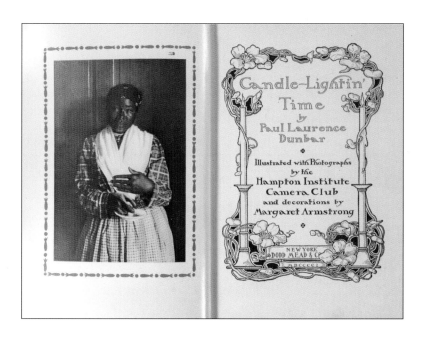

Illustrating poetry
Frontispiece and title page, from Paul Laurence Dunbar, *Candle Lightin' Time*, 1901
This volume of Dunbar's poems was the third illustrated by the Hampton Camera Club. *Virginia Historical Society*

Hampton student
Platinum print on mount, by F. Holland Day, 1905
The young man wears a Hampton Institute uniform. Day's visit to Hampton in 1905 was probably coordinated through a member or members of the camera club, which had previously exhibited his work. *Library of Congress, Prints and Photographs Division, Louise I. Guiney Collection*

From a camera club album
Two cyanotypes, by "WLB," 3.5 x 7.4 in. and 3 x 7 in., mounted on album page, c. 1890–1900
Most of the Hampton Camera Club members were white faculty and staff, and much of their work made use of the waterfront setting. These two images, mounted one above the other on their album page, are here placed side by side (the right image cropped) to present a winter panoramic view across Hampton Creek toward the campus. *Hampton University Archives*

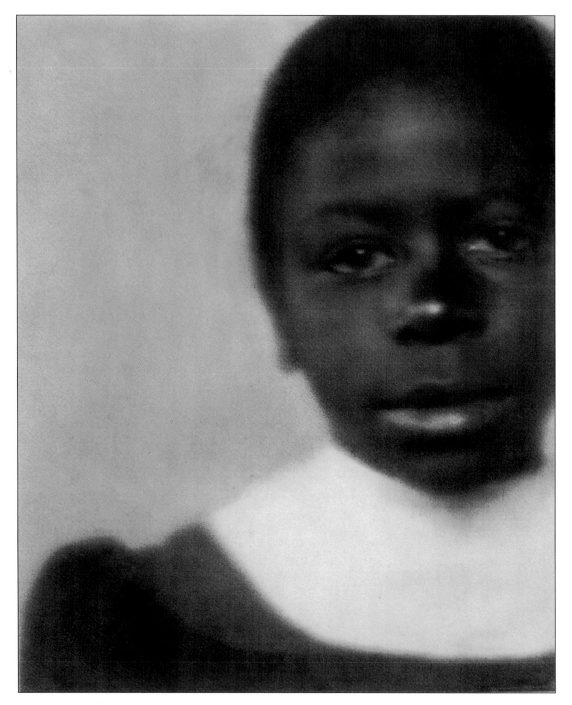

Girl in white collar
Gum bichromate print, by F. Holland Day, 1905
The young girl in a dress with a white collar was a student at the Whittier Elementary school associated with Hampton Institute. *Library of Congress, Prints and Photographs Division, Louise I. Guiney Collection*

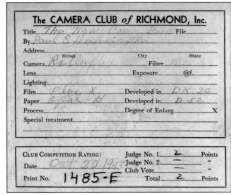

Competition print
Silver Gelatin print on mount, by Paul E. Dunnington, 9.9 x 13.3 in., 1943
The label on the reverse (above) indicates that Dunnington entered "The New Comic Book" (left) in the competition held by the Camera Club of Richmond on 20 Oct. 1943. *Virginia Historical Society, Gift of Mr. and Mrs. Paul E. Dunnington*

The Camera Club of Richmond. The Camera Club of Richmond was established in 1932, initially meeting in the homes of members. Meetings then moved to a series of public rooms in downtown Richmond: in 1934 to the YMCA and then to the Richmond Academy of Arts; and in 1935 to the new Virginia Museum of Fine Arts at the invitation of the director, Thomas C. Colt. In 1936 the club was using a studio on North Third Street. Over the years the meeting place shifted periodically and in 2005 relocated to the Science Museum of Virginia.[17]

The camera club early on adopted a competition format, in which an invited judge ranked submissions by members using a point system to evaluate prints. Soon after their introduction, a new category was created for color slides in the late 1930s. In 1937 director Colt and the Virginia Museum of Fine Arts worked with the camera club to organize the first Virginia Photographic Salon. The catalog noted that "Virginia is experiencing what might easily be termed a photographic renaissance. Within the last few years no less than four active camera clubs have been organized in the state." A jury of four selected from work submitted from across the state, which was exhibited at the museum for three weeks. The salons continued annually until the Ninth Virginia Photographic Salon which was exhibited for two weeks in April-May 1945, at the close of World War II, and which proved to be the last one.

William Edwin Booth. In the 1920s William Edwin Booth (1907–1998) took a summer job with the Metropolitan Engraving Company but kept working and never finished his senior year of high school. Booth became a "freelance roving photographer" in the early 1930s and had some pictures published in the newspaper, which led to Douglas Freeman hiring him in 1933 for a stint as a photographer for the *Richmond News Leader*. In 1934 Booth began many years of work for the Miller & Rhoads department stores, producing advertisements and catalogs until he retired in 1973. He joined the Photographic Society of America in the 1930s, and his photographs were used as cover images for *Newsweek* in 1936 and the *Saturday Evening Post* in 1940. He was a founder of the Camera Club of Richmond in 1932 and active in the Virginia Photographic Salons from 1937 to 1945. In addition to his lifelong interest in the camera club, from 1960 to 1987 Booth wrote a weekly column on photography for the *Richmond Times-Dispatch*.[18]

Looking at prints
Silver gelatin print, 8 x 10 in., c. 1930–40
Members of the Camera Club of Richmond review prints. Ed Booth is at far right. *Virginia Historical Society, Gift of William Edwin Booth*

Hampton Institute, before 1880
Albumen print, by William F. Larrabee, 3.4 x 3.5 in., mounted in album, c. 1870–79
Larrabee was a Union camp photographer and after the war stayed in the area, establishing a studio in Phoebus. The image is labeled: "Library in Academic 1870–79." The Academic building burnt in 1879. *Hampton University Archives*

Hampton Glee Club
Cyanotype, by Robert Russa Moton, 5.8 x 7.9 in., on mount, 1890
Moton was a Hampton graduate, class of 1890, who stayed to become commandant of cadets. The date of this image suggests he began to photograph before the formation of the camera club, of which he was one of the few African American members. Later, in 1915 Moton succeeded Booker T. Washington as head of Tuskegee Institute. *Hampton University Archives*

PROMOTIONAL PHOTOGRAPHY

The most obvious kind of "promotional" photography is not even discussed here, that which is used in advertising. "Promotional" is more descriptive of the use of the photograph than the visual appearance. These images are intended to influence the viewer's perception of a subject, whether to sell a product or to enhance the public image of a travel destination or an institution. Promotional photographs can have the look of practical or pictorial photographs, with the difference being how the images are edited and the context in which they are seen. The real estate agent uses the photograph of a house that shows it at its best, or a label on a package shows the product in optimal conditions. These are not untrue photographs, for they gain their impact directly from the veracity of photographs, but they are selected to support a chosen message about their subject. To make an analogy, if a vegetable garden was photographed from the sowing through the harvesting, a practical series would record what happened to the plants, whether they flourished or drooped, and how they produced. A pictorial series would show the garden to best advantage with lighting and viewpoints, but wouldn't necessarily show how the vegetables turned out. A promotional series would show the most successful plants from a favorable vantage and depict the smiling gardener displaying the best produce.

SCHOOLS

Before effective means of reproduction, when photographs were rather expensive, their primary application in promotion was for displays in public places. A photographic gallery displayed samples in a shop window or in a glass case by the stairway door, with a full collection in the waiting room. Other businesses showed photographs in their offices or in hotel lobbies and other public rooms.

In the era before media and reproduction, fairs and expositions offered a valuable opportunity to present a message to the public. Such events were of many sizes, from local commercial expositions, to annual state fairs, to one-of-a-kind national and international exhibitions. In the exhibition rooms at these events, companies and organizations would present displays that often included large collections of photographs.

An early adopter of this kind of photographic exhibition was Hampton Institute. From its founding in 1868, Hampton Normal and Agricultural Institute was active in publicizing its purposes and activities, to attract both financial support from donors and support for its mission from the public. Its first fair was the 1876 Centennial Exposition in Philadelphia. There the school's display at a "good place in the Main Exhibition Building" included "over twenty imperial photographs" that were "taken by Mr. Larrabee, photographer of Mill Creek." S. H. Larra-

For the Paris Exposition of 1900
Photographic print on mount, by Frances Benjamin Johnston, 1899–1900
The scene is a Hampton Institute class in "repairing and constructing telephones." This print was in the set exhibited in Paris; several copies of the set were provided to the school. *Library of Congress, Prints and Photographs Division, LC-USZ62-132386*

bee had been a photographer at Camp Hamilton in Hampton during the Civil War and stayed in place after the war to establish a practice. The subjects of the photographs included buildings, classrooms, and other interiors, "the Working Squad, Farm hands, brickmakers, Senior Class, pictures of negro cabins, and some of the 'old folks at home,' to illustrate the progress of the times."[19]

An excellent opportunity came when Hampton was invited to exhibit at the Paris Universal Exposition of 1900. With some 50,000,000 visitors, the fair proved to be one of the best attended ever. In 1899 the Rev. Hollis B. Frissell, the head of the school, hired Frances Benjamin Johnston of Washington, D.C., to make photographs for the display. Johnston spent the month of December 1899 and part of January 1900 on the job and produced a set of photographs that has become very well known. For each of 150 views, Johnston provided three prints and a negative, at a fee of $1,000, plus living expenses for herself and an assistant. The *Southern Workman* stated "this collection of pictures, arranged by subjects and mounted on the movable leaves of a large upright cabinet, will form part of the Negro exhibit at Paris." There were many favorable reports from Paris on the photographs, which were also shown at several places in the U.S. Notably in 1900, the year the exhibit appeared, contributions to the Hampton Institute endowment increased dramatically. Such success apparently left the school ready to go to new fairs. A Hampton photographic inventory dated 1905 mentions not only "the set taken for the Paris Exposition," but also "the additional negatives taken for Charleston and St. Louis," likely referring to the Inter-State and West Indian Exposition in Charleston, S.C. (December 1901–May 1902), and the 1904 St. Louis World's Fair, the Louisiana Purchase Exposition (April–December 1904).[20]

Watercolor class
Photographic print on mount, by Frances Benjamin Johnston, 1899–1900
In this view, shown in Paris, of a Hampton Institute class in watercolor painting, the instructor is Leigh Richmond Miner, who became the school photographer in 1907. *Library of Congress, Prints and Photographs Division, LC-USZ62-127364*

Hampton carpentry class
Silver gelatin print, by Leigh Richmond Miner, 7.5 x 9.5
in., on mount, 1913
The careful arrangement of figures is a hallmark of
Johnston's Hampton work, and here of Miner's as well.
Hampton University Archives

Leigh Richmond Miner. Leigh Richmond Miner (1864–
1935) was on the faculty at Hampton Institute and served
as the school photographer for a quarter-century. A native
of Connecticut and a graduate of the Academy of Design
in New York, Miner came to Hampton in 1898 as an
instructor of drawing. He appears in that role in two 1899
Johnston photographs of students sketching. Whether he
provided any assistance to her work at the school is not
known, but as an artist with a New York background who
also knew the students, he could have been a helpful liai-
son. Miner had joined the camera club soon after arriving
at Hampton, and it is likely he was involved in convincing
Johnston to exhibit her photograph collection there.[21]

During 1903 Miner was active in the camera club
project to provide photographs for Paul Laurence Dunbar's
When Malindy Sings. When it was published late that year,
it was the third book of Dunbar's poetry that the club had
illustrated. For the next Dunbar book, *Li'l Gal,* published
1904, Miner provided all the photographs. That year too

Miner resigned from Hampton and moved to New York to operate a photographic
studio. While there he illustrated two more Dunbar books, *Howdy, Honey, Howdy!*
of 1905, and *Joggin' Erlong,* published soon after Dunbar's death in 1906. [22]

In 1906, anticipating the 1907 Jamestown Exposition, Hampton principal
Frissell hired Miner to return to Virginia and make new photographs for exhibition.
Frissell wrote to Miner, "You know the work that Miss Johnston did, something of
the same sort would be needed now." Miner followed closely indeed to Johnston's
model, creating classroom tableaus with posed students that derive quite directly
from her photographs. Although the Hampton Institute exhibit at the Jamestown
Exposition's Negro Building is not documented, it is safe to presume Miner's photographs were among those displayed. Some did appear in a 1907 publication from
Hampton Institute Press, *The Jamestown Exposition and Hampton Institute.*

Miner's photographic work led him to rejoin the Hampton faculty in 1907.
He served as director of applied art, official school photographer, and landscape
designer until his retirement in 1933.[23]

Hampton cooking class
Silver gelatin print, by Leigh Richmond Miner, 7.3 x 9.4 in., on mount, 1913
Principal Hollis B. Frissell suggested that Miner use Johnston's photographs
as his model when the school needed new images for exhibition. Miner had
worked with Johnston in 1899–1900 and produced pictures with much the
same look. *Hampton University Archives*

EARLY TRAVEL

An early use of photography for promotion was to encourage travel and tourism. The chief promoters were the conveyers—the railroads and steamship lines—and the destinations—the hotels and resorts. Displays in the waiting areas of depots and in hotel lobbies were probably the first applications of travel-promotion photography. Once the halftone made reproduction feasible, printed pieces were produced, at first simple handbills and then more elaborate circulars and booklets.

MONS HOTEL, BEDFORD CITY, VA.

Hotel postcard
Photograph in halftone, mounted on postcard, hand-colored, by Heuser & Co., c. 1910
The Mons Hotel was located at the site of today's Peaks of Otter Lodge, on the Blue Ridge Parkway. It closed in 1936. *Virginia Historical Society*

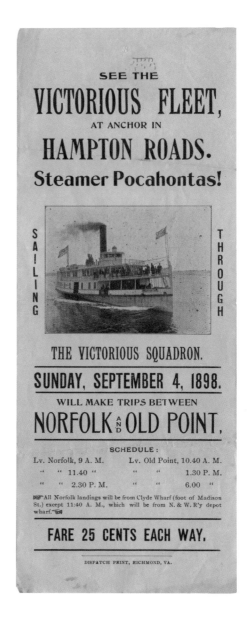

Steamer!
Photograph in halftone, image 2.5 x 3.2 in. on sheet 11 x 4.2 in., 1898
The flyer was printed in Richmond, which suggests it may have been for distribution there and other inland locations. *Virginia Historical Society*

Railroad travel
Photo-lithograph, booklet cover, 6 x 9 in., c. 1906
Looking out the windows when traveling by railroad was a big part of the experience. The Norfolk & Western Railway's booklet used photographs in halftone to illustrate picturesque scenes along its routes and is representative of numerous such publications issued by railroads. *Virginia Historical Society*

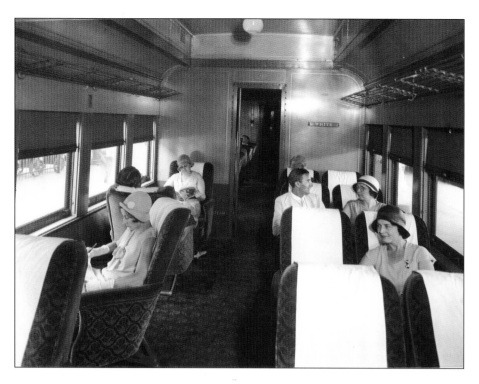

Travel in comfort
Silver gelatin print, by Dementi Studio, 7.9 x 10.1 in., c. 1930–40
Another message was that travel by railroad was comfortable and exclusive, as seen in this car interior for the Richmond, Fredericksburg, & Potomac Railroad. *Virginia Historical Society, Gift of Richmond, Fredericksburg, & Potomac Railroad*

Depot display
Silver gelatin print on mount, hand-colored, 20 x 23 in.,
c. 1920–50
Large handsome photographs of places worth traveling to visit were a familiar feature of railroad stations, hotel lobbies, and other travel facilities for the first two-thirds of the twentieth century. The view is of Claremont, Surry County. *Virginia Historical Society, Gift of Richmond, Fredericksburg, & Potomac Railroad*

JAMESTOWN

The Jamestown Ter-Centennial Exposition of 1907 took place when photography was migrating to a variety of formats. The exposition celebrated the 300th anniversary of the Jamestown landing, and its site was in north Norfolk facing Hampton Roads. The chief source of photography was the Jamestown Official Photograph Corporation, which employed as many as eight photographers on a staff of over twenty. The corporation occupied a two-story building on the grounds where it operated a portrait studio and a retail outlet for souvenirs and keepsakes. On display in the shop windows for viewing "without charge" were seventy-two "historical transparencies" of Jamestown and colonial Virginia sites. At the shop, noted the *Official Guide*, "Kodak films are developed and printed by experts, and all kinds of camera supplies are on sale."[24]

The Jamestown Official Photograph Corporation had "the exclusive concession for all photographic work on the Exposition Grounds and the press department was largely dependent on it for material advertising the Fair." Its cameramen "photographed every Convention and State day group and most of the important exhibits" and "all of the principal events." In the words of the *Official Blue Book*, "Few expositions have been so bountifully supplied with pictorial material for exploitive purposes." The output included photographic prints; official postcards based on photographs and photolithographed in color; other postcards printed in black and white halftone from photographs; stereographs issued by at least four companies; an illustrated book, *The Jamestown Exposition, in Photo-gravure*; scrapbooks of original prints, probably made for Exposition officials, including banquets and social events; and the *Official Blue Book*, an authoritative account of the fair published after it was over and illustrated with many halftones.[25]

Jamestown official photographers
Photograph in halftone, in *The Official Blue Book of the Jamestown Ter-centennial Exposition, A.D. 1907*, 1909
The caption states, "Headquarters of Jamestown Official Photograph Corporation." In front, twenty-one staff members pose with seven cameras. The "display and sales room" on the first floor offered official photographs, view books, and post cards, and the upper floor was offices and work rooms. *Virginia Historical Society*

Jamestown postcard
Color photo-lithograph postcard, by A. C. Bosselman & Co., printed in Germany, 1907
The caption reads, "Powhatan Oak, Jamestown Exposition, 1907." Companies that had not paid the exposition for a concession could not use the imprimatur "official souvenir post card" and probably could not sell at certain shops. They could still issue fair-related postcards. *Virginia Historical Society*

POWHATAN OAK, JAMESTOWN EXPOSITION, 1907. 5587.

Jamestown stereo

Stereograph, by Keystone View Company, 1907

At least four different companies issued stereographs for the exposition. The caption states, "Pocahontas Pleading for the Life of John Smith—Enacted by the Survivors of the Pamunkey Indian Tribe at the Jamestown Exposition." *Virginia Historical Society*

Jamestown souvenir album

Photogravure mounted on thick paper cover, by Jamestown Official Photograph Corporation, 1907

The "official" album *The Jamestown Exposition* includes twenty-four 10 x 12 inch pages. The photogravures were produced by The Albertype Co., with most about 6 x 8 inches and two larger foldout panoramas. *Virginia Historical Society*

Photo exhibition at Jamestown

Photograph in halftone, in *The Official Blue Book of the Jamestown Tercentennial Exposition, A.D. 1907*, 1909

Seen in this image is part of the exhibition of photographs in the Negro Building by A. P. Bedou. The New Orleans photographer won a gold medal. Many of the exhibits at the exposition used photography. At an auditorium built inside one of the exhibition halls, an hourly show presented "motion pictures and colored stereopticon slides" of a "Trip from Jamestown to the National Cash Register Factory at Dayton, Ohio." *Virginia Historical Society*

Jamestown portrait I
Photographic print in folder, by Brooks-Photo, 1907
From the "Jamestown Exposition" imprint, one imagines that the photographer may have had a concession to operate on the grounds. *Virginia State University Archives*

Jamestown portrait II
Silver gelatin print on postcard, 1907
For this portrait, the negative of the individual subject was printed in the oval in the middle, and separately the imagery framing the subject was printed from a prepared copy negative.
Virginia Historical Society

VIRGINIA CHAMBER OF COMMERCE

The Virginia State Chamber of Commerce was founded in 1924 with one of its purposes to undertake "a consolidated statewide promotional program." When the publicity program was enlarged in 1927, a photography section was added, and photography became an official department in 1932. "For thirteen years," stated a report in 1937, the publicity department "has been flooding the nation with material on Virginia."[26]

By 1937 the State Chamber had accumulated more than 20,000 negatives of Virginia subjects and was producing 13,000 photographic prints a year. These were sent to news photo distribution agencies, book publishers, newspapers, magazines, and newsreel film producers. When Scripps-Howard Syndicate or another large agency sent a photographer on assignment to Virginia, the chamber would often provide a staff member to accompany and assist. In addition "State Chamber photographers were furnished wherever a Virginia event was happening that offered a chance for national publicity," explained the 1937 report, "where no other photographic service was covering." By 1954 the chamber's negative collection had grown to 50,000, and the two staff photographers were distributing 15,000 photographic prints a year. The primary photographer for the chamber through these years was Philip I. Flournoy, who started in 1926 at age sixteen. In 1966 Flournoy reported that he had an active file of 125,000 negatives.[27]

The chamber issued its own publications beginning in the 1920s with *Virginia, First in the Heart of the Nation*, an oversize illustrated quarterly that was packed with photographic halftones. Included were pictorial scenic views, images of industrial progress, and aerials. The *Virginia* quarterly was superceded in 1934 by a monthly, *The Commonwealth*, that by 1954 had a monthly press run of 10,000. *The Commonwealth* contained a higher ratio of text and also took advertising. The chamber published *The Commonwealth* until September 1979, when another publisher took over the magazine and issued it until March 1985.

Beautiful industrial view

Photograph in halftone, in *Virginia, First in the Heart of the Nation*, Autumn 1929

At its inception in the 1920s, the Virginia State Chamber of Commerce had an enthusiasm for economic development that seems somewhat single-minded today. The caption for the image says: "The Virginian Railway power plant at Narrows, Virginia, one of the hundreds of beautiful industrial views to be enjoyed in Virginia." *Virginia Historical Society*

Peanut princess

Silver gelatin print, by Flournoy, 8 x 10 in., 1941

The Virginia State Chamber of Commerce took on the job of making the state's agricultural festivals into successful marketing ventures. As a way of getting newspapers to run promotional photography, the VSCC used festival princesses as a hook, especially in the period from the late 1920s to 1941. The festivals were suspended during World War II, and such promotion by princess seems not to have resumed afterward. The first National Peanut Festival was held in Suffolk in January 1941, and a second larger one was held in October the same year; this image was likely produced for one of those. *Library of Virginia*

Tobacco princesses
Silver gelatin print, by Flournoy, 8 x 10 in., c. 1929–41
The National Tobacco Festival was held in South Boston from 1935 to 1941. Promotion using young women in tobacco leaf garments had started by 1929. *Library of Virginia*

Apple princess
Silver gelatin print, by Flournoy, 8 x 10 in., 1940
The Shenandoah Apple Blossom Festival in Winchester began in 1924. Except for a suspension during 1941–45, it has sustained as an annual event into the twenty-first century. *Library of Virginia*

Potato blossom princess
Silver gelatin print, 8 x 10 in., 1938
It was likely the State Chamber that spearheaded the Potato Blossom Festival, on Virginia's Eastern Shore. *Library of Virginia*

For the chamber publicity and photography programs, the two main pushes were attracting visitors to Virginia and promoting Virginia industries and commodity producers. A series of festivals were held around the state to promote particular products, including the National Tobacco Festival, the Suffolk Peanut Festival, the Shenandoah Apple Blossom Festival, and the Rockingham Turkey Festival. The chamber's role in marketing the festivals was among its most successful efforts. Perhaps the most distinctive of the festival publicity materials were the princess images, produced in the 1930s and until 1941. Young women posed in costumes or activities related in some way to the festival theme. The hook for the target editors was an image of a wholesome young female to put into the newspaper.

In 1935 the chamber assisted *National Geographic* on a photo shoot at Colonial Williamsburg. The published result displayed the strength of the chamber's photographic program but also exposed a weakness. The week-long shoot was in color, a new thing then for magazines, and for it the chamber hired and costumed twenty-three models. Grouped with articles about Colonial Williamsburg by John D. Rockefeller, Jr., and William A. R. Goodwin, the photographs appeared in the April 1937 *National Geographic*, in a special color section titled "Virginia's Colonial Heritage." On the one hand, these photographs with a Hollywood-like polish reached a big, ideal audience. Less happily, at the middle of the picture spread was a genre scene in the "pickanniny" style, showing two black children eating watermelon. Presumably it was included as a light-hearted comic touch, but some would have seen the image as a deliberate signal to potential visitors.[28]

The photographs that the chamber circulated on behalf of Virginia represented a point of view that could be seen as progressive in respect to business development but on social matters did not challenge the prevailing status quo and in fact helped to sustain it. The people who inhabit the chamber photographs tend to be either paid models, vacationers, or workers who appear as cogs in the economic machine. Seen from today's perspective, it is noticeable that neither African Americans nor women are presented as achievers or doers. Although it might not be realistic to expect a business-oriented organization to have been an advocate for civil rights, or for equal rights, or for workers, the omission of such concerns at the conceptual level produced a photographic collection made with blinders. Eventually the chamber closed its photography section and donated to the Library of Virginia 31,599 photographic negatives dating 1922–72. The chamber collection is large and wide-ranging but is not a full and complete portrait of the state.[29]

Turkey princess
Silver gelatin print, 8 x 10 in., 1941
The Virginia Turkey Festival was held in Harrisonburg from 1939 to 1997. *Library of Virginia*

1939 WORLD'S FAIR

At the 1939 New York World's Fair, the theme was "the world of tomorrow." Virginia wished to participate but looked for a way to do it inexpensively. At the end of the 1930s, times remained difficult for many, and the state would not authorize much money toward the project. The concept of a low-key oasis for the visitor was presented by John Stewart Bryan, president of the College of William and Mary, and met approval. Things worked out for the state and its treasury when space was obtained in a building shared with other exhibitors, and the idea emerged of offering photo albums as a pleasant sitting activity. Later, "Lieutenant Governor Saxon W. Holt, as head of the state World's Fair Commission, defended the room and its photo collection as appropriate considering the hard times."[30]

The head of the William and Mary Fine Arts Department, Leslie Cheek, Jr., was commissioned to design the exhibit. Over the 1939 season of the fair, the Virginia Room averaged 4,500 visitors per day, for a total of about one million. The Virginia Room offered comfortable seats, a calm atmosphere, and "a complimentary glass of ice water served by a white-jacketed waiter." Available on bookshelves and tables were 227 photograph albums, which were so well perused that the binders had to be replaced twice. Because of the outbreak of war in Europe in September 1939, the second year of the World's Fair in 1940 was much diminished. Like many of the exhibitors, Virginia did not return for 1940.

The editor and organizer of the photograph albums was Virginia man-of-letters T. Beverly Campbell, who also served as on-site manager for the Virginia Room in New York. Campbell had edited *Black Swan: The Magazine of Virginia* from 1929 to 1931 and was the author of *Virginia Oddities: A Scrapbook* (1933), the historical pageant *Liberty or Death* (1936), and productions for the National Tobacco Festival in South Boston. Also assisting on the preparation of the albums were the

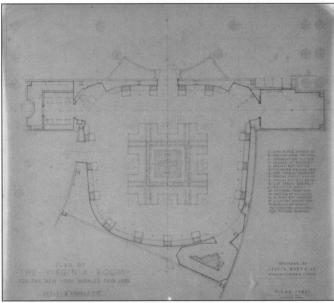

The Virginia Room
The Virginia Room offered a place to sit, drink a glass of water, and look at photographic albums featuring a variety of state subjects. *Virginia Historical Society*

1939 New York World's Fair
Virginia shared the curved building at the end of the pool with other states. Its section was just to the right of the dome. The state participated only for the first year of the World's Fair, 1939. *Virginia Historical Society*

Plans for the Virginia Room
Architectural drawing, by Leslie Cheek, 1939
Seating was at the center of the room and around the outer walls; shelves for the photograph albums were around the outside walls. *Virginia Historical Society*

State Chamber's publicity and photography department staffs. The 227 albums used 5,675 photographic prints, all black and white. The Library of Virginia has preserved the collection and made about 3,000 of the images available online.[31]

A survey of the album images as represented online suggests that the content reflected the social attitudes of the day in much the same way as the State Chamber's photographic program. The aim to attract visitors to Virginia explains much of the included material, the historic sites and beautiful places. There was also an intention to portray the state more broadly and in this a modern viewer notices both a heavy hand on the positive message sauce and the omission of many subjects. For all the historic homes, there are few if any lived-in dwellings in the collection. People appear more as a representative of a designated category than as an individual. Women rarely participate in anything more significant than recreation. Except in the context of an educational institution, adult African Americans appear in the collection only as laborers and never as professionals or entrepreneurs. As a product of their time, the albums today are historical, and much of the state is in them, but a good portion has been selected out.

Living Uncle Sam
Silver gelatin print, by Mole & Thomas, 13.5 x 10.8 in., 1919
In the period around World War I, the photographers Mole & Thomas produced a series of photographs looking down on American troops arranged into patriotic motifs. The text at lower-right states: "The Living Uncle Sam, 19000 Officers and Men, Camp Lee, Va., Major General, Omar Bundy, Com'd'g." At lower-left, the image is dated 13 Jan. 1919. *Virginia Historical Society*

ARRANGED EVENTS

Once photographic reproduction in halftone became an expected part of the mix in newspaper content, editors looked for picture material on a daily basis. To fill the need, new businesses for supplying photographs arose, including picture services, press agents, and publicity offices. The State Chamber's publicity department was typical of such image suppliers. One way for organizations to attract attention or to get a message out was a staged public relations event or media event.

Photo-op: Grip and grin
Silver gelatin print, c. 1950–53
The standard publicity photograph consists of one person handing something to another person, usually shaking hands—the grip—and acting as if pleased—the grin. In the event pictured here, engineered by a trade association, Governor John S. Battle receives the prop, an ordinary object with a celebratory label: "The 200 Millionth Case of Virginia Canned Food." *Virginia Historical Society, John S. Battle papers*

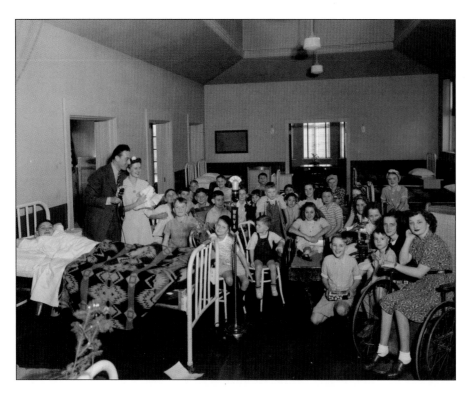

Publicity photo: Christmas 1944
Silver gelatin print, 1944
WRVA broadcasters Harvey Hudson and Ruth Lamlet visit the Crippled Children Home on 25 December 1944. The photograph may have been taken for a release to newspapers or to file for future use. *Library of Virginia, WRVA Radio Collection*

Photo-op: Groundbreaking
Silver gelatin print, 1961
At the groundbreaking ceremony for a new state building in Richmond, Governor Lindsay Almond discovered when he leaned forward that the speaker's stand was not well constructed. *Virginia Historical Society, Henry R. Gonner papers*

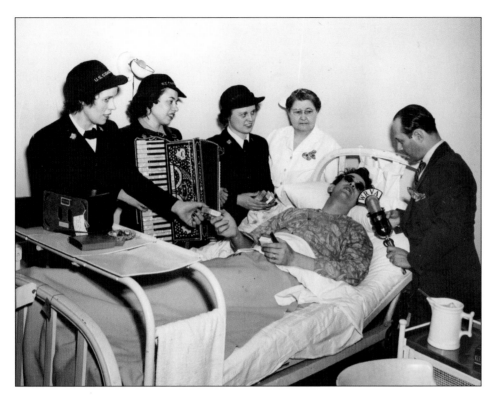

Publicity photo: Smokes for the wounded
Silver gelatin print, 1942–45
The photograph documents a radio station's help with the war effort. A WRVA announcer interviews a wounded soldier while a trio featuring Sunshine Sue serenades. *Library of Virginia, WRVA Radio Collection*

Photo-op: Governor's motorcade
Silver gelatin print, c. 1950–53
Events in which politicians are participants have long been organized so that photographers will be able show them in a favorable setting that will catch interest. *Virginia Historical Society, John S. Battle papers*

DOCUMENTARY PHOTOGRAPHY

An important type of media presentation today is "news." Ideally, news is objective reporting on events. Photography is a big part of modern news reporting. In many ways, news photography had its beginnings in the entrepreneurial Union photography of the Civil War, but news photography is different from simply photography of events. One factor is timeliness. In addition, news photography appears in the context of, and provides a useful balance to, journalists' accounts. Modern news photography really begins with the introduction of halftone reproduction in weekly papers in the 1890s and in daily newspapers after 1900. Then in the 1930s photographs surged to a more central role in news reporting with the rise of such picture magazines as *Life* and *Look* and the movie newsreels.

News photography is one of those subjects worthy of its own volume that here is only skimmed over. The idea of an objective point of view that is truthful to its subject is also found in documentary photography. The word documentary was originally used to describe a kind of movie that is not fictional and considers a subject at some length. In still pictures, the expectation for both documentary photographs and news photographs would be factual reporting without manipulation. News would tend to be a briefer record of a more topical event, while documentary would be a more sustained consideration of a subject seen in a longer perspective.

Whereas practical photographs are made to show a step or condition within a particular discipline, and promotional photographs convey the point of view of their sponsor, documentary photographs in theory aim for an accurate and whole concept of their subject matter. If news photography is the stuff of newspapers and weekly magazines, documentary photography is seen in longer-form magazines and books and exhibitions, as likely today online as in a gallery. In such contexts, groups of images can be presented, as essays or collections, that support each other in conveying their subject.

In Virginia as in American photography in general, the best-known examples of documentary photography are the photographs

Fire

Photographic postcard, c. 1912
Words in the image at lower-left read: "Fire of Riverton Mills, July 5, 1912. Riverton, Va." The site is in Front Royal. The card was mailed in Sept. 1912. *Virginia Historical Society*

Wreck

Silver gelatin print, 1922
The U. S. Army purchased the semi-rigid, 412-foot dirigible *Roma* from Italy in 1921 and based it at Langley Field. On a 21 Feb. 1922 flight to test new engines, the hydrogen-filled *Roma* struck electrical wires over Norfolk, caught fire, and crashed. Thirty-two of the airship's forty-five man crew were killed. *Mariners Museum*

Hurricane

Silver gelatin print, 7.5 x 9.5 in., 1936
Inscribed on reverse: "7:30 am, during height of Hurricane at Willoughby Spit, Sept 18/36, made under great hazard." Willoughby Spit extends out from the Norfolk side of Hampton Roads toward Old Point Comfort. *Virginia Historical Society*

made under the aegis of the Farm Security Administration in the 1930s. The photographs showed the lives of regular people during the Depression with a famously "warts and all" approach. Another set is the Port of Embarkation photographs that documented the port of Hampton Roads during World War II.

UNPLANNED EVENTS

Sometimes it is known in advance when and where an important event will take place, other times things happen unpredictably, and mostly there are indications something will happen but no set time. In each case photographs can be a witness to the occurrence. With a scheduled event, there is time to pre-select angles of view and to ensure that all necessary materials are at hand. The photographer who wishes to capture the unplanned event must stand by in readiness, like an emergency responder, for a storm, fire, crash, or conflict.

Ice
Silver gelatin print, 1936
On the James River at Richmond, the view looks downstream with the City Intermediate Terminal to the left. *Virginia Historical Society*

Flood
Silver gelatin print, by Richmond Newspapers, 1972
Rain from Hurricane Agnes in 1972 caused the James River to rise to its highest level of the twentieth century, flooding communities including Scottsville, Albemarle County. *Virginia Historical Society*

Tornado
Silver gelatin print, by W. Edwin Booth, 1951
The view of the 1951 tornado was made looking west from downtown Richmond. The Carillon bell tower at Byrd Park is visible in the distance; the radio transmission tower no longer stands. *Virginia Historical Society*

Terrorism
Digital print, 2001
Pentagon, Arlington, 11 Sept. 2001. *Virginia Historical Society*

NORFOLK IN 1919

In November 1919 an unknown photographer documented the interiors of forty-six businesses in downtown Norfolk. The purpose is not known, however the proprietors of the stores, repair shops, and restaurants appear to have cooperated with the photographer. The glass plate negatives were collected by a Norfolk resident and rediscovered many years later. In 1986–87 an edition of contact prints from the negatives was produced by a group affiliated with Old Dominion University, including photographer David E. Johnson, who oversaw the printing, photographer Wallace E. Dreyer, and historian Peter Stewart. When the negatives were found, there was no accompanying information, and no contemporary prints are known. A date of November 1919 for the photographs has been assigned based on "calendars displayed in some of the photographs." Research has identified a few of the businesses and enough clues to suggest that "all of the photographs were taken in the East Main Street area, especially between Commercial Place and the Union Station," an area of Norfolk that has since been totally transformed. The cross-section of city life represented in the photographs is of a different character than can be gathered from census data, city directories, or tax records.[32]

Norfolk 1919: Bike repair shop
Silver gelatin print, contact print from 1919 glass negative, image 6.5 x 8.5 in., 1986–87. *Virginia Historical Society*

Norfolk 1919: Restaurant
Silver gelatin print, contact print from 1919 glass negative, image 6.5 x 8.5 in., 1986–87. *Virginia Historical Society*

Norfolk 1919: Tailor shop
Silver gelatin print, image 6.5 x 8.5 in., 1986–87
The image is a contact print made from a glass negative, one of a set of forty-six. The negatives were rediscovered in 1968, and an edition of ten copies each was produced in 1986–87 by David E. Johnson, Peter Stewart, and Wallace E. Dreyer of Old Dominion University. The views are all of shops, mostly interiors, in downtown Norfolk, dated Nov. 1919 from calendars in some of the scenes. Only a few of the businesses could be identified. *Virginia Historical Society*

Norfolk 1919: New York Lunch Room
Silver gelatin print, contact print from 1919 glass negative, image 6.5 x 8.5 in., 1986–87
The New York Lunch Room was located at 728 E. Main St., Norfolk, and the proprietor was Demetrious Feleros, possibly the man standing behind the counter. *Virginia Historical Society*

FSA PHOTOGRAPHS

In May 1935 the federal government created the Resettlement Administration to combat rural poverty. Roy Stryker, a Columbia University economics professor, was named head of its Historical Section, a department intended to document and promote the work of the agency. For that purpose Stryker supervised the initiation of a photography program. In 1937 the agency was transferred to the Agriculture Department and renamed the Farm Security Administration, or FSA, one of the New Deal alphabet agencies. It is as the FSA photographs that the results of Stryker's program have come to be known.[33]

From 1935 to 1944, The FSA produced about 170,000 negatives and about 1,600 color transparencies. The Library of Congress holds about 77,000 prints made under Stryker's direction, and another 30,000 from other sources. Presumably the number of prints made and distributed over the life of the agency was at least that large. Of this total output, research by Brooks Johnson in the files at the Library of Congress, Prints and Photographs Department, in the early 1980s found about 2,000 prints of Virginia. An online search of the FSA/OWI collection of scanned negatives finds about 3,000 Virginia items.

The best known of the FSA photographers, Walker Evans and Dorothea Lange, each took only a handful of photographs in Virginia. The chief photographers of Virginia were Arthur Rothstein, especially in 1935 and continuing until 1940; John Vachon, who worked from 1937 to 1943, with his peak year 1941; Marion Post Wolcott, who covered the state 1939–41, with 1941 also her peak; and Jack Delano, who worked from 1940 to 1942. Other photographers included Paul Carter, mainly in 1936; Russell Lee in 1938; John Collier from 1941 to 1943; Ben Shahn in 1941; Gordon Parks in 1942; and Marjory Collins in 1942.[34]

When the FSA photographs were made, particularly in the first several years, there was a political content to them that is less apparent today than it was then. The Democratic administration elected in 1932 was pushing a legislative agenda to address joblessness and economic distress caused by the Depression. The prescriptions of the New Deal met considerable resistance, and many New Deal supporters felt that not all of the nation's press—at that time, primarily the newspapers—was doing enough to illustrate the conditions that needed correction. The purpose of the photographic project was specifically to provide visual argument for the FSA relief programs, and more generally to show the conditions that required government action. In his study of Virginia FSA photography, Brooks Johnson writes of the time that "agricultural reforms were needed" and "the New Deal offered the best hope for change," and states of the photographs that they were "politically inspired and as such must be considered propaganda."

Whether documentary is a good term for these photographs has been a much-discussed question. Brooks Johnson notes that neither Walker Evans nor Dorothea Lange were satisfied with the term, and photographic historian Beaumont Newhall proposed instead the word "humanistic," which Johnson also

F.S.A.: Urban
Silver gelatin print, by John Vachon, March 1941
The caption card describes the subject as "Singing hymns at evening service of Helping Hand Mission, Portsmouth, Virginia." *Virginia Historical Society*

F.S.A.: Rural
Silver gelatin print, by Jack Delano, May 1940
The caption card describes the subject as "Tenant family and part of his family in field ready for tobacco planting, nine miles north of Danville, Pittsylvania County, Virginia." *Virginia Historical Society*

favors. George Allen Young in 1937 described the FSA work as "Documentary, Propaganda or Sociological Photography." He went on, "Pictures of this type are usually made by the Candid Camera technique. The attempt is made to reveal the injustices and the unhealthy aspects of our society. These pictures are political and economic comments."[35]

One person's objective or documentary point of view is another observer's political point of view or propaganda. A question arises similar to those in other fields: whether a photograph that advocates a point of view can at the same time be objective. Regarding the treatment of 1930s Virginia photography in the present study, it would be fair to ask why the State Chamber photographs have been categorized as promotional, and the FSA photographs as documentary, given that in the late 1930s each would have been used to support (differing) political policies. One part of the answer is that the categories are not intended to be exclusive, and an individual image might well fit into more than one. Another part is that these descriptive categories are based both on the image content and on the use of the image. A single photographic image can be used quite differently in one situation compared to another. Another aspect, especially in looking at a group of photographs, is not so much what they do but what they do not show. Perhaps the key point of the FSA photographs was to bring balance into the national visual discourse. In T. Beverly Campbell's selection of photographs for the World's Fair albums, for instance, there was no poverty. Not that Virginia necessarily wished to highlight that topic, but FSA photographs documenting it in Virginia were available.

ARCHITECTURAL SURVEYS

At least two New Deal programs started to provide employment for white-collar workers had a photographic component and compiled valuable photographic records of Virginia architecture. In recent years the files of these research projects, previously accessed only with difficulty, have become available online.

In 1933 the Historic American Buildings Survey, known as HABS, began to document "America's antique buildings" and continues as an ongoing program today. HABS grew from a proposal by Charles E. Peterson of the National Park Service that architects and draftsmen be employed to make accurate records of important structures, including photographs. Frances Benjamin Johnston had initiated in Virginia in the late 1920s a personal project to document buildings that was likely part of Peterson's inspiration. The Historic American Buildings Survey started under one of the New Deal alphabet agencies and today is administered through the National Park Service. New records continue to be added to the HABS files, which have been available online since 1997 through the catalog of the Library of Congress Prints and Photographs Department.[36]

A second New Deal survey was the Virginia Historical Inventory Project. It operated from 1935 to 1938 as a section of the Works Progress Administration, or WPA, which also administered the Federal Writers' Project, the Federal Theatre Project, and other arts programs. The Virginia Historical Inventory Project, or VHI, was federally funded and state-administered. Researchers employed at the county level collected material on sites of local historical interest through interviews and photographs. The files of the VHI are another collection that the Library of Virginia has made available online.[37]

PORT OF EMBARKATION

By the time the U.S. entered World War II, photographic documentation was becoming a regular practice in many government agencies. A body of photographic work that showed the activities of an agency could be drawn upon for many applications: training programs, public relations, departmental reports, and for internal newsletters and display. Many military organizations (but not all) set up photographic sections during World War II.[38]

Virginia became home to a number of military facilities in the period before the war and in the early years of the conflict, including most famously the Pentagon. One such wartime organization was the Hampton Roads Port of Embarkation, run by the Army Transportation Corps from June 1942 until after the war in 1946. Its function reprised the role of the Hampton Roads area in World War I. Based in Newport News, HRPE managed several sites around Hampton Roads where troops and supplies were gathered and prepared for shipment to

WAC photographer
Gelatin silver print, by U.S. Army Signal Corps, 8 x 10 in., c. 1942–45
The photographer is identified as WAC Corporal Dorothy Baker. *Mariners Museum, HRPE collection*

Impromptu dance
Gelatin silver print, by U.S. Army Signal Corps, 8 x 10 in., c. 1942–45
Mariners Museum, HRPE collection

foreign theaters, primarily across the Atlantic. Convoys of ships were loaded for the invasions of North Africa in 1942 and of Sicily in 1943, for example. In addition, injured soldiers and prisoners were disembarked at the port.

Photographers from the Signal Corps documented much of the activity at HRPE. "The services of the photographic laboratory were extensively used by the Post Commander and Port Historian, to compile a pictorial history of a Port of Embarkation, which is unique in the history of the Army. During the life of the photo laboratory it built up a file of more than fifteen thousand accurately captioned prints."[39] The HRPE had a significant Women's Army Corps contingent, and at least one of the Signal Corps photographers was a WAC, PFC (later Corporal) Dorothy Baker.

The file of the Hampton Roads Port of Embarkation photo laboratory was transferred to the Mariners Museum in Newport News, which holds about 16,000 images with two prints of each, one 8 x10 and one 4 x 5 contact. Another collection of HRPE photographs at the Library of Virginia includes "nearly four thousand photographs bound in thirty-five albums." Called the U. S. Army Signal Corps Photographs, about 3,500 have been made available online.[40]

PERSONAL PHOTOGRAPHY

There are two sides to "personal" photography. First is the portrait, the predominant image of photographic practice in the nineteenth century. Although the portrait became less central to the trade in the twentieth, no mode of photography extends more broadly. Who among us has not sat for one? The portrait is, however, one of those big categories of twentieth-century photography that will be only touched upon here.

A second kind of personal photographs are images that people make for themselves. The migration of cameras into many hands has been a hallmark of the age of modern photography. When it first occurred in the twenty years after 1890, a new group of people became photographers, especially women. Some of them recorded subjects that had not been much depicted before, and in ways that did not necessarily resemble previous images. The standards that had come to govern how photography should be undertaken for commercial or official purposes, or for a client or an editor, did not have to apply to pictures made for personal reasons.

Embarking on pier
Gelatin silver print, by U.S. Army Signal Corps, 8 x 10 in., c. 1942–45.
Mariners Museum, HRPE collection

Because the circumstances of their taking make personal photographs prone to accidents and unplanned occurrences, even people aiming for conventional images of family and friends were forced to accept mistakes in order to preserve special moments. In time the sheer mass of snapshots—the sum of blurs and crops, mid-expressions and half-gestures, missed opportunities and lucky shots—forced a loosening up of rules of composition, not only in casual photography but also in formal photography. Sarah Greenough writes of "photographs that are casually made, usually by untrained amateurs, and intended to function as documents of personal history" that became "a rich reservoir of antirational activity, where chance and contingency reigned supreme." In many respects, variance from the norm in personal photographs became a norm itself. And that variability was not all bad. At times, happy accident can cause a snapshot to come together in a way that transcends intention.[1]

WOMEN PHOTOGRAPHERS

A group that greatly benefited when the means for making photographs became more accessible was women. Only a few women had worked as photographers before 1900. From 1891 to 1896, Mrs. Emeline Turner operated a gallery in Portsmouth, in association with photographer Augustus M. Turner (apparently kin but not her husband), who for a time was listed as manager. In 1900, Mrs. Mary W. Tennant was a photographer in Newport News, but judging from directory listings not a proprietor; she might have worked at the branch gallery there owned by Joseph Faber of Norfolk. Another woman who began early in the century was Bessie Gwendola Brown, daughter of George O. Brown of Richmond.

Brandon exterior
Albumen print, by Edyth Carter Beveridge, 1902
Beveridge published this photograph and the interior in *The Pilot*, a magazine distributed by the Old Dominion Steamship Line, which operated passenger vessels in Chesapeake Bay and along the middle Atlantic coast.
Virginia Historical Society

Brandon interior
Silver gelatin print on mount, by Edyth Carter Beveridge, 1902.
Virginia Historical Society

When her father died in 1910 she and her brother, George W. Brown, became partners in the business and ran it as "The Browns."[2]

Two women photographers who practiced photography as independents—perhaps the pioneers in the state—were Edyth Carter Beveridge and Frances Gibboney. Beveridge (c. 1862–1927) grew up in Richmond as the youngest daughter of a merchant, attending good schools and achieving notice for her art. She began photographing in the 1890s and worked at least through 1907, shooting architecture, events, portraits, and contributing to the illustrated Saturday section of the *Richmond News*. Her notable publications included a photo essay on the White House of the Confederacy, featuring views of each of the fourteen rooms dedicated to a state, which appeared in *Ladies Home Journal* in 1906, and photographs for James A. Harrison's 1903 *Life and Letters of Edgar Allan Poe*. Historian Stacy Gibbons Moore finds no evidence that Beveridge, who never married, worked in photography after 1907: "she may have found it increasingly difficult to find work in a profession that was staunchly and overwhelmingly male dominated. She may even have abandoned photography altogether." Certainly the likelihood is that she was not paid as well as a male would have been for the same work.[3]

Frances Gibboney (1867–1941) grew up in Wytheville, lived for periods in Tazewell and Marion, and by 1900 moved back to Wytheville where she lived the rest of her life. Known to her family as Fannie, Gibboney began photographing by the time she was twenty, mostly portraits and groups of her family and friends. She also photographed patients at Southwestern State Mental Institute in Marion, where Gibboney

Family portrait

Silver gelatin print, from glass negative, by Frances Gibboney, c. 1889–90

Frances Gibboney made this group portrait of her family, including her mother Sallie seated right, her father Albert standing left, her sister Kate standing middle, an unknown lady seated left, and Frances standing right with her palette by the easel. The print is a modern one made from the original negative. *Wytheville Museum*

lived on the grounds with her parents when they worked as caretakers from 1887 to about 1894. She operated a photography studio in Wytheville in 1900 with Susie Fox, but little more is known about it; presumably the main product would have been individual and group portraits. Gibboney also painted, practiced taxidermy, and late in life created an art of carved scenes on tree fungus. She never married and when older lived with her sister in a house that is now the Haller-Gibboney Rock House Museum in Wytheville.[4]

It is noticeable that three women who worked as photographers in early twentieth-century Virginia—Beveridge, Gibboney, and Frances Benjamin Johnston—were all unmarried, which would suggest that marriage or family was a hindrance for a woman to making a livelihood in the field. Other women who made photographs were amateurs. With the introduction of roll-film field cameras, photography became accessible to people who were never going to get involved in chemical processing or elaborate camera set-ups. At first, because processing was not inexpensive, many if not most of the new practitioners were well-to-do. The Natural Bridge Photo Co. issued a photograph by Mrs. Jeannette M. Appleton, a Massachusetts photographer active 1890–91 who was of sufficient means to travel to further her art. A photograph of Monumental Church in Richmond is also credited to Appleton.

Sarah Landon Rives (1874–1957), sister of author Amelié Rives Troubetzkoy, had originally studied drawing and painting. Their home was Castle Hill in Albemarle County. About 1903 Landon, the name she used, "became interested in the camera," and made "studies of the thoroughbred animals on the home estates at Castle Hill, Virginia, as well as favorite views of local scenery, and informal portraits of personal friends." For the winter of 1904–05, Landon stayed in New York

Taxidermy still-life

Silver gelatin print, from glass negative, by Frances Gibboney, c. 1890–1900

The negative is inscribed at upper-left: "Fannie Gibboney, Tazewell, Va., Taxidermist." One presumes that the thirteen mounted birds and four mounted mammals are all examples of the photographer's work, as well as the painting on the easel at right. *Wytheville Museum*

and became "an assiduous worker at the Camera Club, where she has received the benefit of much oversight and encouragement from that sincere and brilliant artist, Alfred Stieglitz." Edward Steichen made a portrait of her, and in 1905–06, Rives's work was included in the first exhibition at Stieglitz's gallery "291." By the 1920s Rives was primarily an oil painter; she had built a darkroom at Castle Hill, but it is not known how seriously she continued to make photographs after leaving New York.[5]

These women all worked in the early 1900s; nonetheless for most of the century, a woman photographer was an exceptional case in most branches of profes-sional photography. It is only since perhaps 1970 that women have become more nearly represented among portrait photographers, journalists, and other kinds of professional photographers. Earlier in the century, the kind of photography that was most open to female participation was personal family pictures. As the pro-cessing of negatives and prints for customers became less of a boutique trade and more a mass-market industry, prices came down, more families made pictures for themselves, and more women became photographers. Personal photographs were a creative outlet for many kinds of people and especially, with the social limita-tions that existed, a means of visual expression for women.

Portrait of Amélie Rives Troubetzkoy
Photographic print, by Landon Rives, 9.6 x 7.7 in., c. 1905
The photographer, Landon, was Troubetzkoy's younger sister. Both lived at the family estate, Castle Hill, in Albemarle County. In 1905 Landon studied under Alfred Stieglitz at the Camera Club in New York. This portrait is reproduced in the 17 Oct. 1905 issue of *The Photographer*. The sisters traveled back and forth between New York and Virginia in this period; it is not known where the photograph was made. *Virginia Historical Society*

Portrait of Amélie Rives Troubetzkoy
Photographic print, probably by Landon Rives, 9.5 x 7.5 in., c. 1905–15
First, the subject is identified based on provenance and the fact that there is a companion portrait of her husband, Pierre Troubetzkoy. Second, the photograph is attributed to Landon Rives based on the fact that she took other portraits of her sister, the look of it is in keeping with her style, the print has the same thick paper and cold tones, and the intimacy of the pose suggests a trust rarely seen in the much-depicted Amélie. *Virginia Historical Society*

THE AMATEUR

As the number of photographers increased, the trade in photographic supplies evolved. In the nineteenth century a photographer might travel to New York or another large city to buy a half-year's supplies, or once a relationship was established, have the supplier ship the chemicals and other basic materials. When photographers began purchasing manufactured products like dry plates and photographic printing paper, a system of regional distributors and local sales outlets arose. By 1900 in cities like Richmond and Baltimore, companies that dealt in related products opened photographic supply departments. A new business venture was to offer services for developing film and making prints. Sometimes a processing service started as a sideline for an existing photography business and sometimes as a dedicated photo lab, but before World War II such labs in Virginia tended to be short-lived. After the war, retail stores appeared that sold cameras, film, and supplies, took in developing, and handled repairs. This became the camera shop business model. Photo labs found that by taking in work from a number of outlets, enough volume could be created to support machine-processing and achieve pricing advantages, and this became a parallel business model.

A survey of the camera shops in two communities can serve to illustrate photographic retail in the twentieth-century. In Alexandria, in 1942 Thrifty Photo Service offered 24-hour film developing and also sold some supplies. Thrifty had closed by 1950 when Henry's Camera Center on King Street began a long run. By 1960 the 700 block of King Street was a photographic center, offering Henry's, Bob's Camera Supply, and Duke Camera Shop. Henry's remained in business into the 1970s; by 1975 the location had become Fotoshop of Alexandria, and then by 1980 National Camera II. Bob's stayed open through 1980.

In Charlottesville, the first camera shop was the Camera Center, open by 1950 and at its long-time Main Street location by the mid-1950s. Cary's Camera opened in 1959 at the Barracks Road Shopping Center. The Camera Center was a small, packed shop, and Cary's catered to the suburban amateur. In the early 1970s, Cary's expanded into three drive-up kiosks under the name Snappy's. By 1985 the Snappy's outlets had been taken over by Colorcraft, a division of

Instruction book

Cover, *The Amateur Photographer*, 1887

The book by W. F. Carlton was subtitled, "A complete guide for beginners in the art-science of photography." Likely a photographic wholesaler enabled its customer, Sol. J. Binswanger, a Richmond dealer in photographic goods, to distribute copies bearing its imprint. *Virginia Historical Society*

Street advertisement

The painting on the wall of a Fredericksburg business was photographed by FSA photographer John Vachon in April 1938. *Library of Congress, Prints and Photographs Division, LC-USF34-008407-C*

Kodak. These kinds of stand-alone kiosks were undercut by the minilabs that became common in drug and other stores in the 1990s. In the mid-1970s Dicky's Darkroom, a black-and-white rental darkroom, operated for several years. Several chains came to Charlottesville in the 1980s: Kelly Camera briefly about 1981, a Richmond Camera outlet that primarily took in processing for the regional firm's lab, and Ritz Camera, a big chain, by 1985. Along with the latter two, the original two stores, the Camera Center and Cary's, kept abreast of change sufficiently to remain active into the late 1990s.[6]

THE ALBUM

The name "album" is from the Latin word for white. It originally referred to a (white) tablet on which names or edicts were written, then later to a book of names, of either attendees to an event or of autographs. An autograph being a personal representation, it is easy to see the evolution to portrait photographs.

Albums to hold cartes de visite were introduced around 1860, not long after the format appeared. Because of the Civil War and the hard times afterward, albums came to Virginia more slowly than other places in the U.S. and primarily at first to wealthier people. Postwar carte de visite albums would typically include a mix of family, including cousins, friends such as classmates, men who served in uniform, copies of portraits of men killed in the war, community leaders such as ministers, and commercially produced images of Confederate leaders. The pages had slots to hold the cards, and when the larger cabinet cards became popular around 1880, pages with bigger slots came out.

Whereas albumen paper was very thin, and prints were almost always supplied mounted, by 1905–10 photographic paper had become thicker and prints usually came unmounted. In addition, because there was no standard size of print, instead of prepared pockets albums used flat blank pages of thick paper on which prints were either glued or attached using photo corners. (One style that did come pre-sized was the postcard album, popular in the 1910s.) The period from about 1900 to 1930 was the great era of the photographic album. People took time to assemble and label them, and one presumes they spent time looking through the albums as well. They were often filled up over time, with the accumulation of images creating a chronological narrative, but not always—the flow of these volumes can be quite original.[7]

Camera shop interior
Silver gelatin print, c. 1935–44
The view of a camera shop was in a lot of unclaimed property dated 1944 from the Danville area. It is likely that the image was shot a few years earlier, in the 1930s, because behind the enlarger on the shelf at upper-right is an advertisement for the German company Agfa. After the U.S. entered the war in late 1941, Agfa products were removed from stores. *Library of Virginia Archives #31473*

Snapshot: Circus parade
Albumen print, by Charles W. Hunter, Jr., 3.4 x 3.7 in., c. 1895–96
View looking down on Richmond's Broad Street, where a crowd watches a circus parade make a turn. *Virginia Historical Society*

Album page: Ship dedication
Five silver gelatin prints, each about 3.2 x 3.2, on page 10 x 11.5 in., c. 1905
The page presents visual notes from a journey, probably by steamer, to Hampton Roads
and the dedication of a ship at Newport News Shipyard. *Virginia Historical Society*

Album page: Personal editing

Five silver gelatin prints on album page, each about 2.3 x 2.3 in., on page 6.5 x 9 in., 1905–06

Inscribed under each print is "Petersburg, Va. 1905." Other identified locations in the album are Amherst, Va., and Columbia, S.C. A woman wearing a light coat and dark hat appears in all but the lower-left photo. In three images, someone has deliberately obscured her face: it is marked out by pen in the upper-left and center photos, and marred in the upper-right photo by a small gouge. (At lower-right, the subject's face was already hidden by shadow.) Also obscured, by pencil marks, is the face of the adult in the lower-left photo, presumably female, based on the type of hat worn, and possibly the same "marked" woman. *Virginia Historical Society*

Album pages: Millboro, Va.
Three silver gelatin prints on left album page, two on right, images about 2 x 3 in., pages 5.5 x 7 in., 1915
Accompanying the album is a guide titled "Index of Kodak book of Sarah Powers Trapnell from about 1908 to 1916." In it these pages are described as: "Watermellon at Millboro. Henry was the porter do not know whose car, maybe Charlies. Katharine H. Land at right of last picture." *Virginia Historical Society*

Album page: 1918 display
Two silver gelatin prints, 2.5 x 4 in., on album page 7 x 10 in., 1918
Much of the album shows student life at Randolph-Macon Women's
College, Lynchburg, c. 1916–22. Inscribed under the first image
is: "The Flag we made–1918." The second image speaks for itself.
Virginia Historical Society

Album page: Jazz Age
Silver gelatin print, 4.2 x 2.3 in., c. 1920–30
A modern young woman sits on the steps of an old-fashioned house. *Virginia Historical Society*

Album pages: Winter scenes
2 photos on left page 2.2 x 3.2 in., one on right page 3.2 x 5.2 in., pages 5.5 x 7 in., c. 1920–30
Ice skating on the Mattaponi River, near Aylett, and a view of the fields at Burlington, King William County. *Virginia Historical Society*

Snapshot: Gobbler on a leash
Silver gelatin print, 3.1 x 5.4 in.,
c. 1920–30
View at football game, Virginia Polytechnic
University. *Virginia Historical Society*

Snapshot: Football
Silver gelatin print, 2.9 x 5.3 in.,
c. 1920–30
View at football game, Virginia Polytechnic
University. *Virginia Historical Society*

Snapshot: Student antics
Silver gelatin print, 3.2 x 5.4 in.,
c. 1920–30
View at campus of Virginia Polytechnic
University. *Virginia Historical Society*

Snapshot: Snow fun
Silver gelatin print, 2.9 x 5.2 in.,
c. 1920–30
View at campus of Virginia Polytechnic
University. *Virginia Historical Society*

Album pages: Beach vacation
Eight silver gelatin prints, 2.3 x 4.2 in., on pages 7 x 11 in., 1925
Inscribed at the top of each page is: "Virginia Beach, July 4th, 1925." On the left page, the sign in the top-right image reads "O'Keefe's Casino." On the right page, the lighthouses in the lower-left image are at Cape Henry. The album is dated 1924–25 and belonged to Ruth E. Saffer of Richmond. *Virginia Historical Society*

PORTRAIT VARIETIES

The portrait was photography's first big subject and has never ceased to be important to its practice. Virginia in the twentieth century saw great variety in portraits. The formal studio portrait continued (and continues) to be produced but without as central a position as it once had. People approach sitting for a portrait in many ways and for varying reasons. Some feel comfortable in a setting outside their normal path and others prefer a familiar place.

1890s snapshot
Albumen print, by Charles W. Hunter, Jr., 3.4 x 3.7 in., c. 1895–96
In the taking, developing, and printing, this print took considerably more effort than a modern photograph. Nevertheless the result is recognizably a snapshot, of the sort made daily by the millions today. Glimpsed beyond the subject is the Lee monument in Richmond. *Virginia Historical Society*

Babe Ruth
Glass negative, by Walter W. Foster, 8 x 10 in., 1921
Ruth's sister, said to have been his only kin, lived in Richmond. The portrait was likely made during an off-season visit, but not known is whether it was before or after the 1921 season, Ruth's second with the New York Yankees and one of his best. *Virginia Historical Society*

Children, 1900
Cyanotype, probably by Frances Benjamin Johnston,
6.4 x 7.4 in., 1900
The four children seated in front of a backdrop
attended Whittier School, an elementary school
operated by Hampton Institute, and likely were
photographed by Johnston in her coverage of the
school. *Hampton University Archives*

Cook family
Black and white glass negative, by De Lancey W. Gill,
7 x 9 in., 1899
Gill photographed the family of George Mayor Cook and
Theodora Octavia Cook at the Pamunkey Reservation,
King William County, in Oct. 1899, as part of a
survey of American Indians collected by the Bureau
of American Ethnology. *National Anthropological
Archives, Smithsonian Institution*

Portrait of Lucille Turner
Silver gelatin print, c. 1928–40
Lucille Turner was apparently a stage name that the performer used when she appeared on WRVA radio. *Library of Virginia, WRVA Radio Collection*

Lucille Turner as Aunt Sarah
Silver gelatin print, c. 1928–40
The period that is most likely for her blackface performance on radio would have been at the end of the 1920s and the early 1930s, following the success of the nationally syndicated *Amos 'n' Andy* show. *Library of Virginia, WRVA Radio Collection*

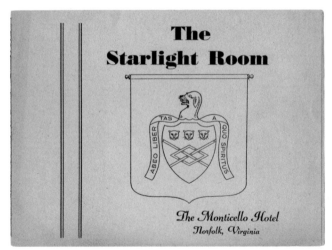

Radio performer

Silver gelatin print on postcard, 5 x 3 in., 1942

Typed on the reverse is "Mystery Melody," and inscribed is "Willie Coleman," presumably the autograph of the subject. The card was sent to a Mrs. Fix in Fordwick, Va., postmarked Harrisonburg, 1942, and was likely the response by radio station WSVA to a contest submission. *Virginia Historical Society*

Memento

Silver gelatin print, 4.7 x 6.5 in., c. 1940–50

At some of the clubs where people went to dance and socialize, a photographer worked the room offering patrons a keepsake. Once the convivial moment was captured, the film was processed quickly and a print in a folder was delivered to the subjects before they left. This couple posed at the Starlight Room, at the Monticello Hotel in Norfolk. *Virginia Historical Society*

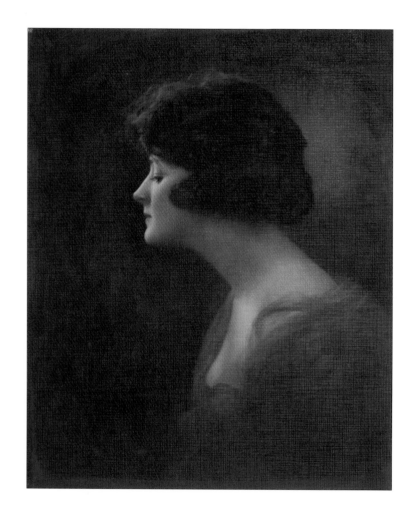

Civilian defense
Silver gelatin print, c. 1942–45
The truck driver was a member of the Volunteer Service Motor Corps, a group organized during World War II as part of the Office of Civilian Defense in Richmond. *Virginia Historical Society*

As if painted
Photographic print, hand-colored, 10.1 x 8 in., c. 1920–1925
A photographic print on paper with a canvas-like texture was hand-colored to resemble an oil painting. The subject is Maria L. Tucker, probably related to the Bird or Randolph families.
Virginia Historical Society

"Mike"

Two gelatin silver prints, in leather display folder, images 9.1 x 7.2 in., 1944

"Mike" was a Doberman-Pinscher whose owners presented him to the U.S. Marine Corps for K-9 duty in June 1944. "Mike" was assigned to handler Private Edward Garland Bernard, of Portsmouth. The pair trained together in the U.S. and were sent to the Pacific theater. On 19 Mar. 1945, "Mike" was killed by enemy mortar fire on Iwo Jima. *Virginia Historical Society*

Confederate veteran

Two silver gelatin prints, mounted on pages, each 4.4 x 6.2 in., by Norfolk Newspapers, Inc., 1951

The photographs are two of the eighteen in an album titled "Last Reunion of Confederate Veterans, Norfolk, Virginia 1951." Left, a veteran is surrounded by well-wishers; right, workers prepare for one of the events. *Virginia Historical Society*

CONCLUSION

This study leaves off at about the two-thirds mark of the twentieth century. By that time photography was a big part of daily American life, especially through broadcast television. Virginia was no different from the rest of the country. Only a minority held out from the media-influenced lifestyle. People saw photographs in newspapers, magazines, movies, advertising, and packaging.

Because film and television were so influential, what before had been known as photography became "still photography." Through the twentieth century the annual volume of stills rose steadily. Color slide film helped build the popularity of photography in the 1940s and 1950s, and the spread of the 35mm camera, especially accelerated with the single-lens reflex in the 1960s, expanded the number of skilled picture-takers. Advertising and journalism flourished. Automated photography found many applications. New kinds of amateur cameras were introduced, and photo-finishing became quicker and easier. In the 1960s, color photography moved past black-and-white.

From the beginning of the century to 1970, the number of Virginia residents who were capable of making a photograph grew by a very large factor. In 1900, when the population was about two million, the U.S. Census counted about 250 professional photographers in the state. Including amateurs the total in 1900 might have been about 2,000 Virginia photographers. By 1970, when the state population was 4.7 million, the number of capable photographers was probably more in the range of 200,000. These numbers are far from precise, but their suggestion of a one-hundred fold increase from 1900 to 1970

Road to Martinsville.

Road to Martinsville
Silver gelatin print, by Harry Bagby, 8.9 x 7.1 in., c. 1930–40
Virginia Historical Society

does capture the scale of the growth in photography. If all of the photographs ever taken in Virginia are taken as a group, the "median photograph" can be defined as the one that was taken after half of them and before half of them. In 2008, the median photograph was probably made about 1978. So much work was produced in the late twentieth century, of such variety, that the idea of trying to survey it is daunting, to say nothing of trying to gather it. That is the main reason this work stops when it does.

The digital world has brought new perspectives. "In this day of DVDs, HD, and Blue-Ray media," states a 2008 website comment, "there is nothing that replaces the warmth of a black and white photo to stir the memories of the past."[1] Digital photography has displaced analog photography because the images are instant, easier to handle, and useful in more ways. The same source image can be displayed on a computer, distributed on a website, published in a book, edited into a movie, placed in a slide show, and printed and framed. That's handy. Such versatility brings photography closer to being a means for recording expression like writing.

In 2000, Virginia's population had increased to 7 million. Today, if every citizen capable of pointing and clicking a digital camera or camera-equipped phone were counted as a photographer, there would be in the neighborhood of 4 million Virginia photographers.

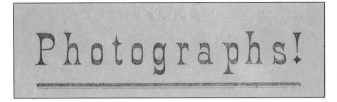

NOTES

CHAPTER ONE: EARLY PHOTOGRAPHY IN VIRGINIA

1. Helmut Gernsheim and Alison Gernsheim, *The History of Photography* (New York, 1969), pp. 17–29.

2. See Lucia C. Stanton, "Jefferson and the Amusements of Science," *Antiques* 144 (July 1993): 92–99. See also "Camera Obscura" at www.monticello.org.

3. List of "Mathematical Apparatus," Massachusetts Historical Society, cited in Stanton, "Jefferson and the Amusements of Science," p. 97.

4. Thomas Jefferson to David Rittenhouse, 6 Sept. 1793 (Historical Society of Pennsylvania), cited in Stanton, "Jefferson and the Amusements of Science," p. 97.

5. See "Camera Obscura," http://explorer.monticello.org/text/index.php?id=76&type=4 (accessed 13 Apr. 2007).

6. Ellen G. Miles, *Saint-Mémin and the Neoclassical Profile Portrait in America* (Washington, D.C., 1994), pp. 39–45, 163–65. Saint-Mémin came to Richmond from Philadelphia and left to Washington and Baltimore.

7. Charles Balthazar Julien Fevret de Saint-Mémin, Account, Richmond, 31 May 1808, with Dr. Charles Everett, Virginia Historical Society (hereafter cited as VHS).

8. "Saint Mémin," *Appleton's Cyclopedia of American Biography* (6 vols.; NewYork, 1888), 1:372.

9. Donald Fleming, *John William Draper and the Religion of Science* (Philadelphia, 1950), pp. 10, 8. Fleming's work is the source for biographical information otherwise not cited, pp. 9–19.

10. Ibid., pp. 15–17.

11. John William Draper, *Scientific Memoirs: Being Experimental Contributions to a Knowledge of Radiant Energy* (1878; New York, 1973), pp. 197–203. One of the chapters is called "An Account of Some Experiments on the Light of the Sun, Made in the South of Virginia."

12. John William Draper to Marcus A. Root, 18 Mar. 1863, rough draft marked "private," Draper Papers, Library of Congress (hereafter cited as LC), cited in Howard R. McManus, "It Was I Who Took The First," *The Daguerrean Annual 1996*, pp. 70–100, quotation on p. 74.

13. J. W. Draper, "Who Made the First Photographic Portrait," *American Journal of Photography and the Allied Arts & Sciences*, n.s., 1 (1859–60): 4, cited in Fleming, *John William Draper*, p. 17.

14. Draper, "First Portrait," p. 3, in Fleming, *John William Draper*, p. 16.

15. Ibid.

16. Draper, "First Portrait," p. 4, in ibid., p. 17; Gernsheim and Gernsheim, *History of Photography*, pp. 52–56, 63–69.

17. Prof. S. F. B. Morse, "The Daguerreotipe," 9 Mar. 1839, letter to the editor, *New York Observer*, 20 Apr. 1839, in *The Farmer's Register* (Petersburg, Va.) 7:9 (May 1839): 258.

18. The argument that Draper was indeed the first to make a photographic portrait in America is made by Howard R. McManus (McManus, "It Was I Who Took The First," pp. 70–100). From the earliest period of the portrait, there are accounts of daguerreotypers using glass containers of blue water to filter the light during exposure. The purpose was to reduce the discomfort of the sitter in the glare of the bright light during the long exposure. This technique touched on two areas of Draper's scientific investigation: first, the study of absorption of spectrum by colored solutions, and second, the particular sensitivity of silver salts to blue light. There should be little doubt that this technique was based on Draper's experiments and teaching. Those cited in early accounts as using the blue water filters, however, were Alexander S. Wolcott and John Johnson, also working in New York, later Draper's rivals in the controversy McManus writes about. One concludes that in the earliest period there must have been an atmosphere of cooperation before things became more competitive.

19. *Washington Globe*, 7 Mar. 1840, cited in Clifford Krainik, "National Vision, Local Enterprise, John Plumbe, Jr., and the Advent of Photography in Washington, D.C.," *Washington History* (fall/winter 1997–98): 5, 12–13, 92. Krainik suggests the daguerreotypist was likely a Mr. Sexias (possibly a French student of Daguerre), who presented a similar exhibition in Baltimore the following month.

20. *Richmond Whig* (semiweekly), 23 July 1841. Italics in original. The name featured in the ad is E. Daws, Jr., but that surname may have been a miscopy of Davis, and the daguerreotypist may have continued south. In May 1842 a Dr. Davis was in Halifax, N.C., at William Pride's hotel offering daguerreotypes for $6.00 (*Roanoke Advocate and States Rights Banner* [Halifax], 2, 11 May 1842, cited in Stephen E. Massengill, *Photographers in North Carolina, The First Century, 1842–1941* [Raleigh, 2004], p. 18).

21. *Richmond Enquirer* (semi-weekly), 12 Oct. 1841.

22. Ibid.

23. *Richmond Compiler*, 3 Dec. 1841. The ad began 2 Dec. and ran through 31 Dec.

24. Ibid., 23 Mar. 1843; *Petersburg Republican*, 26 May 1843.

25. *Norfolk American Beacon*, 28 Oct. 1843.

26. *Lynchburg Virginian*, 2 Sept. 1844.

27. In *Craig's Daguerrean Register*, a biographical compendium, half the daguerreotypists with a Virginia connection were situated in Richmond. In part this ratio may be because of the greater availability of documentation, especially newspapers, for that city.

28. The causes of this fluidity may have been several: the economic instability of a non-essential product; rural versus urban settlement patterns; the daguerreotypers' exposure to mercury vapor; or the nature of the practice as a service in which personality mattered greatly. (There is a similar unrootedness to certain modern jobs too, such as cooks, carpenters, or hairdressers.)

29. "Henry Bryant," *Craig's Daguerrean Registry*, at www.daguerreotype.com. In the early 1850s Henry Bryant was reported to be back in Hartford as a painter.

30. *Norfolk American Beacon*, 18 Apr., 13 July 1845. Jewelers were similar to daguerreotypists in offering precious objects made of silver, often treated by "galvanic" methods and similarly appealing to female consumers. In Petersburg in November 1843, an advertisement offered "Colored Daguerreotype Miniatures, by the Parisian process, taken in the room over Mr. Lumsden's Jewelry store." The daguerreotyper is not named, which suggests it was Lumsden who was behind the venture (*Petersburg Republican*, 14 Nov. 1843).

31. *Ball's Splendid Mammoth Pictorial Tour of the United States* (Cincinnati, 1855), pp. 7–8; reprinted in *J. P. Ball, Daguerrean and Studio Photographer*, ed. Deborah Willis, (New York, 1993), pp. 249–50. If any of Ball's Richmond daguerreotypes are extant, they are not known.

32. *Richmond Times and Compiler*, 3 Jan. 1846; *Richmond Daily Republican*, 28 Oct. 1846. Zachrisson had a competitor, S. E. Dove, who advertised "To Daguerreotypists, Distilled Mercury and Chloride of Gold."

33. *Lynchburg Virginian*, 28 May 1846; *Charlottesville Virginian Advocate*, 16 Oct. 1847; *Charlottesville Jeffersonian*, cited in *Photographic Art Journal* 5 (Jan. 1853): 64; *Fredericksburg Virginia Herald*, 8 July 1852.

34. *Thomson's Mercantile and Professional Directory, 1851–52* (Baltimore, 1851); *Alexandria Gazette*, 4 June, 20 Dec. 1853, and 2 Aug. 1855.

35. Gernsheim and Gernsheim, *History of Photography*, p. 128; "Artists and Daguerreotypists from the United States Census of 1850," *The Daguerrean Annual 1993*, p. 116. There were also fifteen artists in 1850 in Virginia, and in that Census "some daguerreotypists were listed as 'artist.'"

36. *Norfolk City Directory*, 1851–52, p. 1. John Plumbe, Jr., earlier built the most extensive American chain of daguerreotype galleries, but it had fallen apart by 1848.

37. "Obituary" by "A Relative," Norfolk, *The Norfolk Landmark*, 23 Sept 1875; William S. Forrest, *Historical and Descriptive Sketches of Norfolk and Vicinity* (Philadelphia, 1853), pp. 395–98, quotation on p. 397. The online *Craig's Daguerrean Registry* (www.daguerreotype.com) reports that in February 1844 Whitehurst opened a gallery in Charleston, S.C., with a partner named Manning. Forrest placed a portion of his account about Whitehurst in quotation marks, suggesting he was copying a newspaper article, which in turn sounds as if it was published in Baltimore and Whitehurst himself was the primary source.

38. Forrest, *Historical and Descriptive Sketches of Norfolk*, p. 397; *Richmond Times*, 10 June 1845; *Norfolk American Beacon*, 10 Sept. 1845. Because temporary engagements were usually advertised by transient means such as handbills, or by one- or two-day newspaper items, tracking them can be difficult. An 1845 Norfolk advertisement for "Daguerreotype Portraits" gave a location that sounds much like the one for Whitehurst mentioned in the 1875 obituary: "at the corner of Main and Talbo[t] Streets up Stairs, next door to J. M. Freeman, Jeweller." The name in the ad is not Whitehurst's, however, but F. W. Burwell, who appears in other ads as a Norfolk watchmaker. Likely these rooms were suited for daguerreotyping, and Whitehurst and Burwell each rented them temporarily at different times (*Norfolk American Beacon*, 18 Apr. 1845).

39. *Richmond Daily Republican*, 23 Aug. 1848; *Norfolk Southern Argus*, 15 Jan., 19 Feb. 1848. Norfolk does not seem to have been as active a town for daguerreotypes as Richmond, judging from the limited number of advertisements found for them (in the newspapers that are available). Whitehurst's Richmond gallery at 77 Main was between 14th and 15th streets, a block west of Shockoe Creek and in a rather mixed section of immigrants and their shops, tobacco factories, iron foundries, the slave trading houses a block away, and First Market on the other side of the creek. It was a less elevated location than the galleries up the hill in the printing and newspaper district.

40. *Petersburg Daily Republican*, 10 Nov. 1848; *Lynchburg Virginian*, 7 Aug., 6 Nov., and 11 Dec. 1848.

41. *Lynchburg Virginian*, 14 May 1849.

42. *Petersburg Republican*, 1 Jan. 1850; *Richmond Daily Republican*, 24 Aug. 1850. If Whitehurst's five galleries were open 300 days a year and averaged ten portraits a day apiece, that would have been an annual rate of 15,000 likenesses a year; his claim does not seem much out of line.

43. *Richmond Daily Republican*, 23 Aug. 1848; *Photographic Art Journal* 1 (Mar. 1851): 189–90; 2 (Sept. 1851): 154; and 6 (Sept. 1853): 193.

44. Massengill, "Photographers in North Carolina, 1842–1941," pp. 19–20, 211. Harrison was Whitehurst's cousin.

45. *Photographic Art Journal* 2 (Sept. 1851): 189; *Petersburg Daily Express*, 14 May 1852; *Lynchburg Virginian*, 14 June 1852, 28 Apr. 1853.

46. *Norfolk American Beacon*, 10 Sept. 1845; *Petersburg Daily Republican*, 10 Nov. 1848; *Lynchburg Virginian*, 6 Nov. 1848, 14 May 1849.

47. *Richmond Daily Republican*, 14 Oct. 1848; *Lynchburg Virginian*, 14 May 1849; *Petersburg Republican*, 1 Jan. 1850.

48. *Petersburg Republican*, 1 Jan. 1850. No patent appears to have been awarded to Whitehurst for this device.

49. *Richmond Daily Republican*, 23 Aug. 1850; *Lynchburg Virginian*, 19 Aug. 1852; *Petersburg Daily Express*, 17 Aug. 1853; *Richmond Whig*, 21 Jan. 1853.

50. *Petersburg Daily Express*, 17 Aug. 1853; *Richmond Whig*, 21 Jan. 1853; *Norfolk Southern Argus*, 5 Jan. 1856.

51. *Petersburg Daily Express*, 17 Aug. 1853.

52. *Norfolk Landmark*, 23 Sept. 1875.

53. Massengill, "Photographers in North Carolina, 1842–1941," p. 211; *Petersburg Daily Express*, 24 Apr. 1856; *Norfolk Southern Argus*, 12 June 1856, 16 Mar. and 25 Nov. 1857; *Norfolk City Directory*, 1859; *Richmond Daily Dispatch*, 4 Feb. 1857; *Richmond City Directory*, 1859; and *Norfolk Landmark*, 23 Sept. 1875. For a period in the nineteenth century, guano, manure from sea birds, was harvested from far-flung islands for fertilizer.

54. On Plumbe, the primary account is Krainik, "National Vision, Local Enterprise," pp. 4–27. Not only did Pratt and Plumbe have a British background in common, Plumbe had worked as a civil engineer in the field at eighteen, as did Pratt (ibid., p. 7).

55. A Norfolk and a Petersburg location are noted, neither with a street address, in an 1846 advertisement headed "Plumbe National Daguerrean Gallery and Photographic Depots" (*Norfolk American Beacon*, 12 May 1846). C. S. Middlebrook was an operator at Plumbe's Gallery, Petersburg, located in Mechanic's Hall, North Sycamore and West Tabb Sts. In April 1847 Middlebrook announced that he "intends moving to Richmond." In Nov. 1848, Mr. Broadbent was "engaged for a few days, at Mr. Middlebrook's room" (*Petersburg Republican*, 2 Apr. 1847, 8 Nov. 1848; *Craig's Daguerrean Registry*).

56. *Scientific American*, 11 Sept. 1845; "Card of National Publishing Company," *The Plumbeian*, 6 Jan. 1847. In the standard presentation of a daguerreotype in a case, over the plate is a mat, a decorative window that hides the edges of the plate and separates the surfaces of the plate and the cover glass. Notably, in looking at the type of mat seen in Plumbe and in early Pratt daguerreotypes, there is a correlation, for both employ similar simple window shapes and the same textured gilt surface (for Plumbe examples, see Krainik, "National Vision, Local Enterprise," pp. 10, 15). Like many of Plumbe's branches when his chain dissolved, the New York City distribution center, presumably the source for those mats, may have continued to provide them under new management. Another Alexandria connection is through John S. Grubb, one of the witnesses for Pratt's patent application. In 1850–52 he worked at Pratt's gallery in Richmond. Inscribed on the case of a pair of daguerreotypes of James

Sharples's portraits of George and Martha Washington is: "Daguerreotyped from the Arlington pictures by John S. Grubb, Alex. Va. Sept. 1849" (*Semi-Annual Catalogued Auction of Antiques, Americana, and Decorative Arts, June 24 & 25, 2005*, Green Valley Auctions, Mt. Crawford, Va.).

57. Richmond City Personal Property Tax Records, 1846–50, Library of Virginia (hereafter cited as LVA); *Richmond Daily Republican*, 23 Aug. 1848.

58. Thomas Dimmock, *Century Magazine*, June 1895, p. 315. The account concludes, "Three weeks later he was dead in Baltimore." One of the daguerreotypes from this session is held at Columbia University Libraries, Special Collections. See http://www.columbia.edu/acis/textarchive/rare/77.html (accessed 7 Jan. 2008).

59. *Richmond Daily Republican*, 23 Aug. 1848; *Richmond Whig*, 31 May 1849, 21 Dec. 1850; *Photographic Art Journal* 1 (Mar. 1851): 190. The Langenheim brothers of Philadelphia had purchased the rights for Talbot's process in May 1849 but were able to sell almost no licenses. (According to the Gernsheims, the Langenheims sold none at all, but Pratt certainly seems to have struck a deal.) The Langenheims, unable to make their contracted payments to Talbot for the rights, offered to trade him rights to their albumen-on-glass process—the hyalotype—but Talbot declined, and the Langenheims' business went into bankruptcy (Gernsheim and Gernsheim, *History of Photography*, pp. 186–87).

60. *Richmond Whig*, 18 Feb. 1851. "The proceeds of the first day," 18 Feb. 1851, were "devoted to the Richmond Poor, under the auspices of the ladies" of the Union Benevolent Society. Mary Wingfield Scott states that Pratt designed two houses on North 5th Street in Richmond. Just north of 621 N. 5th St. "formerly stood [in 1950] a pair of houses built in 1848 by William A. Pratt, who lived in one of them before he built the Castle on Gamble's Hill. Judging by that edifice and his Daguerrian Gallery called 'At the Sign of the Gothic Window,' this vanished 'Cottage ornée,' as he called it, would probably have been a valuable item in the study of Richmond architecture" (Mary Wingfield Scott, *Old Richmond Neighborhoods* [Richmond, 1950], p. 280).

61. *Elliot & Nye's Virginia Directory, and Business Register* (Richmond, 1852); W. A. Pratt, letter, in *Photographic Art Journal* 1 (Mar. 1851): 190.

62. W. A. Pratt, letter, 10 Oct. 1851, in *Photographic Art Journal* 2 (Oct. 1851): 235–36.

63. *The Loom*, 29 May 1846. Plumbe was not the first to mount groups of daguerreotypes together, but he did it in a big way and his subjects were important. The Grand National Fair was initiated by members of Congress and organized as an expression of nationalist zeal (and probably a little bit of Whig party platform). *The Loom* was a newspaper published in Washington, D.C. for the duration of the National Fair.

64. *Richmond Daily Republican*, 23 Aug. 1848; *Richmond Whig*, 10 Feb. 1852. In the 1848 ad, Pratt's list of subjects on display includes "U. S. Senate of 1846"; one wonders if he acquired any of the images that Plumbe had shown at the National Fair in May 1846.
It is likely that Pratt, with his canal engineer experience, created another framed set of daguerreotypes that predated these sets, titled "Employees and Directors of the James River and Kanawha Company." This piece, apparently a commemoration of his tenure, was produced for James Carrington Cabell, president of the canal until his ouster on 12 February 1846. The twenty-six plates arrived framed at VHS in the 1920s, but only the plates were saved and the rest discarded.

65. *Photographic Art Journal* 1 (Mar. 1851): 189; 2 (Sept. 1851): 154; Gernsheim and Gernsheim, *History of Photography*, p. 128. The daguerreotypers were Brady, Lawrence, the Mead brothers, Pratt, the Roots, Whitehurst, and Babbit.

66. W. A. Pratt letter, 10 Oct. 1851, in *Photographic Art Journal* 2 (Oct. 1851): 236; *Richmond Whig*, 30 Jan. 1852; *Virginia State Directory*, 1852.

67. *Richmond Whig*, 20 Jan. 1852.

68. Ibid., 10 Feb. 1852.

69. Ibid., 30 Mar. 1852. The actual dimensions of the framed work are 20 x 23 inches, less than four square feet. Most of the House members are laid out alphabetically, but on the bottom row nine portraits appear after William B. Zinn, likely the late sitters. A delegate from Clarke County, John W. Luke, won the drawing and took home the frame.

70. Naturally a structure such as Pratt's Castle would be very costly, and to defray the debts incurred Pratt attempted to raise funds by offering a house he owned in a sweepstakes. Chances were being offered through the gallery in April 1855 (*Richmond Dispatch*, 16 Apr. 1855).

71. Under an agreement to cover his expenses, before delivery Pratt exhibited "The School of Athens" in London and at various sites in the U.S., including the Mechanic's Institute Fair, Richmond, in Oct.-Nov. 1856. At the university the large canvas was hung in the auditorium of the Rotunda Annex. When it was lost in the 1895 Rotunda fire, a new copy was obtained that is extant in the auditorium of Old Cabell Hall. Remaining from Pratt's university tenure are the infirmary, opened Oct. 1858, at the south end of the east range, and a plan of the university grounds c. 1858. The gatekeeper's lodge, a residence built by Pratt c. 1856, was demolished in 1937 for Alderman Library. His obituary (uncited photocopy from Waynesboro Public Library files) states that he became, using his dual-citizenship with Britain, a gunrunner during the Civil War. He remained at the university until 1865, and that year also sold Pratt's Castle. He purchased an estate near Waynesboro, Walnut Grove, and practiced architecture there until his death in 1879.

72. *Richmond Dispatch*, 21 Nov., 20 Dec 1856; *Richmond Semi-Weekly Examiner*, 6 Nov. 1857.

73. Gernsheim and Gernsheim, *History of Photography*, pp. 194–97.

74. The glass negatives most suitable for ambrotypes were "thin," meaning more transparent and less dense, which the photographer achieved by leaning toward underexposure and by reduced development.

75. *Richmond Dispatch*, 14 Apr. 1855; *Alexandria Gazette*, 2 Aug. 1855; William Welling, *Photography in America, The Formative Years* (New York, 1978), p. 111.

76. *Richmond Dispatch*, 14 Apr. 1855.

77. *Lynchburg Virginian*, 29 Aug. 1855; *Richmond Dispatch*, 9 Jan. 1856.

78. *Richmond Dispatch*, 13 Dec. 1855.

79. Ibid., 18 Oct., 20 Nov., 13 Dec. 1855.

80. Laurie A. Baty, ". . . and Simons." Montgomery Pike Simons of Philadelphia (c. 1816–1877)," *The Daguerreian Annual 1993*, pp. 183–200; *Craig's Daguerrean Registry*; *Photographic Art Journal* 4 (Nov. 1852): 319–22. See Joe Strubel, "The Passions Series Daguerreotypes: Valentine's Project to Know Himself," *The Daguerrean Annual 2001*, pp. 98–108. In 1853 Simons prepared "A Short Dissertation on the Daguerrean Art," in which he argued provocatively that "The sun, although an indispensable agent, has no more to do with making a daguerreotype that it has to do with writing a book" (*Photographic Art Journal* 5 [Jan. 1853]: 66).

81. Cited in Welling, *Photography in America*, p. 111.

82. *Richmond Dispatch*, 29 Dec. 1855 (lower-right of advertisement: de 20).

83. Ibid., 21 Dec. 1855.

84. Ibid., 22 Dec. 1855.

85. Ibid., 11 Jan. 1856 (lower-left of advertisement: de 31).

86. Ibid., 8 Jan. 1856; Welling, *Photography in America*, p. 118.

87. *Richmond Dispatch*, 9 Jan. 1856.

88. Ibid., 10 Jan. 1856.

89. Ibid., 12 Jan. 1856.

90. Ibid., 14 Jan. 1856.

91. Ibid., 15 Jan. 1856.

92. Welling, *Photography in America*, p. 118. Simons had one more sally for "The Patent

Right Man." Although he had been critical of one of Gibbs's notices, declared Simons, "to find fault with him for it, would be equivalent to finding fault with a hog for grunting, or an ass for braying. It is natural for them" (*Richmond Daily Dispatch*, 26 Jan. 1856).

93. *Lynchburg Virginian*, 17 Apr., 20 June, 10 Oct. 1856; *Norfolk Southern Argus*, 6 Jan. 1857; *Richmond Daily Dispatch*, 11 Dec. 1856.

94. Floyd Rinhart, Marion Rinhart, and Robert W. Wagner, *The American Tintype* (Columbus, Ohio, 1999), pp. 9–26. Hamilton Smith and Peter Neff, Jr., were primarily responsible for the melainotype; and Victor Griswold for the ferrotype.

95. *Petersburg Daily Express*, 3 Apr. 1855, 24 Apr. 1856, 4 Aug. 1857, 23 Feb. 1858.

Chapter Two: Civil War

1. Keith F. Davis, "'A Terrible Distinctness,' Photography of the Civil War Era," in *Photography in Nineteenth-Century America*, ed. Martha A. Sandweiss (New York, 1991), p. 135.

2. Gernsheim and Gernsheim, *History of Photography*, pp. 141–44.

3. *Humphrey's Journal*, 1 Oct. 1862, p. 123. The term used today for carte de visite, "CDV," is probably of more recent coinage and likely originated among collectors. One advantage of the CDV was efficiency in production: a number of images would fit on one 8 x 10 glass-plate negative and thus could be developed and then printed at the same time. Cameras were equipped with lens boards holding four or six lenses, each to expose a separate section of the plate, to make CDV negatives. By uncovering one lens at a time, different images could be assembled on the plate, or a negative could include multiples of the same image to facilitate mass production for subjects such as a hero's portrait.

4. *Richmond Whig*, 18 Jan. 1859. A typical publicity effort for a traveling show in this period would have the top performer visit newspaper offices and be introduced to the editors, who thereby flattered would see fit to mention the performance in their columns. The newspaper does not describe the photograph as a carte de visite, but the term was not yet a familiar one and no alternative format is more likely, given the date and its European origin.

5. Gernsheim and Gernsheim, *History of Photography*, pp. 294–95, 253–62; *Norfolk Southern Argus*, 4 May 1860; *Williamsburg Weekly Gazette and Eastern Virginia Advertiser*, 13 Feb. 1860; *Richmond Enquirer*, 30 July 1861. Stereo daguerreotypes by M. P. Simons of Richmond are held at the Valentine-Richmond History Center and at VHS.

6. *Alexandria Gazette*, 9 May 1860. Once a term enters popular culture, it is often adopted as a name for things similar to but not quite the same as the original thing the term referred to. For instance, another kind of print called an "Imperial" that emerged after the Civil War was a sun-powered photographic enlargement enhanced with India ink or other media. Both versions of the Imperial were also called "Life Size" portraits.

7. *American Journal of Photography* (hereafter cited as *AJP*), new ser., 1 May 1861, p. 367; new ser., 1 Sept. 1861, p. 168.

8. *Humphrey's Journal*, 15 Feb. 1862, p. 319; Coleman Sellers, letter of 23 Mar. 1862, *British Journal of Photography*, 15 Apr. 1862, p. 157, cited in Davis, "A Terrible Distinctness," p. 146. With the South's limited metal fabrication facilities, and the need for military production, even making small iron plates enameled in black for tintypes was a challenge for the Confederacy. See Rinhart, Rinhart, and Wagner, *The American Tintype*.

9. *Richmond Daily Dispatch*, 16 Feb., 14 Mar. 1863; *Richmond City Directory*, 1860.

10. *Richmond City Directory*, 1859, 1860; *Richmond Daily Dispatch*, 1 Nov. 1860, 21 Feb. 1861.

11. *Richmond Daily Republican*, 28 Oct. 1846; Margaret Vannerson, *The Family History*, (Redwood, Calif., 1971), pp. 18–19; Brooks Johnson, "Mr. J. Vannerson . . .

remarkably successful in the matter of likenesses," in *Chrysler Museum Journal* 1 (1994): 15–25; *Petersburg Daily Express*, 4 Aug. 1857.

12. *Directory for the City of Richmond for 1859*; *Second Annual Directory for the City of Richmond 1860*; *Richmond Daily Dispatch*, 3, 21, 23 Nov., 18 Dec. 1860. In the 1859 directory, J. Thomas Smith was at 215 Main Street. His advertisement promised "Genuine Double Glass Ambrotypes" at Corinthian Hall and claimed "Lowest Prices Ever Known." Vannerson was not a discount portraitist, and the conflicting instincts over price may have been a reason that the partnership was short-lived.

13. In 1853 Minnis & Watson opened "newly and neatly fitted up rooms" at 146 Main St., Richmond (*Richmond Morning Mail*, 21 May 1853). Then in 1854 Minnis opened a branch in Lynchburg and ran it for a few years before selling it in 1856 to his operator there, N. S. Tanner, who in 1860 remained in business (*Richmond Daily Dispatch*, 14 Feb. 1861).

14. *Fredericksburg Virginia Herald*, 24 Mar 1860. On Routzahn, see Ben Ritter, "The Widow's Favorite," *Civil War Times Illustrated* (hereafter cited as *CWTI*) 17 (Feb. 1979): 36–39.

15. *Alexandria Local News*, 28 Jan., 22 Jan. 1862.

16. Ibid., 15 Jan. 1862. The *Local News* was a Union paper that in October 1861 took over the press of the *Alexandria Gazette*.

17. *Alexandria Gazette*, 15 Feb. 1861. VHS has an imprinted "Woolf, Alexandria" carte de visite that has a likely date of 1864 or 1865 (based on the inscription on the reverse).

18. Alexandria *Local News*, 23 Oct. 1861; *Alexandria Gazette*, 12 June 1862; Josephine Cobb, "Photographers of the Civil War," *Military Affairs* 26 (autumn 1962): 132, 127–35. Among the fourteen or so photographers given permits by the provost marshal to work in Alexandria were D. Hass (1862–65), Peter Mc Adams (1862–65), G. W. Rosebery (1863–65), and August & J. C. Opperman (1862–65). Other permits were for specific local facilities: A. Stacy at Fort Ramsey (1862–65), Harry Clarke at Round House (1865), Frank Harman (or Herman) at Fort Seminary (1863), and John Jones at Camp Convalescent (1863) (Ross J. Kelbaugh, *Directory of Civil War Photographers, Vol. One* [Baltimore, 1990], pp. 87–101).

19. Seller's letter of 25 May 1862, *British Journal of Photography* 9, 16 June 1862, cited in Davis, "A Terrible Distinction," p. 239.

20. *New York Tribune*, 20 Aug. 1862, in Cobb, "Photographers of the Civil War," p. 128. Among permit recipients in northern Virginia were William Maul in Arlington (1864), Frederick Gein in Fairfax (1863), L. A. Crump at Falls Church (1862–63), Cross & Pierang at Fort Lyon (1863–65), and D. G. Alexander at Vienna (1864). Kelbaugh, *Directory of Civil War Photographers, Vol. One*, pp. 87–101.

21. Cobb, "Photographers of the Civil War," pp. 131–32; Kelbaugh, *Directory of Civil War Photographers, Vol. One*, pp. 87–101; Frederic E. Ray, "The Photographers of the War," in *Shadows of the Storm*, Vol. 1 of *The Image of War 1861–1865* (Garden City, N.Y., 1981), pp. 412–13.

22. *Yorktown Cavalier*, 3 Mar., 14 Apr. 1863; Cobb, "Photographers of the Civil War," p. 130. James G. Barney had a permit to bring in chemicals to Yorktown from Baltimore (Kelbaugh, *Directory of Civil War Photographers, Vol. One*, p. 87).

23. *Norfolk & Portsmouth Old Dominion*, 25 Dec. 1863; J. Cobb, "Photographers of the Civil War," pp. 127–35; Norfolk City Directory, 1860.

24. *Norfolk & Portsmouth Old Dominion*, 30 Jan. 1864.

25. J. Cobb, "Photographers of the Civil War," pp. 127–35; Kelbaugh, *Directory of Civil War Photographers, Vol. One*, pp. 87–101. "Kern" might have been "Kerr," or "Kein."

26. *Humphrey's Journal*, 15 Feb. 1862, p. 319; *Richmond Daily Dispatch*, 24 July 1861.

27. *Alexandria Soldiers' Journal*, 27 Apr. 1864.

28. "Editorial Miscellany," *AJP*, 15 Mar 1861, p. 320; 1 May 1861, p. 367. The writer,

probably the editor Charles A. Seely, was not enthusiastic about the prospect of war. The somewhat arch tone of his March 1861 commentary must be read against the background of that moment's intense patriotism and even eagerness for war: "There will be little danger in the active duties, for the photographer must be beyond the smell of gunpowder or his chemicals will not work."

29. "Editorial Miscellany," *AJP*, 15 Mar. 1861, p. 320.

30. One author makes the passing comment that "these men, whether independent or not, were de facto employees of the Anthony company (no matter how free lance they may have considered themselves)." In photography the difference between an "independent" and an "employee" is not small, because it has bearing on how the photographer selects and treats his subjects. When an independent is hired, his point-of-view and style come with the package (William A. Frassanito, *Grant and Lee, The Virginia Campaigns, 1864–1865* [New York, 1983], p. 21).

31. "The popular market for relatively inexpensive stereo and portrait photographs stimulated a complex interchange in the early 1860s between three important parties: Mathew Brady, Alexander Gardner, and Edward Anthony. The quality and quantity of American Civil War photography is a direct result of the overlapping personal, artistic, and commercial interests of these men" (Keith F. Davis, *George Barnard, Photographer of Sherman's Campaign* [Kansas City, Mo., 1990], p. 53).

32. William Marder and Estelle Marder, *Anthony, the Man, the Company, the Cameras* (Amesbury, Mass., 1982).

33. William A. Frassanito, *Antietam, The Photographic Legacy of American's Bloodiest Day* (New York, 1978), p. 29; *Humphrey's Journal*, 1 Sept. 1861, p. 133.

34. Frassanito, *Antietam*, pp. 32–35.

35. Davis, "A Terrible Distinction," p. 139; Frassanito, *Antietam*, p. 35. At the maps division of the Library of Congress (hereafter cited as LC) is the item, "Map exhibiting the approaches to the city of Richmond prepared for Maj. Gen. Geo. B. McClellan," by E. J. Allen, which has the credit "J. F. Gibson, Photographer. Head Quarters, Army of the Potomac, May 31st, 1862."

36 *Southern Illustrated News*, 11 Oct. 1862. The prints and photographs department at LC has in its collection two May 1862 views at Yorktown credited jointly to John Wood and John F. Gibson and two June 1862 views of bridges over the Chickahominy River credited to David B. Woodbury.

37. Civil War collection, prints and photographs division, LC, searched at http://lcweb2.loc.gov/pp/cwpquery.html.

38. *Humphrey's Journal*, 15 Oct. 1862, p. 143; *New York Times*, 20 Oct. 1862.

39. Davis, "A Terrible Distinction," p. 139. Gardner, Knox, and Reekie appear in the photograph "Officers of the St. Andrew's Society," by Alexander Gardner, Nov. 1865, Brooks Johnson, *An Enduring Interest, the Photographs of Alexander Gardner* (Norfolk, 1991), p. 4.

40. *Humphrey's Journal*, 15 Sept. 1861, p. 158.

41. Susan E. Williams, "'Richmond Again Taken,' Reappraising the Brady Legend through Photographs by Andrew J. Russell," *Virginia Magazine of History and Biography* (hereafter cited as *VMHB*) 110 (2002): 444.

42. Application, 6 Nov. 1880, to U.S. Treasury Department for position, reproduced in James D. Horan, *Timothy O'Sullivan, America's Forgotten Photographer* (New York, 1966), p. 314; Civil War collection, prints and photographs division, LC, searched at http://lcweb2.loc.gov/pp/cwpquery.html.

43. Ray, "The Photographers of the War," p. 410; *Humphrey's Journal*, 1 Jan. 1862, cited in Davis, "A Terrible Distinctness," p. 147.

44. Davis, "A Terrible Distinctness," p. 147; *AJP*, 15 Oct. 1861, p. 240.

45. The South had the potential to produce tintype blanks, which were iron plates with a black baked-enamel surface, but all indications are that its limited number of metalcrafters turned to military supplies.

46. "Editorial Miscellany," *AJP*, 15 Oct. 1861. See for instance advertisements for "Window glass" at W. W. Wooldridge, 15th St., and W. Peterson & Co., Main St., *Richmond Daily Whig*, 5 Mar. 1862 and for "Plate glass" at R. Wendenburg & Co., Main St. "under Spotswood Hotel," *Richmond Southern Punch*, 12 Dec. 1863.

47. *Richmond Examiner*, 8 Jan. 1862.

48. *Richmond Enquirer*, 19 Sept. 1861; *Lynchburg Virginian*, 5 Sept. 1861.

49. *Richmond Sentinel*, 8 Oct. 1863.

50. *Lynchburg Virginian*, 15 July 1861. The photographer George S. Cook of Charleston, S.C., (and post-war of Richmond) was an active importer and reseller of photographic supplies until 1864, first from a Philadelphia supplier by way of New York, and later from England. Jack C. Ramsay, Jr., *Photographer . . . Under Fire, The Story of George S. Cook (1819–1902)* (Green Bay, Wis., 1994), pp. 54, 61, 64–67. In order to be right with southern patriotism, Tanner's Lynchburg ad surely misrepresents the source of the material. While it may have been true in a sense that the packages in Tanner's order traveled south of Lynchburg on their path to delivery, in shipment to Norfolk or to Charleston, and thus in that sense came "from the South," there can be little doubt that the stock itself originated in the North.

51. *Richmond Daily Dispatch*, 9 Dec. 1861.

52. *Richmond Sentinel*, 30 Sept., 7, 10 Oct. 1863; *Richmond Daily Dispatch*, 7 May 1864. Also listed in September 1863 were "two superior cameras, complete; Metallic and glass plates, preservers; Picture Frames and cases," and in October 1863 "Head-rests, Stands, Cyan. Potash."

53. In Petersburg no advertisement was found after the Minnis Gallery in September 1861 (*Petersburg Daily Express*, 17 Sept. 1861). In Lynchburg, N. S. Tanner advertised into July 1861 and George W. Kyle until February 1862 (*Lynchburg Virginian*, 15 Jul. 1861, 27 Feb. 1862). The Auction Gallery in Winchester, despite being in the midst of the ebb and flow of armies, advertised into March 1862 (*Berryville Conservator*, 12 Mar. 1862). R. J. Rankin in Staunton ran the same advertisement from January 1859 until September 1863 (*Staunton Spectator*, 18 Aug., 1 Sept. 1863). Wm. Roads, ambrotypist, advertised in Charlottesville at least until April 1864 (*Charlottesville Daily Chronicle*, 7 Apr. 1864).

54. Jeffrey Ruggles, "Lithographic Views of Virginia," unpublished manuscript.

55. *Richmond Whig*, 7 July 1862. The one type of imagery that does seem to have had C.S.A.-wide success throughout the war was the lithographic cover-art of sheet music. In its case the music made the difference, tapping into a distribution system already in place of music stores and people accustomed to purchasing music by mail.

56. *Richmond Daily Dispatch*, 27 Aug., 21 Sept. 1861; *Richmond Examiner*, 30 Jan., 25 Feb. 1862. From J. W. Randolph's advertisement in the *Examiner*: "for sale a large lot of handsome Photographs, 50 cts. Each—Davis, Stephens, General Johnson, Beauregard, Garibaldi, Simmons, Jones, Ripley, Jamison and Bartow, Cols. Preston, Wigfall, and Bartow; Major Anderson; Captains Ingraham, Harston and Packman; Dr. Gibbs; Governors Brown, Adams, Pickens and Meau; Prince Napoleon; Princess Clotilde; Hayre, Rhett and others."

57. *Southern Illustrated News*, 7 Jun., 29 Aug. 1863. From the 29 August issue: "Let the pictures of our gallant leaders in this contest for independence be preserved in every household in the Confederacy and handed down to the generations coming after us as valuable *souvenirs* of the present struggle."

58. *Richmond Daily Dispatch*, 7 Mar. 1864. As discussed in chapter three, most of the prints from wartime negatives were produced after the war.

59. Ibid., 1 Nov. 1860; *Richmond City Directory*, 1860; Confederate War Tax Returns, National Archives (hereafter cited as NA), RG109, chap. 10, vol. 190, box 44, Virginia, District 11, Feb., Apr. 1864.

60. *Richmond Daily Dispatch*, 10 Apr., 7 Nov. 1861, 8 Jan 1863; Confederate Papers Relating to Citizens or Business firms, NA, M346, Roll 845. In August 1863 Rees

paid tax on a gross income of $11,856, presumably for the first half of 1863. In April 1864, representing probably the second half of 1863 and possibly the first quarter of 1864, his reported gross income was $32,000, which does seem high but could represent accelerating inflation. It is possible that Rees had non-photographic income that was enlarging his volume, but there is no indication of it (Confederate War Tax Returns, NA, RG109, chap. 10, vol. 190, box 44, Virginia, district 11, Aug. 1863, Feb., Apr. 1864).

61. *Southern Illustrated News,* 7 June 1863; S. H. M. Byers, 5th Iowa, to his brother John, 11 Dec. 1863, reprinted in *National Tribune,* 29 Dec. 1891, at http://www.mdgorman.com/Written_Accounts/National_Tribune/national_tribune_12291891.htm (accessed 18 Jan. 2008). Rees's view of Libby Prison is known from copies of it, such as the 1882 lithograph, *Libby Prison. The Only Picture in Existence, as it Appeared August 23, 1863,* by A. Hoen & Co., Richmond. A collection is online at http://www.mdgorman.com/Photographs/CR%20Rees%20Photos.htm (accessed 18 Jan. 2008). See also Ray, "The Photographers of the War," p. 413.

62. Confederate War Tax Returns, NA, RG109, chap. 10, vol. 190, box 44, Virginia, district 11, Apr. 1864; *Richmond Daily Dispatch,* 15 Aug. 1864. There would have been no place perceived as safer for Rees than his gallery located in the heart of the city; the Evacuation Fire was unimaginable before it occurred. Besides, moving large quantities of glass negatives in wagons over bumpy roads would have been both a formula for breakage and next to impossible logistically.

63. *Richmond Daily Dispatch,* 11 Nov. 1861, 20 Feb., 10 Mar. 1862; *Richmond Whig,* 24 Feb. 1862.

64. *Southern Illustrated News,* 1 Nov. 1862; War Dept. Collection of Confederate Records, NA, RG109, chap. 10, vol. 190, box 44, Virginia, district 10, Aug. 1863; vol. 202, Sales Tax Register, Dist. No. 10, Richmond, Va. Aug-Oct 1863; vol. 205, Sales Tax Register, Oct. 1863-Jan. 1865; vol. 203, Jan. 1864–Jan. 1865; vol. 204, Jan.-Feb. 1865; Confederate Papers Relating to Citizens or Business Firms, NA, M346, roll 1051; *Richmond Daily Dispatch,* 19 May 1864. For the war tax that the Confederate government imposed on businesses beginning in mid-1863, in August 1863 Vannerson paid the specific tax, a professional tax, of $50, and a $120 tax on gross sales through July 1 of $4,800. That return also noted he had a capital investment of $1,000. In January 1864 he paid the $50 photographer tax. In April 1864 he paid gross sales tax of $165, which if it was a late payment for the second half of 1863 would have shown an increase in the dollar amount of sales over the first half, but with inflation probably reflected the same or slightly lower sales. For "4 Photographs of Lt. J. M. Jarrett" at General Hospital No. 4 Vannerson charged $50. That February he invoiced $15.00 each for "2 photographs of John Wyatt," at General Hospital No. 1. No wartime records have been found for Vannerson after May 1864. There is no evidence that Vannerson entered into any partnership during the war. In the 1866 city directory, the brothers were living at the same Richmond address, 714 N. 9th St. The *Richmond Evening Whig,* 5 Apr. 1865, describes the Evacuation Fire "burning down to, but not destroying M. L. Jacobson's store, No. 77 Main Street, south side, halfway between 14th and 15th streets." Vannerson's gallery was at that address above the store.

65. David Bendann, Richmond, letter to Daniel Bendann, Baltimore, 13 Oct. 1857, Acc.42709, LVA; *Richmond Daily Dispatch,* 1 Nov. 1860; *Southern Illustrated News,* 4 Oct. 1862.

66. *Southern Illustrated News,* 21 Mar., 11 July 1863.

67. Ibid., 29 Aug. 1863; Confederate War Tax Returns, NA, RG109, chap. 10, vol. 190, box 44, Virginia, district 11, Sept. 1863, Feb. 1864.

68. Confederate Papers Relating to Citizens or Business Firms, NA, M346, roll 693; *Richmond Daily Dispatch,* 11 Apr., 9 May 1864.

69. D. Mark Katz, *Witness to an Era, The Life and Photographs of Alexander Gardner* (New

York, 1991), pp. 26–31; *Richmond Daily Dispatch,* 18 July 1861; *New York Illustrated News,* 22 July 1861, p. 177. See "Infernal machines discovered in the Potomac," drawing by Alfred Waud, online at LC-P&P.

70. *Boston Journal,* reprinted in *Alexandria Soldiers' Journal,* 13 Jul. 1864.

71. Richard W. Stephenson, "An Unfamiliar Country: The Commonwealth During the Civil War," *Virginia In Maps* (Richmond, 2000), pp. 189–206, esp. 196–99.

72. Richmond City Directory, 1859, 1860; *Richmond Daily Dispatch,* 24 Dec. 1860, 13 Jun. 1861. By 1860 Charles R. Rees was renting the former Pratt's gallery location at 145 Main.

73. *Richmond Daily Dispatch,* 25 Feb., 19 Aug. 1862; 26 Nov. 1863.

74. Albert H. Campbell, "The Lost War Maps of the Confederates," *Century Magazine* new ser., 34, Jan. 1888, p. 480. Sanxay wrote instructions to Jedediah Hotchkiss, describing the photographic copy process in detail, found in the Hotchkiss Papers, LC (Stephenson, "An Unfamiliar Country," *Virginia in Maps,* p. 199).

75. *Richmond Daily Dispatch,* 16 Feb., 14 Mar. 1863; Confederate Papers Relating to Citizens or Business Firms, "Sanxay & Gomert," NA, M346, roll 901. Documents confirm Adolph Gomert's employment by the Engineer bureau from late February to 30 June 1864; and Sanxay & Gomert's, 1–31 October 1864. In addition Julian Vannerson was employed as a photographer from 13 April to 31 May 1864. A. J. Riddle had come to Richmond early in the war, and was still there in March 1863, advertising for a substitute "to go in the City Battalion." The same month that Sanxay and Gomert were printing his negatives, August 1864, Riddle was photographing at Andersonville, the notorious prison camp for Union soldiers in Georgia.

76. *Richmond Daily Dispatch,* 21 May 1864; Confederate Papers Relating to Citizens or Business Firms, "Sanxay & Gomert," NA, M346, roll 901.

77. Davis, "A Terrible Distinctness," pp. 157–59; Williams, "Richmond Again Taken," pp. 437, 444–45. According to Davis, Russell paid Fowx out of his own pay for the instruction.

78. Davis, "A Terrible Distinctness," pp. 158–59; Williams, "Richmond Again Taken," p. 448.

79. Frassanito, *Grant and Lee,* pp. 40–198.

80. Ibid., pp. 49–60; Williams, "Richmond Again Taken," pp. 448–49. Regarding Guy Fox, see Josephine Cobb, "Mathew B. Brady's Photographic Gallery in Washington," *Records of the Columbia Historical Society,* 1953–56 vols., 53–56 (Washington, D.C., 1959): 52. The principle archives that hold Civil War glass negatives are the Prints and Photographs Dept at LC and the Still Photographs Department at NA. These collections are a mostly undifferentiated mixture of negatives from all the major Union producer groups: Brady, Anthony, Gardner, and Russell. A number of scholars have contributed to identifying negatives by subject and photographer, including archivists at the institutions and William Frassanito in his publications. Recently Susan E. Williams, by measuring the actual sizes of the glass plates held by LC and NA, and tracking in particular the unusual 6½ x 8½ inch plates of Fowx, has enabled a number of additional images to be sorted by their makers.

81. Frassanito, *Grant and Lee,* pp. 88–94, 172–97; Williams, "Richmond Again Taken," pp. 448–49.

82. Frassanito, *Grant and Lee,* pp. 292–330; Williams, "Richmond Again Taken," pp. 450–52. The only views from the Gardner group on the Richmond/Petersburg front in this period were a few by John Reekie.

83. A. J. Russell, "Photographic Reminiscences of the Late War," *Anthony's Photographic Bulletin* 13, July 1882, pp. 212–13, cited in Frassanito, *Grant and Lee,* pp. 336–37. From Russell's transcription, it sounds as if Roche was another Scot. The duplicated view from Fort Mahone is of a young soldier frozen in death with head back, a log at a diagonal across the foreground. Roche's view was a stereo-plate issued by Anthony, and Russell's an 8 x 10 plate, a print in the VHS collection.

84. *Richmond Evening Whig*, 14 Apr. 1865.

85. Frassanito, *Grant and Lee*, p. 379; Civil War collection, Prints and Photographs Division, LC, searched at http://lcweb2.loc.gov/pp/cwpquery.html (accessed 18 Jan. 2008); *Philadelphia Photographer* 2, Sept. 1865, p. 154, at http://www.mdgorman.com/Written_Accounts/Other_Papers/philadelphia_photographer_91865.htm (accessed 18 Jan. 2008). The article noted that "Messrs. Levy & Cohen publish both carte and whole size" of the Richmond views.

86. *Richmond Evening Whig*, 21 Apr. 1865; Williams, "Richmond Again Taken," p. 456. The little-heralded Guy Fowx thus shares the photography credits for some of the most seminal portraits of the Civil War, of Grant at Cold Harbor and Lee at Richmond.

87. A Washington reporter commented, "A bird's-eye view from Gamble's Hill, an abrupt buff just above the city, was worth to me the journey from Washington" (*Richmond Times*, 26 Apr. 1865).

88. Gardner and Gibson had issued a panorama of Camp Winfield Scott near Yorktown in 1862. George Barnard produced a series of panoramas in 1864 of Tennessee scenes and of Atlanta, which Gardner prepared and issued (Civil War collection, Prints and Photographs Division, LC, searched at http://lcweb2.loc.gov/pp/cwpquery.html). Some of the individual photographs in the panoramas, framed to be part of a larger whole, when viewed individually were quite stark and unlike the usual notions of the picturesque of the period. Beaumont Newhall used one such photograph in his 1964 *History of Photography* to suggest a sort of early modernist look in the depiction of Richmond's ruins, without mentioning that it was extracted from its intended placement by appearing alone.

CHAPTER THREE: THE COMMUNITY PHOTOGRAPHER

1. *Richmond Evening Whig*, 7 Apr. 1865; *Richmond Times*, 21 Apr. 1865; Cobb, "Photographers of the Civil War," pp. 131–34. None of these galleries lasted long in Richmond. In the 1866 directory, John H. Pein at 188 Broad had added Frederick Bannasch, who had been with him at Bermuda Hundred, as a partner; by September 1866, the gallery was no longer listed, although both men were Richmond residents in 1869 (Cobb, "Photographers of the Civil War," p. 134; *Richmond City Directory*, 1866–69). By early May 1865 James Coleman requested that "all who have paid for Negatives to get them," sounding as if he were about to move on (*Richmond Whig*, 4 May 1865). No listing for Harris or Bancroft appeared in the 1866 directory.

2. Kelbaugh, *Directory of Civil War Photographers*, 1:95; *Richmond Times*, 21 June 1865.

3. Lynchburg city directory, 1859, *Lynchburg Virginian*, 17 Apr. 1856; North Carolina Photographers, at http://www.lib.unc.edu/ncc/pcoll/phgrs.html; "Adam H. Plecker," Clement Anselm Evans, ed., *Confederate Military History* (1899; Atlanta, 1987), 4:1118–19; Louis Ginsberg, *Photographers in Virginia, 1839–1900: A Checklist* (Petersburg, 1986), p. 13; transcript of interviews with Henry Miley, by Harrison Waddell, 1941 (hereafter cited as Henry Miley transcript), Michael Miley papers, Rockbridge Historical Society, Leyburn Library, Washington & Lee University (hereafter cited as WLU), pp. 1–2.

4. "Photographed by Wm. Roads," unpublished work-in-progress by Antoinette W. Roades; *Charlottesville Daily Chronicle*, 7 Apr. 1864; Ben Ritter, "Jackson's First Wartime Portrait, The Widow's Favorite," *CWTI* 17:10 (1979): 36–39; Virginia George Redd, "C. H. Erambert, photographer," *The Southsider* (Charlotte Court House, Va.) 7:1 (1988): 4–6.

5. *Richmond City Directory*, 1866–87.

6. *Petersburg City Directory*, 1865–1901; *Petersburg Telephone Directory*, 1898.

7. Robert K. Krick, "Treasure-Trove, Photographer's Archive Yields Previously Unseen Post-Civil War Views of Fredericksburg," *Fredericksburg Free-Lance Star*, 17 Dec. 2005.

8. Craig's Daguerreian Registry online; *Richmond City Directory*, 1866–80; A. Lawrence Kocher and Howard Dearstyne, *Shadows in Silver, A Record of Virginia in Contemporary Photographs Taken by George and Huestis Cook with Additions from the Cook Collections* (New York, 1954), p. 3. See also Jack Ramsay, Jr., *Photographer . . . Under Fire: The Story of George S. Cook (1819–1902)* (Green Bay, Wis., 1994). Among those who worked for Anderson was photographer Charles Lumpkin, who just after the war had his own gallery and towards the end of his career in the early 1900s photographed for the *Richmond News*.

9. Cartes de visite and cabinet card credits, VHS museum collection; research on W. E. Eutsler by descendant Mary Byrd Blackwell, Woodstock, Va.; *Wise Hoover of Carloover*, ed. Hoover B. Lide and Dougas P. Smith (Richmond, 1991), pp. 42, 44–45, 53, 59, 62.

10. "Joseph H. Faber," in Philip Alexander Bruce, ed., *Virginia: Rebirth of the Old Dominion* (Chicago, 1929), 3:228–30; *Fredericksburg City Directory*, 1880; *Norfolk City Directory*, 1886–1911.

11. Sara B. Bearss and Patricia D. Thompson, "The Eye of a Master, Foster's View of Richmond, 1900–1925," *VMHB* 98 (1990): 641–44. See also Sara B. Bearss and Patricia D. Thompson, *Foster's Richmond* (Richmond, 1991). Dementi bought out partner William H. Faris in 1928. His son Robert Dementi joined the business after 1940. In 1972 a merger created Dementi-Foster Studio. About 1990 the studio name changed back to Dementi Studio. In September 1972 Foster Studio glass plates were donated to VHS by W. Foster Orpin, and in 1992 Foster Studio film negatives were donated to VHS by Mrs. M. Elisabeth Dementi. Frank A. Dementi (1905–1986) worked for three years in his brother's studio, leaving to work at a Richmond newspaper. In 1942 he opened Colonial Studio in Williamsburg, and after World War II moved the business to Richmond. When he closed in 1984, he donated a collection of photographs to the Valentine Museum.

12. David Moltke-Hansen, "Seeing the Highlands, 1900–1939: Southwestern Virginia through the Lens of T. R. Phelps," *Southern Cultures* 1:1 (1994): 23–49.

13. "The Holsinger Studio Collection," at http://www.lib.virginia.edu/small/collections/holsinger/index.html. See also F. T. Heblich, Jr. and Cecile Clover Walters, *Holsinger's Charlottesville, 1890–1925: Selected Photographs from the Collection of Rufus W. Holsinger* (Charlottesville, 1978).

14. Elizabeth M. Gushee, "Christopher Ethelbert Cheyne," *Dictionary of Virginia Biography* (hereafter cited as *DVB*) (Richmond, 2006), 3:202–3; "Notes on the Cheyne Family," at http://www.lva.lib.va.us/whatwehave/photo/cheyneabout.htm.

15. Norfolk and Portsmouth directories, 1883–1908; *Virginia State Directory*, 1900; U.S. Census 1900, Newport News. For 1891, the first year Emeline Turner was listed as photographer, Augustus Turner was listed as manager at the same address, and she was also listed as a grocer at the corner of Glasgow and Armstrong streets. By 1908 Augustus was listed as a photographer and Mrs. Turner was listed only as a widow, both living at the same address, and the 208 High St. studio had been taken over by William Stertzbach.

16. Keith F. Davis, "A Terrible Distinctness," p. 168. See Alexander Gardner, *Photographic Sketch Book of the Civil War* (reprint, New York, 1959). Each volume contained fifty 8 x 10 prints each, presented in chronological order with printed captions, and with both negatives and positives credited and dated. Selected from the work of photographers associated with Gardner, the prints were mostly of the Eastern theater and largely of Virginia. Davis estimates that about 100 copies were produced, "or at most 150."

17. Williams, "Richmond Taken Again," pp. 438–40, 458–60. See *Russell's Civil War Photographs, 116 Historic Prints by Andrew J. Russell* (reprint; New York, 1982).

18. Jeana K. Foley, "Recollecting the Past, A Collection Chronicle of Mathew Brady's Photographs," in Mary Panzer, *Mathew Brady and the Image of History* (Washington, 1997), pp. 189–207.

19. Foley, "Recollecting the Past," pp. 190–96. Among the Department of War's Brady acquisitions were several hundred daguerreotype portraits, which were transferred to

the Library of Congress. The National Archives collections of Civil War photographs are held at College Park, Md. A large portion are scanned. See http://www.archives.gov/research/civil-war/photos/ (accessed 25 Jan. 2008).

20. Foley, "Recollecting the Past," pp. 190–91, 197–202. Anthony & Anthony's reissue imprints included "Photographic History" and "The War for the Union." John Taylor's imprints included "The War Publication and Exhibition Company," and "Taylor & Huntington." The Library of Congress Prints and Photographs Department has scanned and made available online about 7,000 images from Civil War negatives. See http://lcweb2.loc.gov/pp/cwphtml/cwpabt.html (accessed 25 Jan. 2008).

21. As previously discussed, Confederate photographers faced shortages of materials, lack of money by potential customers, and the unavailability of portraits of many figures.

22. *Richmond Times*, 8 June 1865; *Richmond City Directory*, 1866; *The Magnet* (Richmond) 1:5 (Sept. 1866); *The Magnet* (Richmond) (Aug./Sept. 1867). As previously mentioned, Vannerson had worked for Minnis in Petersburg in 1857 (*Petersburg Daily Express*, 4 Aug. 1857).

23. *The Magnet* (Richmond) (Aug./Sept. 1867); *Richmond City Directory*, 1869–1892. The Cook Collection at the Valentine/Richmond History Center would probably contain any surviving negatives.

24. See chaps. 1 and 2. The names of the other African Americans who worked at daguerreotype or ambrotype galleries are not known.

25. *Richmond City Directory*, 1869–1909. That Hill was working for Cook in 1882 suggests that Hill may have previously worked for D. H. Anderson, whose gallery Cook purchased in 1880. In the 1910 Census, a Thomas Hill was sixty-five years old and a widower living in the city home.

26. *Petersburg City Directory*, 1870–71, 1876–77, 1877–78, 1888–89; U.S. Census 1880; *Lynchburg City Directory*, 1888.

27. Giles B. Jackson and D. Webster Davis, *The Industrial History of the Negro Race of the United States* (Richmond, 1908), pp. 216, 246; *Norfolk City Directory*, 1909–11.

28. *Richmond City Directory*, 1875–88. The several Davis galleries were among those on the 800 block of East Broad.

29. *Richmond City Directory*, 1886–87–1903. In that era's directories, an asterisk was often used to denote a black person or business. There may have been a short-lived black gallery at 813 E. Broad St. in 1897, when two black photographers were listed as working at that address, Horace S. Davis and Wilson Brown. No business listing at that address appeared in the directory, but the gallery may have expired in the time between the residential canvas and the business survey for the directory.

30. G. F. Richings, "J. C. Farley," *Evidence of Progress Among Colored People* (1900; Chicago, 1969), pp. 495–96. George W. Davis, the proprietor, did more managing than picture-making, with two or more galleries open at any time.

31. William J. Simons, "James C. Farley, Esq.," *Men of Mark: Eminent, Progressive and Rising* (1887; New York, 1968), pp. 800–4.

32. *Richmond City Directory*, 1882–92; *Richmond Planet*, 21 Feb. 1885, 11 May 1895. James C. Farley and his wife Rebecca P. Robinson of Amelia County (married 1876) had seven daughters. Farley's work was exhibited at the 1884 Colored Industrial Fair in Richmond, and the 1885 World's Exposition New Orleans.

33. *Richmond Planet*, 11 May 1895; *Richmond City Directory*, 1897–99. In the city directories the Jefferson gallery was not asterisked as "colored" until 1901. Possibly given the era and the gallery's location, the principals had reason to be circumspect about the ownership situation. The Brown family papers include a three-year partnership agreement between George O. Brown and Rebecca P. Farley, James Farley's wife (Gregg D. Kimball, "George O. Brown," *DVB*, 2:291–92).

34. *Richmond City Directory*, 1899–1910.

35. *Richmond City Directory*, 1889–1905; U.S. Census 1880.

36. *Richmond City Directory*, 1899–1910; Gregg D. Kimball, "George O. Brown," 2:291–92.

CHAPTER FOUR METHODS & FORMATS

1. Gernsheim and Gernsheim, *History of Photography*, pp. 332–34, 420; Beaumont Newhall, *The History of Photography: From 1839 to the Present Day* (New York, 1964), pp. 139–40. The definition of instantaneous evolved over the years, from several seconds in the 1850s to 1/100,000 of a second in the 1920s. The Henry Miley quotation is from the primary source about him and his father, Michael Miley. This source is the corrected transcript of interviews conducted in 1941 with Henry Miley by Harrison Waddell, a Lexington educator. "Upon Henry Mackey Miley's return from Catawba sanatorium where he had been undergoing treatment for a tubercular condition, he was importuned by Waddell to preserve his memories of his father's work and their experiments in color photography. Miley was hesitant about doing this for unknown reasons. However, Waddell suggested that with Miley's aid he (Waddell) might be able to give the random thoughts of Miley some permanent form. He suggested that he come and talk with Waddell in the presence of his secretary who would make notes which Waddell would later put in the form of a paper. After several visits, Miley became quite interested, and the papers of the conversation in Miley's own words still exist in Waddell's possession" ("The Waddell Paper," Miley papers, folder 8, WLU). Based on the interviews, Waddell wrote a paper in December 1941, "The Mileys and Color Photography," which appeared in the *Rockbridge County News*, 1 Jan. 1942 (Waddell's manuscript is in the Rockbridge Historical Society papers, WLU). On a return visit to Lexington in February 1951, Henry Miley reviewed the interview transcripts, made some corrections—the first page of the transcript is inscribed "Notes made by Henry Miley"—and "stated that everything contained herein was (so far as he knew) correct and substantiated" ([Mame Warren], *Michael Miley, American Photographer and Pioneer in Color*, n. 5, p. 3 [catalog to exhibition at DuPont Gallery, 8 Jan.–8 Feb. 1980, WLU]).

2. Gernsheim and Gernsheim, *History of Photography*, pp. 407–9.

3. With daguerreotypes or wet plates, long exposure times could cause plates to lose sensitivity or to dry out. An 1880 article, for instance, noted that when extending exposure "unusually long," a consequence could be the "very annoying spots, so-called 'dry spots' upon the collodion layer" (Fritz Haugk, "Wet Plates for Long Exposures," *Photographic Times* 10 [1880]: 77; other articles in *Photographic Times* that year, when dry plates were coming out, included "Gaslight for taking Photographic Pictures" [Feb. 1880, p. 28] and "Photography by Moonlight" [Nov. 1880, p. 248]).

4. Horace Carter Hovey, *Celebrated American Caverns, Especially Mammoth, Wyandot, and Luray: Together with Historical, Scientific, and Descriptive Notices of Caves and Grottoes in Other Lands* (Cincinnati, 1882), pp. 167–68.

5. Thilo Koenig, "The Other Half: The Investigation of Society," in Michal Frizot, ed., *A New History of Photography* (Cologne, 1998); Michael Pritchard, "Artificial Lighting," in John Hannavy, ed., *Encyclopedia of Nineteenth-Century Photography* (New York, 2007), 1: 83–84.

6. Little heed was given to photographic image rights until the end of the nineteenth century.

7. Thomas Hariot, *A briefe and true report of the new found land of Virginia of the commodities and of the nature and manners of the naturall inhabitants*, illustrated with copper-plate engravings produced by Theodore de Bry (Frankfort am Main, 1590).

8. *Album of Richmond, Va.* (New York, 1882), inside back cover. Louis Glaser was a lithographic printer in Leipzig, Germany. The Virginia titles published by Wittemann Bros., N.Y., and produced with folded images using the Glaser process include: *Centennial Album of Yorktown and of Richmond, Va.* (1881); *Souvenir of Mount Vernon* (1881); *Album of Baltimore & Ohio R. R. Scenery* (1881); *Album of Richmond, Va.* (1882); *The Shenandoah Valley* (1882); *Souvenir of Mount Vernon, Va.* (1885); *Richmond, Va.* (1887); and *Norfolk, Va.* (n.d.).

9. Luis Nadeau, "Collotype," in Hannavy, ed., *Encyclopedia of Nineteenth-Century*

Photography, 1: 313–14. The Albertype Company was based in downtown Brooklyn, N.Y., from 1890 to 1952 and was linked to the Wittemann family. The company published souvenir books, pamphlets, and postcards of locations throughout the United States. The Virginia titles utilizing collotype include: *Richmond Illustrated in Albertype* (1888); *James towne Island* (n.d.); and W. H. Kimberly, *Souvenir of Old Point Comfort and Environs* (1890). Not all of the Virginia titles produced by the Albertype Company were in collotype, however, for the company also printed in photogravure in the 1890s. In the photograph files at the VHS are many Virginia views identified as albertypes, usually in 4 x 5 or 5 x 7 sizes. Why these prints were originally produced is not known; possibly they were production overruns donated after the dissolution of the company.

10. *Richmond, Virginia Illustrated* (Indianapolis, 1891); *Art Work of Norfolk and Vicinity* (Chicago, 1895); *University of Virginia; Photo-gravures* (Charlottesville, 1895); *Art Work of Scenes in the Valley of Virginia* (Chicago, 1897); *Art Work of Lynchburg and Danville, Virginia* (Chicago, 1903); *Art Work of Danville* (Chicago, 1903); *Art Work of Petersburg, Virginia* (Chicago, 1903).

11. Printing with type is relief printing. A measure of the versatility of the halftone is that it can also be used in photogravure, which is intaglio printing; or the halftone can be stripped-in to a film plate, for printing that is lithography-based and therefore planographic.

12. Kocher and Dearstyne, *Shadows and Silver*, pp. 14–15.

13. Ibid., p. 73.

14. *The Home-Maker* 1 (Nov. 1888), p. 1. The previous month's issue used for its frontispiece a photograph of another James River plantation house, Brandon, that was likely by Huestis Cook, but a print of the image has not been examined to confirm that attribution.

15. Kocher and Dearstyne, *Shadows in Silver*, pp. 14–15. Huestis Cook photographs reproduced in Marion Harland, *Some Colonial Homesteads* (New York, 1897) include: p. 25, exterior of Westover river-front (different than in *The Home-Maker*); p. 51, the tomb of William Byrd II, and p. 59, "A Curious Iron Gate," both the same photographs as used in *The Home-Maker*; and p. 61, exterior of Berkeley. Huestis Cook photographs reproduced in John Fiske, *Old Virginia and Her Neighbors* (Boston, 1900) include: 2:163, Westover (yet another river-front view); 2:176, Westover gate; 2:189, the wharf at Upper Brandon; and 2:283, Byrd's tomb at Westover.

16. Sally Nelson Robins, *Gloucester, One of the First Chapters of the Commonwealth of Virginia* (Richmond, 1893); Anna Venable Koiner, *Echoes from the Land of the Golden Horseshoe* (New Market, Va., 1897).

17. The earliest-found editorial halftone in a Virginia newspaper appeared in the *Richmond Planet* on 5 January 1895. In many Virginia newspapers, the use of halftones seems to have begun in advertisements, such as the portrait of a business owner that appeared in the *Manchester Leader* by January 1894 or the Hotel Pocomoke in the *Accomac Peninsula Enterprise* on 9 December 1899.

18. "A Colored Photographer," *Richmond Planet*, 21 Feb. 1885. See references to J. C. Farley and his dealings with John Mitchell in Anne Field Alexander, *Race Man, The Rise and Fall of the "Fighting Editor" John Mitchell, Jr.* (Charlottesville, 2002), pp. 35, 47.

19. The photograph of the interior of the "Police Court" is not credited, but the accompanying descriptive article makes it apparent that the photographer was Mitchell (*Richmond Planet*, 9 Mar. 1895). Three photographs related to the Barnes and Abernathy case are uncredited but in context are surely by Mitchell (*Richmond Planet*, 3 Aug. 1895). In Suzanne Lebsock's account of that last case, she has Mitchell traveling to Amelia County with photographer J. C. Farley, but the citations do not support this conclusion. It is more likely that Mitchell was on his own and took the photographs (Suzanne Lebsock, *A Murder in Virginia: Southern Justice on Trial* [New York, 2003], pp. 165–66). Likely Mitchell had his photographic processing done by George Brown, the leading African American labman in the city.

20. *Richmond News*, 5 Oct. 1899. In that first issue, the *Richmond News* featured at the top of the front page a halftone of Miss May Handy, "a reigning belle," and on inside pages portraits of the Democratic politicians who welcomed the newspaper for its political preference. See also Michael Ayers Trotti, "Murder Made Real: The Visual Revolution of the Halftone," *VMHB* 111 (2003): 333–78.

21. Ibid., 2 Jan. 1900.

22. On Nièpce, see Michal Frizot, "A Natural Strangeness, the Hypothesis of Color," in Frizot, ed., *A New History of Photography*, p. 411.

23. U. S. Patent #4423, issued to William A. Pratt, Alexandria, Mar. 1846. Alexandria was returned from the District of Columbia to Virginia in 1846, so officially Pratt may not have been a Virginian the day the patent was awarded.

24. Discussing color is like philosophy or physics in that no sooner are terms defined than a new level of activity will be introduced that calls all previous assumptions into questions. In reality all color photography is selected color, only in varying ways. The actual light that enters a camera from a subject is not what is captured in a photograph; rather that light triggers a process that, by a different path for each method, results in a dye or other color representation in the photograph. There is no such thing as pure "natural color," but some images certainly have more of the sense of it than others.

25. In particular, the monochromatic "life-size" enlargements that were finished in charcoal, pencil, and wash.

26. See Eric de Maré, "How It Works," *Colour Photography* (Harmondsworth, Eng., 1968), pp. 23–39.

27. The theory of "color temperature" introduces an additional linear scale and thus another level of complexity. Any given light source illuminates with light of a particular color: think of the warm light of an incandescent bulb or the cool light of a skylight. Usually our eyes will adjust to the color temperature of the light where we are, and we will simply see the normal range of colors. When we are in a place illuminated by sources of varying color temperatures, we may notice the difference in light color. An astronomical phenomenon that expresses color temperature is the range of star colors, from the (cooler) red and yellow stars to the (hotter) blue-white stars. Color temperature can be measured. Values on the scale range from 2800°K tungsten light—rather yellow—up to regular daylight at 5500°K, and above that to cloudy sky illumination, electronic flash, and a skylight, in the range of 6000°K. Modern films have been designed to be panchromatic at a particular color temperature. Adjustment to the light source is also a component of high-end digital photography.

28. De Maré, *Colour Photography*, pp. 40–41. In this simplified explanation, a few key elements have been omitted. An alternate method on the same principle would be to expose each negative through a filter of one of the three complementary colors. A fine selection of early color photography, including a reproduction of Maxwell's 1861 "Tartan ribbon," appears in Naomi Rosenblum, "The Origins of Color in Camera Images," in *A World History of Photography* (New York, 1984), pp. 280–95.

29. Frizot cites presentations on the three-color process to the French Photography Society on 7 May 1869 by two independent researchers, Charles Cros and Louis Ducos du Hauron (Michel Frizot, "A Natural Strangeness, the Hypothesis of Color," in Frizot, ed., *A New History of Photography*, p. 413).

30. In France, Becquerd "criticized the results achieved with three-color processes" in 1876, calling them "tinted according to the whim of the operator." Ibid.

31. Gernsheim and Gernsheim, *History of Photography*, pp. 334, 523; de Maré, *Colour Photography*, p. 43. Beaumont Newhall, curator at George Eastman House, Rochester, wrote in 1952: "The question of who made the first successful color photograph in America is difficult to answer because of the definition of a color photograph. I am inclined to give the honor to Frederick Eugene Ives who in 1892 showed color

photographs by means of three lanterns. We have his original apparatus here and show the actual photographs regularly" (Beaumont Newhall to Marshall W. Fishwick, 4 Dec. 1952, Miley papers, special collections, WLU).

32. Henry Miley transcript, pp. [12, 14]. Halation occurs when the negative has fogging around the more heavily exposed parts of the emulsion, which are the bright areas of the subject (see Henry Miley transcript, pp. [3–4]).

33. Ibid., p. [14].

34. Ibid.

35. Ibid., pp. [15–16].

36. United States Patent Office, Michael Miley and Henry Mackey Miley, of Lexington, Virginia, Assignors to Miley Colour Photograph Company, of New York, N.Y., "Color Photograph and Art of Making Same," patent no. 711,875, 21 Oct. 1902.

37. Henry Miley transcript, p. [17]; Miley and Miley, "Color Photograph and Art of Making Same," patent no. 711,875, 21 Oct. 1902.

38. Jas. Lewis Howe, "Miley's Process of Color Photography," *Science* 17 (1903): 193; Henry Miley transcript, pp. [17–18].

39. Henry Miley transcript, pp. [9, 18]; H. M. Miley to Dr. [Marshall] Fishwick, 3 Jan. 1952, Miley papers, WLU.

40. Rosenblum, *A World History of Photography*, pp. 275, 450.

41. Henry Wilhelm, *The Permanence and Care of Color Photographs: Traditional and Digital Color Prints, Color Negatives, Slides, and Motion Pictures* (Grinnell, Iowa, 1993), p. 20.

42. Ibid., pp. 25–26.

43. Ibid., pp. 19–24. Agfa introduced its color negative film, Agfacolor, in 1943, but was not in the position to compete with Kodak internationally then, or for some years following.

44. Ibid., p. 20. The name Kodachrome prints was used after 1955 for prints from slides, made using internegatives or later directly on positive print paper, but the paper was not Kodachrome process as it was pre-1955.

Chapter Five: Twentieth-Century Subjects

1. The commercial photography lab Action Photo stopped offering E-6 sheet film processing in 2007. Labs that had previously ended E-6 service included Richmond Camera Shop and Professional Photographics.

2. Michel Auer, *The Illustrated History of the Camera* (Boston, 1975), pp. 80–81, 186, 196, 203, 212–221.

3. *Richmond Telephone Directory*, The C & P Telephone Co. of Virginia, July 1950, Oct. 1960; *The Black Swan, The Magazine of Virginia*, advertisement Mar. 1930, p. 31; photograph "The Road to Westover," Mar. 1930, p. 19; photograph "The Brook," May 1930, p. 4. About 2,400 black-and-white 8 x 10 inch film negatives by W. Harry Bagby, and a smaller number of prints, are held by VHS.

4. See for example the two bird's eye views of Virginia by John Bachmann, and one of Alexandria issued by Charles Magnus but likely prepared by Edward Sachse, in *Virginia in Maps, Four Centuries of Settlement, Growth, and Development*, ed. Richard W. Stephenson and Marianne M. McKee (Richmond, 2000), pp. 239–41.

5. Rosenblum, "Photography from the Air," *A World History of Photography*, pp. 246–47. See "Balloon view of Boston," 13 Oct. 1860, by J. W. Black, at <www.bpl.org/research/print/collections.htm>.

6. Gary W. North and Richard W. Stephenson, "Modern Mapping: From Saddles to Satellites," *Virginia in Maps*, p. 255. For Virginia State Chamber of Commerce use of aerial photographs, see "Virginia from the Air," photographs by Underwood & Underwood, *Virginia, First in the Heart of the Nation*, Vol. 2, No. 3, Autumn 1927, pp. 2–3.

7. On pictorial photography c. 1890–1912, see Beaumont Newhall, "Photography as an Art," *The History of Photography* (New York, 1964), pp. 97–110; Peter C. Bunnell, "Towards New Photography, Renewals of Pictorialism," *A New History of Photography*, ed. Michel Frizot (Köln, Germany, 1998), pp. 310–26.

8. George Allen Young, "The Aims and Aspirations of Pictorial Photography, Virginia Photographic Salon 1937," *Virginia Museum of Fine Arts Publications 1936–1938*, Vol. 2, No. 9, Feb. 1937, p. 5.

9. Bettina Berch, *The Woman behind the Lens, The Life and Work of Frances Benjamin Johnston, 1864–1952* (Charlottesville, 2000), pp. 14–38, 108–130.

10. Berch, *The Woman behind the Lens*, p. 117.

11. W. Troy Valos, "Harry C. Mann," <http://www.npl.lib.va.us/smrt/dip_website/mann.html>; "Mann's Children, A Gallery of Photographs by Harry C. Mann," *Virginia Cavalcade*, Vol. XXVII, Spring 1978, pp. 175–76. See also "About the Harry C. Mann Photograph Collection," at <http://www.lva.lib.va.us/whatwehave/photo/aboutmann.htm>.

12. Carroll Walker, 12 Sept. 1980, The Oral Histories Collection, Special Collections, Old Dominion University Libraries, Norfolk, Virginia, <http://www.lib.odu.edu/special/oralhistory/tidewater/walkertranscript.html> (29 Feb. 2008). The Virginia State Chamber of Commerce gave its Harry Mann collection to the Virginia State Library, now the Library of Virginia, which holds about 3,000 glass negatives and prints. The Norfolk Public Library also has a large number of Mann prints.

13. A. Aubrey Bodine, *The Face Of Virginia* (Baltimore, 1963), p. 174.

14. Jean Haskell Speer, "Eternal Mountaineer, The Photographs of Earl Palmer," *Virginia Cavalcade*, Vol. 40, No. 2, Autumn 1990, p. 75 (74–83); Jean Haskell Speer, *The Appalachian Photographs of Earl Palmer* (Lexington, Ky., 1990).

15. Speer, *The Appalachian Photographs*, pp. 127–28; Speer, "Eternal Mountaineer," pp. 76, 77.

16. "The Camera Club," [uncredited typescript paper, c. 1997], Hampton University Archives; Camera Club albums, Hampton University Archives; Vanessa Thaxton-Ward, "Hampton's Photographic Collections, An Extraordinary Visual Record," *The International Review of African American Art*, Vol. 20, No. 1, 2005, pp. 58–61; Nancy B. McGhee, "Portraits in Black: Illustrated Poems of Paul Laurence Dunbar," *Stony the Road, Chapters in the History of Hampton Institute*, ed. Keith L. Schall (Charlottesville, 1977), pp. 100–102; Barbara L. Michaels, "New Light on F. Holland Day's Photographs of African Americans," *History of Photography*, Vol. 18, No. 4, Winter 1994, pp. 334–347.

17. Carole Hagaman, "Camera Club of Richmond, Club History," <http://www.cameraclubofrichmond.com/aboutus.html> (25 Feb. 2008).

18. Jeffrey Smith, "Free-lancer often in right place at right time," *Richmond Times-Dispatch*, 5 Jan. 1989; Ellen Robertson, "Photographer, writer Edwin Booth, 90, dies," *Richmond Times-Dispatch*, 18 Sept. 1998; "Photographic Booth," *History Notes*, VHS, No. 4, Autumn 1991, p. 4; W. Edwin Booth, [typescript autobiography], 18 Feb. 1993, VHS Museum Dept. Accession files.

19. "Hampton at the Centennial," *Southern Workman*, May 1876, p. 35, clipping at Hampton University Archives; Ross. J. Kelbaugh, *Directory of Civil War Photographers*, Vol. 1 (Baltimore, 1990), p. 95.

20. Berch, *The Woman behind the Lens*, pp. 46–52; Lincoln Kirstein, "A Note on the Photographer," *The Hampton Album* (New York, 1966), pp. 54–55; "Photograph Department," [typescript document dated Nov. 1905], Hampton University Archives.

21. Vanessa Thaxton-Ward, "Hampton's Photographic Collections, An Extraordinary Visual Record," *The International Review of African American Art*, Vol. 20, No. 1, 2005, pp. 58–61; "The Camera Club," [uncredited typescript paper, c. 1997], Hampton University Archives.

22. Nancy B. McGhee, "Portraits in Black: Illustrated Poems of Paul Laurence Dunbar,"

Stony the Road, Chapters in the History of Hampton Institute, ed. Keith L. Schall (Charlottesville, 1977), pp. 100–102.

23. Letter, H. B. Frissell to Leigh R. Miner, 24 Oct. 1906, Hampton University Archives, cited in "The Camera Club"; *The Jamestown Exposition and Hampton Institute* (Hampton, 1907), pp. 17–22. Photographs by Miner also appeared for example in *The Need for Hampton* (Hampton, 1916).

24. W. H. Bright, *Official guide of the Jamestown ter-centennial exposition, held at Sewell's Point on Hampton Roads, near Norfolk, Va., April 26 to November 30, nineteen hundred seven* (Norfolk, 1907), p. 58.

25. *The official blue book of the Jamestown Ter-centennial Exposition, A.D. 1907: the only authorized history of the celebration; illustrated.* (Norfolk, 1909).

26. Verbon E. Kemp, "Virginia Chamber's Thirty Years," *The Commonwealth, The Magazine of Virginia*, Vol. XXI, June 1954, pp. 25–27; "The State Chamber's First Forty Years," *The Commonwealth*, Vol. XXXI, Apr. 1964, pp. 45–47; Robert F. Nelson, "Report of the Publicity Department of the Virginia State Chamber of Commerce," Reports of Chamber Offices and Committees, etc. 1937, Virginia State Chamber of Commerce, General File, Box 14, Acc. 28252, Library of Virginia.

27. Nelson, "Report of the Publicity Department," 1937, Acc. 28252, LV; Kemp, "Virginia Chamber's Thirty Years," *The Commonwealth*, June 1954, p. 27; "Phil Flournoy's Virginia Album," *The Commonwealth*, Vol. 33, Dec. 1966, p. 23. Not all of the negatives held by the Chamber were taken by its photographers. For many years it was the keeper of the Harry Mann negatives, and after the VHS acquired the Michael Miley negatives in 1941, the Chamber stored them for some years.

28. "Virginia's Colonial Heritage," *National Geographic Magazine*, Vol. LXXI, April 1937, color plates after p. 416.

29. Kemp, "Virginia Chamber's Thirty Years," *The Commonwealth*, June 1954, p. 27; "Phil Flournoy's Virginia Album," *The Commonwealth*, Vol. 33, Dec. 1966, p. 23; "About the Virginia State Chamber of Commerce Photograph Collection," online at Library of Virginia (18 Feb. 2008), <http://www.lva.lib.va.us/whatwehave/photo/aboutvcc.htm>.

30. Mary Tyler Cheek, "'An Island of Quiet in an Ocean of Noise,' The Virginia Room at the 1939 World's Fair," *Virginia Cavalcade*, Summer 1985, p. 33 (pp. 30–37); Edward D. C. Campbell, Jr., "Fair Shadows, Virginia, Photographs, and the 1939 World's Fair," *Virginia Cavalcade*, Vol. 41, Summer 1991, p. 15 (pp. 6–19).

31. Campbell, "Fair Shadows, Virginia, Photographs, and the 1939 World's Fair," pp. 6, 10, 14–15.
The original photographs of the 1939 World's Fair collection are held at Library of Virginia. The prints have been removed from the 1939-era albums and placed into new archival-quality albums that preserve the order of the originals. An explanation of the organization of the World's Fair albums is at the LV website at <http://www.lva.lib.va.us/whatwehave/photo/wfcabout.htm> (20 Feb. 2008).

32. Peter Stewart, "Norfolk in Nineteen Nineteen" [spiral-bound booklet with portfolio], (Norfolk, 1987). "This portfolio of forty-six prints is one of an edition of ten."

33. Brooks Johnson, *Mountaineers to Main Streets, The Old Dominion as seen through the Farm Security Administration Photographs* (Norfolk, 1985), pp. 5–7. In Sept. 1942 the section was transferred to the Office of War Information.

34. "The FSA-OWI Collection," Library of Congress, Prints and Photographs Dept., at <http://lcweb2.loc.gov/pp/fabout.html>. The online search was for "Virginia" (4654 items), less "West Virginia" (1601 items), at <http://lcweb2.loc.gov/pp/fsaquery.html> (3 Mar. 2008).

35. Johnson, *Mountaineers to Main Streets*, pp. 61, 57–58; George Allen Young, "The Aims and Aspirations of Pictorial Photography," pp. 6–7.

36. "HABS/HAER, Scope and Background of the Collections," at <http://lcweb2.loc.gov/pp/hhhtml/hhintro.html> (6 Mar. 2008). Johnston's model could also have inspired Peterson for what it lacked, from an architectural historian's point of view. HABS reports include measured drawings and written information along with any photographs.

37. Edward D. C. Campbell, Jr., and Stacy Gibbons Moore, "Foundation of the Past, The WPA Historical Inventory Project in Virginia," at <http://www.lva.lib.va.us/whatwehave/map/vhiarticle.htm> (6 Mar. 2008). Also architectural and available online at LV is the School Buildings Service Photographs Collection. See <http://www.lva.lib.va.us/whatwehave/photo/schoolabout.htm>.

38. Photographs used to make a government agency look good would certainly seem to fall into the category called here promotional photography. However those photographs could well have been selected to create a point of view, from a larger set of photographs that more neutrally documented the activities of the agency.

39. Capt. John C. Colwell, "The Port Signal Office," *The Road to Victory, A History of Hampton Roads Port of Embarkation in World War II*, ed. Maj. William R. Wheeler (Newport News, 1946), Vol. 2, p. 160.

40. "Port of Embarkation, Signal Corps Photographs of Hampton Roads, 1942–1945," *Virginia Cavalcade*, Vol. 37, no. 2, Autumn 1987, pp. 76 (74–77); "About the U.S. Army Signal Corps Photograph Collection," at <http://www.lva.lib.va.us/whatwehave/photo/sccabout.htm> (29 Feb. 2008).

41. Comment by "mose" at *The Virginian-Pilot* website, 22 June 2008, <http://hamptonroads.com/2008/06/birdseye-view-how-hampton-roads-developed>

ACKNOWLEDGMENTS

In the production of this book—the research, search for images, and realization—many people have provided assistance. We express appreciation to: Vaughn Webb and J. Roderick Moore, Blue Ridge Institute, Ferrum College; Angela Way, the Atkinson Museum, Hampden-Sydney College; Donzella Maupin and Vernon Curtney, Hampton University Archives; Carrie E. Taylor and Liesel Nowak, Thomas Jefferson Foundation; Dale Neighbors, Rebecca Dobyns, Special Collections, Library of Virginia; J. Christian Kolbe and other staff, Archives, Library of Virginia; Tom Moore, the Mariners' Museum; Adam Fielding, Special Collections & Archives, George Mason University; Drury Wellford and other staff, Museum of the Confederacy; Robert Hitchings and Troy Valos, the Sargeant Memorial Room, Norfolk Public Library; Randy Klemm, Pamplin Historical Society and the National Museum of the Civil War Soldier; Michelle Anne Delaney, Photographic History Collection, National Museum of American History, Smithsonian Institution; Meg Glass Hughes, Valentine Richmond History Center; Alex Novak, Vintage Works Ltd.; Jeffrey Allison, Emily Smith, and John Ravenal at the Virginia Museum of Fine Arts; Lucious Edwards, Virginia State University Archives; Aaron D. Purcell and Tamara Kennelly, Special Collections, Virginia Tech; Vaughan Stanley, Special Collections, Washington and Lee University; Amy C. Schindler and Beatriz B. Hardy, Special Collections, Swem Library, College of William and Mary; Frances Emerson, the Wytheville Museum; Richard L. Bland, Richmond; Howard McManus, Salem; and Ross Johnson. Staff members also have been helpful at Special Collections, Alexandria Public Library; the Prints and Photographs Division, Library of Congress; and Special Collections, University of Virginia.

At the Virginia Historical Society, Meg Eastman scanned and prepared images and Ron Jennings made photographs. James Kelly has overseen the project. Others in the museum department who have contributed in various ways are Rebecca Rose, Heather Beattie, William Rasmussen, Lauranett L. Lee, and Andrew Talkov. Drew Gladwell, Dale Kostelny, and Jamie Davis installed the exhibition. Nelson Lankford, Paul Levengood, and Graham Dozier assisted with editing and texts, and Ann de Witt has prepared an online exhibition. The library staff has been unfailingly helpful: Frances Pollard, John McClure, Katharine Wilkins, Greg Hansard, Julie Mannering, Janice Keesling, and Sarah Bouchey. Lee Shepard and Margaret Kidd in the manuscripts and archives department provided quick responses to all requests. Sam Prickett has been the project technologist.

Finally, a note slipped into his briefcase at home suggests that among those to whom the author ought to express appreciation are his indulgent, immediate family: Sandra Lambert, Lula Lambert, Zeph Ruggles, Arabella Ruggles, and Jane Ruggles. Thanks to you all.

JEFFREY RUGGLES

INDEX

Numbers in bold refer to illustrations.

Photography In Virginia was designed by Sara D. Bowersox. Page layout was composed in Adobe InDesign on a Power Macintosh G4. It was typeset in Adobe Garamond 10/12 and ITC Franklin Gothic 10/12. Printed on 128gsm GoldEast gloss paper by Four Color Imports of Louisville, KY and Everbest Printing Co. of Hong Kong, China. The book was produced and published by the Virginia Historical Society.